Colonial Legacies
Contemporary Lens-Based Art and the Democratic Republic of Congo

COLONIAL LEGACIES

Contemporary Lens-Based Art and the
Democratic Republic of Congo

GABRIELLA NUGENT

Leuven University Press

Published with support of the Association for Art History

© 2021 by Leuven University Press / Presses Universitaires de Louvain / Universitaire Pers Leuven. Minderbroedersstraat 4, B-3000 Leuven (Belgium).

All rights reserved. Except in those cases expressly determined by law, no part of this publication may be multiplied, saved in an automated datafile or made public in any way whatsoever without the express prior written consent of the publishers.

ISBN 978 94 6270 299 8
eISBN 978 94 6166 427 3
https://doi.org/10.11116/9789461664273
D / 2021 / 1869 / 45
NUR: 652

Typesetting: Crius Group
Cover design: Anton Lecock
Cover illustration: Georges Senga, *Une vie après la mort*, 2012. Inkjet on Baryta paper, 170 × 60 cm. Courtesy of the artist. (https://www.georgesengart.com/une-vie-apres-la-mort)

Table of Contents

Acknowledgements 7

Introduction 9

Chapter 1. Mining Lubumbashi: Sammy Baloji's *Mémoire* 25

Chapter 2. The Maintenance of Mobutu's Zaire: Michèle Magema's *Oyé Oyé* 49

Chapter 3. The Image of Lumumba: Georges Senga's *Une vie après la mort* 85

Chapter 4. From Kinshasa to the Moon: Kongo Astronauts 119

Coda. Between History and individual histories 151

Notes 155

Bibliography 176

Index 189

Colour Plate Gallery 193

Acknowledgements

This book is indebted to the History of Art Department at University College London. It was there that I learned to think and write about art and the work that art does in the world. My gratitude is owed above all to Tamar Garb for supporting this project from the start and for years of close looking and conversation while she supervised my PhD. Her challenge to a masculinist Eurocentric art history remains a model for me. The research and writing for this book were made possible by a PhD studentship from the History of Art Department at UCL. Additional funding was provided by the Society for French Studies.

During the development of this research, I was able to present my work at Université libre de Bruxelles; University of East Anglia; University of Birmingham; the Institute of Advanced Studies, UCL; the African Studies Research Centre, UCL; the History of Art Department, UCL; the Centre for Multidisciplinary and Intercultural Inquiry, UCL; School of Oriental and African Studies and University of Cambridge. I am grateful to those who invited me and to all the participants and audiences at these events. Portions of Chapter 1 appeared in the article "Mining Time in Sammy Baloji's *Mémoire*" in *African Arts*. Anonymous peer reviewers helped to advance the research presented here. Based on Chapter 3, I wrote the article "Between Camera and Canvas: The Case of Patrice Lumumba and Congolese Popular Painting", published in *Nka: Journal of Contemporary African Art*. I am thankful to the editors and publishers of these articles for their permission to reproduce the material in this book. I also wish to thank my PhD examiners, Debora Silverman and Julian Stallabrass, who provided generous feedback on my dissertation and encouraged its publication. I am grateful to them for their continued support of my career.

Thank you to the artists whose works were the impetus for my writing: Sammy Baloji, Michèle Magema, Georges Senga and Eléonore Hellio and Michel Ekeba of Kongo Astronauts. I would like to thank the team at Leuven University Press, especially Mirjam Truwant for her enthusiasm in the project and for guiding me through all stages of the publication process. Thank you to the two anonymous reviewers whose comments helped to improve my manuscript. I would also like to thank the staff at museums, galleries and archives who have facilitated the reproduction of the included images. The Association for Art History generously provided a grant to support the publication.

ACKNOWLEDGEMENTS

I wish to express a large debt of gratitude to my friends and family. I would like to especially thank Grace Linden, Angelina Volk, Malik Al-Mahrouky and Meret Kaufmann. Lewis Hammond has provided much kindness and joy over the course of this project, and I thank him for all his support. Lastly, I thank my parents, Ina Petrone and Michael Nugent, and my brother, Lucas Nugent, who are always there when I need them, encouraging and assisting my work in infinite ways. The seed of this project was planted when we moved as a family to Belgium, and I dedicate this book to them.

Introduction

For the photomontage series, *The Album* (2013), the Congolese artist Sammy Baloji digitally superimposed contemporary colour photographs of the ongoing conflict in eastern Democratic Republic of Congo onto scanned pages of a colonial-era album that captured a trip to the same area of the Great Lakes in 1911–1913. The latter was assembled by Henri Pauwels (1880–1932), a Belgian colonial officer contracted to supply specimens for the Royal Museum for Central Africa in Tervuren, Belgium, while the contemporary photographs were taken by Congolese journalist Chrispin Mvano. Mvano's images represent the violent struggles in the regions of North and South Kivu, where the fighting, which has killed and displaced several million people since 1996, is rooted in ethnic divisions between the Hutu and Tutsi populations that were exploited by the Belgian colonial administration. In one of the photomontages that comprise *The Album*, Baloji combines photographs of United Nations Blue Helmets, as in the soldiers, police officers and local civilian personnel deployed as peacekeepers in the region, with shots of carefully arranged dead

Figure I.1: Sammy Baloji, *The Album (Pauwels's Album, p.7 installation detail)*, 2013. Digital photograph on archival paper. © Sammy Baloji. Courtesy of Axis Gallery, New York. (Plate 1, p. 194)

animals [fig. I.1]. Hunting was the objective of Pauwels's expedition as evidenced in the black and white trophy photographs whose pictured specimens were taken back to Belgium to construct dioramas at the Royal Museum. In the photomontage, a contemporary onlooker enters a sepia-toned photograph of several slain antelope lined up in a row, while a topless man from Pauwels's album carrying a crocodile over his shoulder steps onto the road patrolled by the Blue Helmets. Below these images, Mvano's photograph of gun-laden soldiers is placed between shots of a lifeless lion, assumingly killed by the colonial officer who poses with it. In Baloji's take on Pauwels's album, historical actors encounter the region's future and contemporary figurations are given a past. The overlaying of temporalities is profoundly disjunctive. For the series conveys the entwinement between the colonial conquest of land, animals and people and the ongoing protracted conflict in eastern Congo.

The Album is in many ways emblematic of the lens-based art that I analyse in this book. In addition to the work of Baloji, *Colonial Legacies* considers a selection of contemporary visual artists born or based in the Congo: Michèle Magema, Georges Senga and the artist collective Kongo Astronauts. *The Album* engages several of the themes shared across the artworks discussed in chapters ahead. For a start, the series combines old, black and white analogue photographs with contemporary colour images taken by a digital camera. Photomontage, as deployed by Baloji, creates transhistorical connections, linking the colonial past and postcolonial present. Multiple temporalities come to exist on the space of the page, from that of Pauwels's and Mvano's to Baloji's own time. The juxtaposition of the photographs troubles the perspective of events and experiences as fixed in time. Furthermore, Baloji's deployment of the album emphasises the way photographs exist as physical objects shaped by time and space as well as social and cultural experiences. They constitute a physical presence in the world, and they are enmeshed with subjective, embodied and sensuous encounters. Private photo albums from the colonial era, like Pauwels's, depicted the privileged life of white European settlers. Their owners carefully arranged photographs and shaped visual accounts in a way that conveyed their own experiences and perspectives. Narratives were constructed by these objects, and yet, in Baloji's series, the album's temporal integrity and purpose is challenged. By strategically juxtaposing Pauwels's photographs with contemporary shots of the longstanding conflict in eastern Congo, Baloji suggests the violence connected to the album. Moreover, the juxtaposition of the two sets of photographs, *then* and *now*, suggests the significance of the camera in constructing perceptions of the Congo.

The title of this book, *Colonial Legacies*, refers to the ways in which Belgian colonialism transformed the structures of everyday life in the Congo. Through the selected artworks, I attend both to these transformations as well as their afterlives and mutations in the post-independence era. Born largely in the 1970s and 1980s, the artists central to this study grew up in the aftermath of colonialism. This generation only experienced the aftereffects of the colonial era rather than actually living through it. Their memory of this time is always already mediated through literature, images and representations.[1] Here, I take up both Andreas Huyssen's concept of the "secondary trauma" of a second generation who grow up in the aftermath of catastrophe and experienced its trauma as citation, as well as what Bogumil Jewsiewicki terms "vicarious memory" as in memory obtained by proxy.[2] Gleaned from their own experiences, the selected artists offer varying perspectives onto the ways in which Belgian colonialism shaped the Congo. Both Sammy Baloji (b. 1978) and Georges Senga (b. 1983) were born and raised in Lubumbashi, a city in the country's mineral-rich southeastern region of Katanga, but today live and work abroad. Their artworks selected for discussion attend to local lived experiences in the city through the global language of photography. Alternatively, Michèle Magema (b. 1977) emigrated with her family from the capital city of Kinshasa, which was then under the governance of President Mobutu Sese Seko, to Paris, France in 1984 when she was six years old, growing up in the diaspora. She returned to the Congo in 2015 after more than a thirty-year absence. Magema's artwork examined in this book addresses the Mobutu era, her last memory of the Congo, through the lens of French feminism. Meanwhile, the Kinshasa-based artist collective Kongo Astronauts was founded in 2013 by French artist Eléonore Hellio (b. 1966) and Congolese artist Michel Ekeba (b. 1984). The work produced by the collective prioritises a certain internationalism through the figure of the astronaut, as well as the connections between Kinshasa and the wider world. This book's focus on artists born or based in the Congo marks a break from previous scholarship that explored the colonial past mainly through white male European viewpoints.[3]

The artists under discussion in *Colonial Legacies* predominantly employ photography and video in a variety of formats, and I therefore wish to foreground medium-specific concerns in this book. The camera carries a specific currency in the Congo. In 1904, E.D. Morel, a British shipping clerk, with Roger Casement, British consul to the Congo Free State, mounted an organised campaign in Britain against Belgium's King Leopold II and the atrocities occurring in his personal colony. Their human rights campaign became the largest humanitarian movement during the late Victorian era and the first to use photographs as a central tool, most famously taken by British missionary Alice Seeley Harris.[4] The photographs foregrounded by the campaign showed the mutilation experienced by the Congolese, many of whom had their hands cut off as punishment in a brutal labour system organised around the extraction of rubber. These images circulated widely in the press and were used to illustrate the lantern slide lectures delivered by the Congo Reform Association in Europe and North America.[5] For many, these photographs created a lasting impression of the colony. The Berlin Conference of 1884–85 had recognised Leopold as the trustee and guardian of the Congo Free State, but due to the global outcry around the atrocities, he was forced to hand over his colony to the Belgian Parliament in 1908. The exceptional violence captured in Seeley Harris's photographs prompted the counter-development of the Congo as *une colonie modèle* ("a model colony") by the Belgian government. This concept gained currency at two historical moments: first, after World War I with the illustrated magazine *L'Illustration Congolaise* and again after World War II with the governmental service InforCongo (1950–1960).[6] The photographic wing of InforCongo was established to testify to the advancements in the Belgian Congo for a local and worldwide audience.[7] It was in this context that, for many Belgians, the colony existed through the visual economy of photography; there were few who actually ventured to it while photographs of it proliferated.[8] The colony was also promoted filmically through newsreel footage, sometimes deployed in the case of colonial propaganda. For example, the visit of Patrice Émery Lumumba (co-organised by the Ministry of the Colonies and InforCongo) to Belgium in 1956 – after which he would lead the Congolese struggle for independence – was captured in a report shot for television and cinema.[9] Four years later, on 2 December 1960, Lumumba's final public appearance before being assassinated on 17 January 1961 was recorded by the foreign press in images and newsreel footage that were disseminated globally.[10] It is in this vein that *Colonial Legacies* turns to photography and video as the technologies of modern history through which the Congo was made visible around the world.

In comparison to the culturally loaded deployment of oil painting as a long-standing "Western" medium, photography and video are often considered the globalised media of contemporary art.[11] As soon as the daguerreotype was introduced publicly in 1839, it was taken up by African photographers.[12] Video alternatively emerged in the 1960s, the era of decolonisation, and it was subsequently adopted by artists around the world. Both mediums are considered truly "global" due to their easy dissemination. Indeed, the selected artists were chosen as their artwork circulates in a global art world. Here I am interested in the transmission of their work and the audiences encountered, and I will shortly discuss the appearance of several of the selected artists on the Belgian art scene. It is also worth noting that the work of Baloji and Kongo Astronauts moves between art and film. Despite globalisation's utopian visions of artists and artworks travelling freely across continents, the popularisation of lens-based art is also due to certain constraints. The shipping of artworks other than photography and video propose a financial and logistical challenge to curators working with limited budgets, as well as artists who struggle with the cost of materials and studio space. Alternatively, the hardware, equipment and know-how of lens-based art are within the reach of many people thanks to the accessibility of digital technologies.

Both photography and video have a special relationship with time, and the artists included in this study make time and the passage of time a subject in their work. Photographs are often described as slices of time, or, in the words of Roland Barthes, "a certain but fugitive testimony", capturing one moment which then enters another.[13] Video is said to be an "art of time"; it is a medium in which time can be manipulated – literally slowed down, sped up, repeated or erased, redefining the boundaries of past, present and future.[14] Photographers who work with juxtapositions and couplings similarly play with the concept of time, reminding us of the then and the now inherent in the still image. There is a further significance to the relationship between these mediums and time in the context of postcolonial Africa. They enable the temporal entanglements that characterise the construct of the "postcolony" theorised by Achille Mbembe. According to Mbembe, the "postcolony" expresses a given (and shared) trajectory – that of African societies emerging from the experience of colonialism with its concomitant violence. One crucial aspect of the postcolony is its construction of time, as Mbembe wrote: "As an age, the postcolony encloses multiple *durées* made up of discontinuities, reversals, inertias, and swings that overlay one another, interpenetrate one another, and envelope one another: an *entanglement*".[15] Photography and video, with its several screens and combinations of visuals and sound, make visible these overlaying temporalities. Through their engagement with time, the selected artists expose the afterlives of Belgian colonialism, capturing the ways in which the past punctuates the present.

Here, a clarification is helpful, this book does not offer a survey of lens-based Congolese art. Rather, it foregrounds several contemporary artists from a specific generation operative in lens-based mediums who work with archives, or a lack thereof. The artworks chosen for analysis in this book can be situated within the "archival turn" in contemporary art. This shift coincided with a theoretical turn, compellingly captured and titled by Jacques Derrida's *Archive Fever* (1996), that submitted archives as historical documents to scrutiny.[16] The philosophical inflection of the archival turn is best attributed to the publication of Michel Foucault's *The Archaeology of Knowledge* (1972). In the text, Foucault defines the archive as "the first law of what can be said, the system that governs the appearance of statements as unique events".[17] The archival turn registers a rethinking of the relationship between power and knowledge production, asking what kinds of truth-claims lie in documentation. This epistemic shift has been defined by Ann Laura Stoler as a move from "archive-as-source" to "archive-as-subject".[18] In 2004, Hal Foster accounted for "an archival impulse at work internationally in contemporary art".[19] In the years since, a large number of exhibitions and publications have addressed the production of art as an exercise in exploring archival materials and techniques.[20] While there are studies on artistic engagement with archives in African contexts, the majority of these accounts concentrate on South Africa.[21] Alternatively, *Colonial Legacies* examines the intersections of artists and archival practices in the context of the Congo. Baloji, Magema and Senga draw on colonial and independence-era photographs, television broadcasts and paraphernalia sourced from both public and private archives, which are subsequently coupled with contemporary imagery. Alternatively, I argue that the work of Kongo Astronauts steps in for an absent archive, creating a speculative counter-archive.

Opening up archives as sites of contested history and practice has led to a desire to reimagine African pasts, presents and futures in artistic practice.[22] Attending to the ways in which images shift the ground on which we establish historical reconstruction and interpretation has been key to scholars interested in writing histories of Africa that privilege the visual over the written record.[23] Scholars have used photographs and archives to contest dominant historical narratives and to produce histories of a different kind.[24] In Eduardo Cadava's words, "the photographic image... interrupts history *and opens up another possibility of history*".[25] The openness of images as "complicated, ambiguous and incongruous historical objects" has simultaneously enabled artists to explore them in creative ways, offering multiple re-readings and blurring the lines of historical and speculative knowledge, documentary and fiction.[26] Baloji, Magema and Senga use archival materials to tell stories that displace official versions of the past and present, contesting old and cliched assumptions. Their artworks shed light on local on the ground experiences, emphasising the gaps and shortcomings of hegemonic accounts. The work of Kongo Astronauts is defined by a similar compulsion: they create new meanings from reusing, re-presenting and recycling second-hand materials and, in doing so, they propose a re-reading of the past and present. Each of the artworks examined in this book centres on people and events occluded from dominant narratives of the Congo: the lives of miners, past and present; women who performed in Mobutu's state-sponsored programme of singing and dancing; ordinary people who collected photographs of Lumumba and watched the arrival of the independent state; and, finally, the global thrill of the Space Age, techno-optimism and the circuits of electronic technologies. By drawing our attention to these different experiences, the selected artworks attest to the everyday ways in which the history of colonialism permeates the post-independence present. They create a new visual record for the future, one that attests to the ramifications of the colonial past across time.

From the Congo to Belgium

The careers of the artists discussed in this book, and the artworks that they produced, coincided with a critical awareness of the colonial era that surfaced in Belgium at the end of the 1990s and grew in visibility over the course of the 2000s and 2010s. This reckoning with the country's past, as argued by Matthew Stanard, is constitutive of "a repeated cycle of forgetting and remembering" that occurred after the end of colonialism in 1960.[27] A new consciousness and awareness of the colonial past emerged in the late 1990s, the effects of which, I would argue, continue to reverberate today. The years that followed, were significant for the predominant role played by the visual arts in addressing the country's colonial history, especially by artists of Congolese origin. The globalisation of the art world and the explosion of biennial culture in the 1990s led to the emergence of a younger generation of artists born or based in the Congo who offered a more critical engagement with Belgium's colonial past, specifically in terms of the alternative perspectives gained from experiencing its aftermath.

In 2005, the Royal Museum for Central Africa, commissioned by King Leopold II in 1904 to showcase the Congo Free State following the success of the Congo pavilion at the 1897 world's fair, staged an exhibition entitled *La mémoire du Congo: Le temps colonial* (*The Memory of the Congo: Colonial Times*) that offered the first comprehensive curatorial survey of the country's history of colonialism.[28] However, as critics observed, the exhibition largely omitted the violence that was waged in the Congo. The Royal Museum's displays and organisation had betrayed a set of widely shared colonialist attitudes for more than a century.[29] The staging of *La mémoire du Congo* was prompted by the publication of two books that had pushed the government to acknowledge the country's brutal colonial past. First was American author Adam Hochschild's *King Leopold's Ghost: A Story of Greed, Terror and Heroism in Colonial Africa* (1998), which described the extent of the deaths in the Congo through Leopold's forced labour system, labelling it as genocide.[30] His account unearthed several previously unknown sources while also turning attention to already published texts such as those of Daniël Vangroenweghe and Jules Marchal from the 1980s and 1990s.[31] Hochschild's controversial book was translated into French and Dutch in 1999. Former Belgian officials who worked in the Congo took to the internet with a 10-page message claiming that only half a dozen people had their hands chopped off and that the punishment was even carried out by local troops.[32] Many Belgian historians challenged the qualification of genocide made by Hochschild and Marchal.[33] Jean Stengers, a leading Belgian historian on the colonial era, commented, "Terrible things happened, but Hochschild is exaggerating. It is absurd to say so many millions died".[34]

In 1999, the year after *King Leopold's Ghost* appeared, Ludo De Witte, a Belgian journalist and sociologist, added to the controversy with his book, *De moord op Lumumba* (*The Assassination of Lumumba*). The text disclosed Belgium's complicity in the assassination of the Congo's first democratically elected prime minister, Patrice Émery Lumumba, in 1961. The book was quickly translated into French (2000), English (2001) and Spanish (2002) and was debated in academic journals and the popular press. In Belgium, the Chamber of Representatives created a commission of enquiry charged with exploring the extent of the country's complicity in Lumumba's death. The committee ended up verifying many of De Witte's findings and offered an official apology to the Congolese people on 5 February 2002.

Concurrently, the Belgian artist Luc Tuymans turned to the theme of Belgian colonialism for the 49th Venice Biennale held in 2001. Prompted by the controversy that had arisen in the country, Tuymans exhibited a new body of work at the Belgian pavilion called *Mwana Kitoko* ("beautiful white man"), taking its title from the propaganda film shot around King Baudouin's visit to the Belgian Congo and Ruanda-Urundi in 1955 by André Cauvin. Nine works were created for the series.[35] Paintings zoomed in and out of the events surrounding the colony's independence from Belgium and the chief protagonists involved in the struggle. On the walls of the pavilion – a structure that was constructed a year before the Congo Free State was handed over from the ownership of King Leopold II to the Belgian state in 1908 – were a life-sized rendering of a 24-year-old King Baudouin arriving on his state visit to the colony, a close-up of Lumumba and a depiction of Moïse Tshombe, Congolese politician and president of the secessionist state of Katanga from 1960 to 1963, with his companions. Memory and its suppression were themes central to the exhibition as suggested in the blurred brushstrokes and ghostly figures, as well as the more elusive and fugitive aspects of the series. For example, the celebrations of Congolese independence on 30 June 1960 are evaded in *Leopoldville* (2000) [fig. I.2]. Tuymans depicts Congolese and Belgian flags draped on a modernist building with several figures standing outside on their balconies, as if they were watching a parade below. Comparable through its omission is the painting *Leopard* (2000). Here the artist turns to a leopard skin, a ceremonial symbol of authority in the Congo, placed on the floor as a witness to these events. However, the suppression suggested by Tuymans is a privilege specific to the Belgian context. The events in the Congo are seen from the perspective of a white Belgian man for whom the colonial era could disappear. Memories of colonialism though persisted for the Congolese, as it had changed the everyday landscape of the Congo in such a way that troubled the ability for it to ever lay dormant.

It was around the same time as Tuymans's *Mwana Kitoko*, or shortly thereafter, that several contemporary artists of Congolese origin started to exhibit on the Bel-

Figure I.2: Luc Tuymans, *Leopoldville*, 2000. Oil on canvas, 54.5 × 83.6 cm. Private Collection. © Luc Tuymans. Courtesy the artist and David Zwirner. Photo: Studio Luc Tuymans, Antwerp.

gian scene in an attempt by the country's institutions to address its colonial past through Congolese voices. Following the suggestion of the Belgian photographer Marie-Françoise Plissart, who had travelled to Lubumbashi in 2005, Baloji exhibited *Vues de Likasi* in 2006 at La Cambre, a renowned visual arts school in Brussels. His photomontage series *Mémoire* (2006) was shown that same year at the Royal Flemish Theatre in Brussels. The work's video component was screened at the Cultuurcentrum in Bruges for the Festival of African Cinema in November 2007, and it was also shown at Yambi, a cultural programme organised by the French Community of Belgium in Brussels from September to October 2007. The photomontage series and video component of *Mémoire* are under discussion in this book's first chapter. In 2008 and again in 2010, Baloji and Congolese writer and artist Patrick Mudekereza were invited to spend several weeks at the Royal Museum's recently developed artist-in-residence programme.[36] Together, they created the project *Congo Far West*, which combined black and white photographs, sketches, drawings and paintings from the Belgian explorer Charles Lemaire's expedition to Katanga (1898–1900) held in the Royal Museum's archives, with contemporary colour photographs and text.[37] Baloji and Mudekereza were simultaneously contributing to the growth of the arts scene back in Lubumbashi through the establishment of the city's own biennial, entitled "Rencontres Picha: Biennale de Lubumbashi", which they had started with other young artists in 2008 through grassroots organisation.[38] As illustrated here, the old colonial centre is impacted upon by the descendants of the formerly colonised, both in the Congo and through travel and migration by the empowered immigrant communities who apply pressure from within Belgium.

As part of the Biennale de Lubumbashi, Baloji and Mudekereza organised a series of educational workshops for artists. Senga was discovered by Baloji and Plissart at one of the ateliers held during the Biennale's inaugural edition in 2008. The advent of biennials on the erstwhile periphery has created alternative centres of production and critical reception, leading to the transformation of the artistic field beyond Europe and North America. The work of Kongo Astronauts similarly turns the eyes of the art world to Kinshasa. Magema's career is also emblematic of this shift: she won the Prix du Président de la République Sénégalaise in 2004 at Dak'Art, Africa's first ever biennial established in 1992, for the video installation, *Oyé Oyé* (2002). This work is the subject of the second chapter. Magema exhibited *Oyé Oyé* at Simon Njami's *Africa Remix*, which opened at Museum Kunstpalast in Düsseldorf in 2004 and went on a three-year tour, and again in 2007 at the *Global Feminisms* exhibition, co-curated by Maura Reilly and Linda Nochlin, at the Brooklyn Museum in New York. Magema also exhibited at the Biennale de Lubumbashi in 2015. This trip marked the first time that she had returned to the Congo since leaving in 1984.

In 2014, the Mu.ZEE, a museum in Ostend specialising in Belgian art from 1830 onwards, hosted *Hunting and Collecting*, a research project and exhibition organised by Baloji that questioned historical amnesia around the colonial era and challenged postcolonial narratives on the Congo.[39] Senga also participated in the project. The exhibition was part of Bato Congo, a multidisciplinary programme presented in Ostend and supported by the Flemish International Cooperation Agency that aimed to explore the relationship between Belgium and its former holdings in the Congo. It invited young Congolese artists to enter a dialogue with their Belgian counterparts. WIELS, a contemporary art centre in Brussels, has also supported artists exploring the country's colonial past. Senga held a residency at WIELS in 2015. His page on the centre's website is illustrated with a photographic diptych from the series *Une vie après la mort* (2012), which centres around the figure of Lumumba. This series, the subject of the third chapter, was originally shown at the Biennale de Lubumbashi in 2013 and again in 2015 at Rencontres de Bamako, sub-Saharan Africa's second ever biennial established in 1994 after Dak'Art and the first dedicated to photography. In 2016, WIELS staged an exhibition by Baloji in collaboration with anthropologist Filip De Boeck, which offered an exploration on the afterlives of colonial architecture in Congolese cities. Senga's participation in the 2019 edition of the Biennale de Lubumbashi was supported by WIELS and Baloji's by Flanders State of the Art.

In 2015, Belgium's Venice Biennale pavilion turned again to the subject of colonialism. Working in close collaboration, Belgian artist Vincent Meessen and Brussels-based curator Katerina Gregos developed a group exhibition that welcomed ten artists from four continents and, for the first time in the pavilion, artists from Africa, including Baloji. The title of the exhibition, *Personne et les autres*, was taken from a lost play by André Frankin, a Belgian art critic affiliated with the Lettrist and Situationist International. The exhibition engaged with the consequences of cultural and artistic connections across Europe and Africa in the 1960s and its aftermath. *Personne et les autres* attempted to trace a series of connections between avant-garde circles, such as Dada, CoBrA and the Situationist International, with pan-Africanism, the end of colonialism and a "Global 68", the lesser known offshoot of May 1968 in the Global South. These connections will be discussed in further detail through the work of Kongo Astronauts.

What had started with the Royal Museum's staging of *La mémoire du Congo* culminated in 2013 when its exhibits closed for an extensive renovation in order to more accurately contend with the country's colonial past. The exhibits reopened to the public on 9 December 2018. Contemporary artworks produced by artists born or based in the Congo, for example Magema's *Mémoires Hévéa, entre Histoire et histoires individuelles*, which was commissioned by the Biennale de Lubumbashi in 2015, had been acquired to address the shared history between Belgium and the Congo. *Mémoires Hévéa* is discussed in the coda to this book. Rebranded as the "AfricaMuseum", its Facebook page shared a photograph of Magema overseeing the installation of the work in November 2018. Artists from the Congo are today invited to the former metropole to provide their perspectives on the country's colonial past and its afterlives in postcolonial Congo. Since the emergence of the debates within Belgium in 1998, the contemporary visual arts have operated as a key site of exploration and crucial discussion of the country's seventy-five years of colonialism, creating new knowledge, perspectives and vantage points.

* * *

Decolonial and anti-racist movements, such as Black Lives Matter and Rhodes Must Fall, have demanded a global reckoning with the enduring historical legacies of colonialism that have profoundly shaped our world. The significance of visual art to these debates can be discussed in terms of the relationship between politics and aesthetics. Politics, according to Jacques Rancière, is a struggle over the "distribution of the sensible", the system of divisions and boundaries that determines what is common to a community.[40] Hegemonic distributions of the sensible are termed by Rancière as "the police", which establish a distribution of the sensible based on exclusion, ensuring that select groups, activities and thoughts are made visible while others are concealed.[41] As Rancière states, some "speech is understood as discourse and another as noise".[42] Politics disrupts the police order by supplementing it with voices previously excluded from participation in the "parcelling out" of the visible and invisible, the audible and the inaudible, the sayable and unsayable.[43] Politics, for Rancière, occurs when the previously marginalised make themselves and their desires known, seen and heard.[44] The artwork included in this book can be thought of in these terms. Contemporary art produced by Congolese artists opens up opportunities for voices that have previously been excluded from discussions around Belgium's colonial past.

Rancière emphasises the parallel between aesthetics and politics in that both reconfigure the distribution of the sensible. Artistic practice is one manifestation of aesthetics, which is capable of proposing alternative perceptions and subjectivities. By "undoing the formatting of reality", visual art disturbs "the meaningful fabric of the sensible".[45] Art, in other words, can change what is visible, audible and sayable. While, in Belgium, the country's colonial past has been subjected to repeated cycles of remembering and forgetting, the selected artists attest to the ways in which it endured in the Congo. Moreover, with its experimental imagination and its speculative possibilities, visual art is uniquely capable of producing alternate imaginaries around the past and present, especially when confronted by a lack of evidence or testimony, the existence of which is determined by colonial histories of power. Édouard Glissant has described both the power and limits of the imagination inherent to artistic practice: while it cannot avert destitution in reality, imagination can change mentalities, leading, however slowly, to political transformation.[46] The artworks included in this study offer a vision of the past and present that might not otherwise exist, and these works come to circulate in both the physical and digital world where they encounter new audiences. Rancière conceives of art's role as working against formations of "consensus" or what is common knowledge.[47] By contrast, art and politics seek paradoxical ways to upend the logics of consensus through what he calls dissensus, "a dissensual re-configuration of the common experience of the sensible".[48] Rancière continues: "Within any given framework, artists are those whose strategies aim to change the frames, speeds and scales according to which we perceive the visible".[49] They question the self-evidence of the visible and make the invisible visible. This framework theorised by Rancière provides a way to conceptualise the artwork included in *Colonial Legacies*.

The chapters

In the Western collective imagination, the Congo largely exists through the "Heart of Darkness" trope. It is the land of Joseph Conrad, where Kurtz lost his mind, but also that of Henry Morton Stanley, David Livingstone, Casement and Morel, Leopold II, the Berlin Conference and the ensuing "Scramble for Africa". Leopold's Congo Free State epitomised the brutal workings of nineteenth-century colonialism. This "discursive landscape", as Kevin Dunn has pointed out, still haunts Western imaginings and re-imaginings of the Congo.[50] Dunn notes that while most people in the Western world know very little about the Congo, they ironically feel as though they know it very well because it was "enveloped in a century of powerful imagery".[51] Following Nancy Rose Hunt, the Congo's violence remains iconic and spectral in public consciousness.[52] The mutilation photographs mobilised by the Congo Reform Association were given a new life by Hochschild's *King Leopold's Ghost* and they continue to circulate today. As Filip De Boeck has observed, many books, films and articles that cater to non-academic audiences suggest that the colonial enterprise produced its ultimate mass grave in the Congo and that the country's postcolonial reality is similarly defined by an endless afterlife, born from the assassination of Lumumba.[53] One notable exception is David Van Reybrouck's *Congo: The Epic History of a People*, originally published in Dutch in 2010 and subsequently translated to English in 2014. The book comprises the testimony of ordinary Congolese people who witnessed the country's major events and it recounts these events through their eyes.[54] Drawing from De Boeck, however, the strength of stereotypical imaginings of the Congo renders its real physical reality invisible.[55] My book is indebted to the scholars, many of whom are anthropologists and historians, who have broken down these circumscriptions, attempting to see things as they actually are, and who, in the words of Hunt, aim for "no heroes, no villains and little haunting" and seek "to move historical imaginations beyond horror and humanitarianism".[56] It is in their footsteps that my book follows. Another vital contribution to my thinking has been work of Black studies scholars, such as Fred Moten, Saidiya Hartman and Tina Campt. Without wanting to conflate complex, diverse and specific contexts, my own research has been galvanised by their innovative approaches, specifically with regards to reconstructing and rearticulating subjectivity in the contexts of archives, care as an antidote to violence and the ever-present (im)possibility of escape from conditions of duress. These scholars have both renewed and deepened my understanding of images.

Colonial Legacies is attentive to the work that artworks do. In my analysis, I offer an incredibly close reading of the selected works. I situate them in the contexts out of which they emerge, while simultaneously attending to their material density, intricate detail and profound emotional economy, which I set in dialogue, and often in conflict, with historiography and theory. The various subject positions occupied by the artists included in this book are emblematic of contemporary art today, as in they operate between the local, or "the particular" as Okwui Enwezor described it, and the global.[57] The selected works are attuned to the concerns of the contemporary and, at the same time, they address place-specific histories and experiences. I convey this sense of multiplicity in my analysis through the frames and references that I bring to bear on them. Moreover, the artworks under discussion attest to the entanglements of our world, defying oppositions of the so-called "West" and "non-West", a distinction which seems to linger in the discipline of art history and its continental frameworks. This false division has been confounded in the work of Debora Silverman whose account of Belgian art nouveau as "imperial modernism" created from Congo raw materials and motifs attests to the immediate presence of the colony in the metropole, and, in many ways, my book explores the reverse in postcolonial Congo through the selected artworks.[58]

With regards to terminology, in *Colonial Legacies*, I take up the shorthand of "Belgian colonialism", but, as Silverman reminds us, it is important to recognise that this entity was defined by two separate phases: imperialism and colonialism.[59] The first phase is the Congo Free State, a non-settler colony privately owned by King Leopold II who funded it as an arena of investment and extraction for commercial interests. This fictional state of about twenty million people, ruled by decree and run from Brussels, was an empire of extraction, one in which the Congolese were turned into customers for Belgian manufacturers. Alternatively, the second phase, known as the Belgian Congo, which begun in 1908 when the state was forced to annex King Leopold's realm, is marked by a paternalistic ideology that sought to transform the Congolese into citizens of empire. The histories of extraction and the continued exploitation of the Congo's natural resources that I address in this book are a product and one of the afterlives of Leopold's Free State. Meanwhile, the transformations in structures of gender can be discussed both in terms of these labour histories and capitalist incentives for profit, as well as the ideological drives of the church and the Belgian administration.

This book's first chapter examines Baloji's photomontage series, *Mémoire*, as well as the video component of the work created in collaboration with the Congolese dancer and choreographer Faustin Linyekula. For the series, Baloji worked with photographs from the archive of the Belgian mining company Union Minière du Haut Katanga and their former sites in Lubumbashi. In my analysis of the series and video, I seek to complicate claims of absence that are often thought to pervade the Congolese landscape. I explore the competing time worlds introduced by Belgian colonialism, but also the ones that result from the forces of neocolonialism and global extractive economies in Lubumbashi.

Photography and video are mediums that travel and are associated with a global set of exchanges and encounters. One of my central concerns is the geographical specificities of photography and video and, in the case of my study, the effects of the Congolese context and the era of Belgian colonialism on these transnational mediums. Most lens-based theory is derived from encounters with the camera in Europe and North America.[60] If globalisation has expanded art worlds (albeit with limitations), then our scholarship should simultaneously widen in scope. There are other theories that can be developed from experiences with the camera elsewhere and the way that specific locales come to weigh on it. In the same vein, I am concerned with the entanglements of photography and video with other traditions of making that characterise the material history of the Congo.

The second chapter considers Magema's double screen video installation, *Oyé Oyé* (2002). Taking up archival footage from the Mobutu era, Magema explores the ways in which Congolese women endured the government's project of *authenticité* from the 1970s onwards, specifically, a cultural policy entitled *l'animation politique et culturelle*, a system of state-sponsored singing and dancing that endured until the end of the 1980s. In doing so, the work engages with an accumulation of changes that had transformed the structures of gender in the country since the era of Belgian colonialism. *Oyé Oyé* considers the extensive tradition of women's labour that constitutes the background of everyday operations, often excluded from accounts of the country that travel through a series of male political figures or from violence to violence.

The third chapter focuses on Senga's photographic diptych series, *Une vie après la mort* (2012), which centres on the figure of Lumumba who was assassinated in 1961. The series engages the intertwined lives of Lumumba; Kayembe Kilobo, an elderly schoolteacher in Lubumbashi whose clothing, lifestyle and opinions had been self-consciously styled on Lumumba since the 1950s and the artist himself, who was taught by Kayembe in school. *Une vie après la mort* explores the legacy of Lumumba in Lubumbashi. In this chapter, I explore the transmission and circulation of photographs of Lumumba and the ways in which they were absorbed and deployed by audiences at the time. I simultaneously consider the afterlives of these images as they endure in Congolese popular painting, cinema and Senga's series, and I ask what it means to look at these photographs of Lumumba today.

The fourth chapter considers Kongo Astronauts, an artist collective based in Kinshasa, specifically their photographs, short films and collaborations. The collective stage landings in the city through an astronaut dressed in a spacesuit constructed from the parts of discarded electronic devices spray-painted silver and gold. By evoking a consideration of the astronaut in Kinshasa, a symbol largely associated with a Euro-American context, I argue that Kongo Astronauts challenge stereotypical and preconceived conceptions of the city, as well as cliched assumptions that circumscribe certain geographies and events. Through the collective's work, I explore the ways in which the Congo connects to and even enables the Space Age in the 1960s and 1970s, as well as the lifecycle of contemporary digital technologies. I contend that the collective captures a sentiment of optimism associated with the end of colonialism, the Space Age and the Internet, all of which purported a more equal and shared world, and yet Kongo Astronauts simultaneously suggest its downfall through e-waste and the global corporations that pillage the Congo's mineral resources.

Colonial Legacies concludes with a brief coda that reads Magema's *Mémoires Hévéa* as emblematic of the work discussed in this book. Magema's work looks back, capturing the lived dimensions of history and the temporal oscillations of photography. Moving beyond the relationship between past and present, I contend that the artworks examined in *Colonial Legacies* look forward to the unfinished work of decolonisation.

CHAPTER 1

Mining Lubumbashi

Sammy Baloji's *Mémoire*

Mémoire, a series of photomontages constructed in 2006 by Sammy Baloji, comprises a set of old, black and white photographs embedded onto contemporary colour images taken by the artist of former mining sites in Lubumbashi, situated in the Katanga province. In the thirty composite images, African men and women and European officials extracted from photographs produced by the Belgian mining company Union Minière du Haut Katanga in the 1920s and 1930s appear around today's abandoned mining complex. [fig. 1.1]. The Congolese dancer and choreographer Faustin Linyekula enters these sites in the video component of *Mémoire*, which was created in the same year as the series of stills. Produced by Baloji in a one-off collaboration with Linyekula, the video is a looped 14 minute and 30 second single screen projection structured around clips of the sites overplayed with the voices of Congolese politicians whose speeches echo over the landscape. This archival soundtrack is accompanied by three separate events centring on Linyekula. Though the photographic series and video piece are grouped together under the same title, they are often exhibited separately, acting as standalone works.

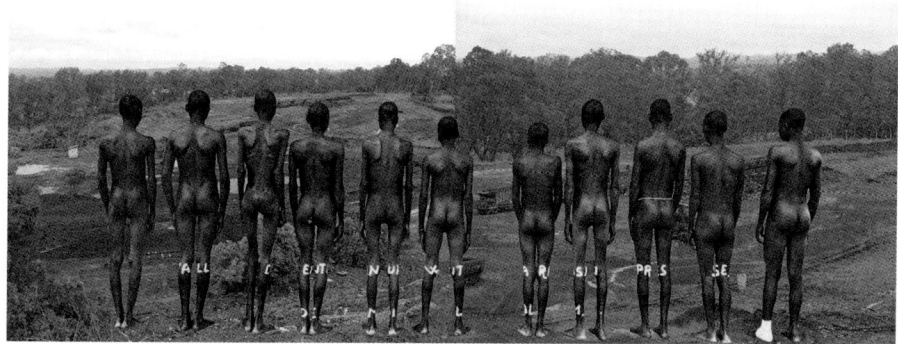

Figure 1.1: Sammy Baloji, *Untitled 3* from *Mémoire* series, 2006. Archival digital photograph on satin matte paper, 60 × 159.38 cm. © Sammy Baloji. Courtesy of Axis Gallery, New York. (Plate 2, p. 195)

The history of Katanga and the contemporary struggles in the region are central to Baloji's work. The Berlin Conference of 1884–85 recognised the sovereignty of King Leopold II over the Congo Free State, including the mineral-rich area of Katanga. Beneath its surface, Katanga concealed the greatest deposit of cobalt, one the largest deposits of copper and other minerals, such as tin, gold, uranium and zinc. Union Minière du Haut Katanga, a company established by King Leopold II in 1906 and backed by Belgium's largest holding company, Société Générale de Belgique, exploited this wealth. The establishment of Union Minière followed virulent criticism of King Leopold II over evidence of atrocities in the Congo Free State.[1] By offering attractive investments through consortiums, such as Union Minière, Leopold had hoped to gain the support of financiers and, through them, to gain sympathy from their governments. When the Belgian Parliament took control of the colony in 1908, the state offered Union Minière continued access to Katanga as it was dependent on taxes produced by commercial enterprises.[2]

In 1910, Union Minière constructed a foundry and started to extract copper in 1911, while, nearby, the city of Elisabethville, today Lubumbashi, was established. Union Minière's system of employment exemplified "industrial paternalism" in its attempt to control every aspect of the African workers' existence, from accommodation and schools to clubs, wives, health care and breastfeeding.[3] Independence in 1960 slowly led to the end of the company, though Union Minière did support the Katangese secession led by Moïse Tshombe from 1960 until 1963 in order to gain continued access to the sites. After the end of Belgian colonial rule, many foreign powers concerned themselves with who would control the country's mineral resources. Union Minière had been crucial to World War II.[4] Following Albert Einstein's warning that Nazi Germany could create atomic weapons, the United States attempted to secure all the uranium in the Belgian Congo, and it was Congolese ore provided by Union Minière that exploded over Hiroshima and Nagasaki.[5] In 1966, President Mobutu Sese Seko took over Union Minière, converting it into the state-owned company, La Générale des Carrières et des Mines (Gécamines). The nationalisation of the mining industry was part of Mobutu's strategy of Africanisation, in addition to renaming the country Zaire. As a result of mismanagement and a dramatic downturn in global copper prices, Gécamines started to collapse in the 1980s as the company fell behind in its payment schedules, started laying off its workers and left its sites in disrepair, a course that accelerated in the 1990s.[6] Unemployment currently overwhelms Katanga where many men are *creuseurs* or "artisanal miners", engaging in strenuous, dangerous activity lacking appropriate safety equipment.[7] This current state of affairs represents a significant break from the colonial past of industrial mining under high finance.

Born in 1978, Baloji grew up in Lubumbashi, while Linyekula was born in 1974 in Kisangani in northern Congo. Both spent the years of their youth under Mobutu's government, which propagated a campaign of *authenticité* that began at the end of the 1960s. The *"recours à l'authenticité"* ("recourse to authenticity") advocated the resumption of an "authentic" African culture after colonial acculturation, rejecting "imported ideologies". Linyekula's early career was defined by years of travelling.[8] Migrating to Kenya in 1993, Linyekula attended a choreography workshop in Nairobi entitled "Towards Contemporary African Dance" led by the Ivorian Alphonse Tiérou, who, amongst others such as Germaine Acogny, was attempting to develop a contemporary African choreography culture.[9] Linyekula later travelled to France in 1998 to train with Régine Chopinot and Mathilde Monnier.[10] Returning to the Congo in 2001, Linyekula established Studios Kabako, a space for dance and physical theatre. He relocated the Studios Kabako to Kisangani in 2006. Meanwhile, Baloji started photographing Lubumbashi in 2004.[11] Hubert Maheux, the then director of the city's French Cultural Centre, provided Baloji with the equipment to take photographs for an architectural guide of Lubumbashi. The photomontage component of *Mémoire* originates from Baloji's experience of photographing the city. The Belgian entrepreneur, George Arthur Forrest, who established the French Cultural Centre, supported Baloji's early career. Forrest is the owner of Groupe Forrest, a conglomerate founded in 1922 around the mining industry in Katanga whose services vary from transport to civil engineering. Forrest was appointed an executive of Gécamines from 1999 to 2001. He took this opportunity to acquire the archive of the former Union Minière, which was subsequently digitised.[12] This archive provided the black and white photographs from which Baloji worked in the series, digitally extracting figures and transposing them with Photoshop onto digital, colour photographs taken by the artist of the sites today.

Pertinent to Baloji's work is Mbembe's influential notion of the "postcolony" as propounded in the 2001 eponymously titled collection of essays. Mbembe opened the collection with a scathing critique of the way in which the West routinely characterises Africa, arguing that the continent is primarily understood through conceptions of "'absence', 'lack' and 'non-being', of identity and difference, of negativeness – in short, of nothingness".[13] However, the "postcolony" as a construction is condemned to the very same "narrative of loss" that Mbembe decried.[14] It has, paradoxically, been taken up by postcolonial scholars and conflated with Mbembe's thinking around "necropolitics and necropower", as summarised by him:

The various ways in which, in our contemporary world, weapons are deployed in the interest of maximum destruction of persons and the creation of *death-worlds*, new and unique forms of social existence in which vast populations are subjected to conditions of life conferring upon them the status of *living dead*.[15]

The postcolony has come to stand in recent theoretical literature for various states of absence, violence and death, and Baloji's work has previously been understood largely through these terms. Bogumil Jewsiewicki, for example, asserted that *Mémoire* expressed the feelings of loss experienced by Congolese youth due to the closure of the once prosperous mining sites.[16] It has become, he writes, a "desolate wasteland" and Baloji, a "photographer of absence".[17] The sites' state of abandonment and disrepair was also foregrounded by Tate Modern's wall text that accompanied the display of *Mémoire* in 2011.[18] Similarly, Elsie McCabe Thompson, the former president of the now closed Museum for African Art in New York, described Baloji's series as picturing a once occupied environment, now characterised by an "absence of humanity".[19]

However, the aesthetics and politics of ruins and ruination are anything but static.[20] The discourse of decline that habitually circumscribes *Mémoire* tells only part of the story. Dystopia, as discussed by Jennifer Robinson, is a profoundly disabling trope, one that overlooks a variety of experiences in search of evidence to support an overarching and one-dimensional dystopic narrative.[21] This search for dystopia has circumscribed the vision of several scholars writing on Baloji's *Mémoire*. Though the sites seen in the series are described by critics as abandoned or empty, on close inspection, it appears that they are actually occupied by some contemporary figures. For example, men of varying ages, alone and in groups, congregate on the site captured in *Untitled 17* [fig. 1.2]. Dressed in casual clothes, they dig, stand by, crouch over and walk across the site. These appearances continue throughout

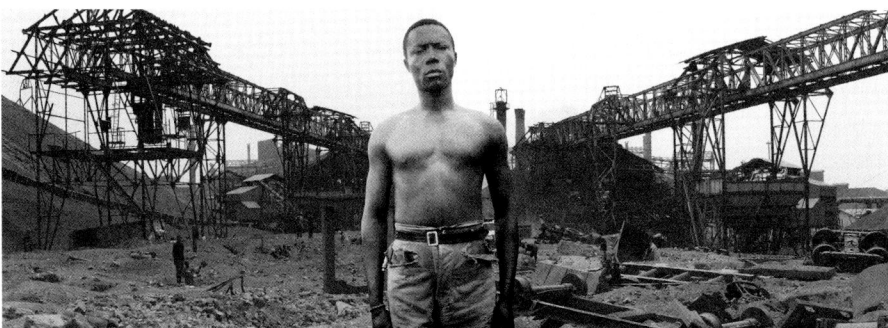

Figure 1.2: Sammy Baloji, *Untitled 17* from *Mémoire* series, 2006. Archival digital photograph on satin matte paper, 60 × 167 cm. © Sammy Baloji. Courtesy of Axis Gallery, New York. (Plate 3, p. 196)

the series, asserting the environment as an occupied or populated one. Given that people continue to live in such environments, it is vital that we think more carefully about the terms of their existence.

Thinking through time

Two colour photographs of contemporary Lubumbashi are adjoined to compose the background or site in *Untitled 3* onto which a group of men extracted from an earlier black and white photograph are transposed [fig. 1.1]. Naked with arms by their sides and buttocks exposed, the group is lined up for a physical examination on their arrival at Union Minière. Medical inspection was essential to the recruitment process.[22] Union Minière required examinations both on enlistment and on arrival at the place of work. Only robust and healthy individuals were admitted to the compounds. Death and suffering had defined the camps where the workers lived in the early years of the company. Union Minière was even described by Marchal as a "Man-Eating Corporation".[23] However, in the 1920s, the company attempted to stabilise its workforce by offering longer contracts with the attraction of advance bride-wealth payments, accommodation, schools and care.[24] Many Africans sought employment with the company, which, in turn, fed, clothed and educated generations in Katanga, a clear change from today's *creuseurs* who struggle on the sites for scraps.[25] Through these archival photographs and their superimposition over the dilapidated landscape, Baloji conveys a specific experience: the economic advantages Union Minière workers enjoyed that were taken away after the end of colonialism.[26] These advantages are occluded in several accounts on Union Minière.[27] For example, John Higginson suggested that the concerns of the workers were in continuous opposition to the company, clearly challenged by Baloji in several of the works.[28] Higginson's assertion seems to constitute a larger trend in scholarship that overlooks the experience of Union Minière workers; the administration of the company is often more of a concern.[29] Returning to *Untitled 3*, the examinations cited by several of the archival photographs in *Mémoire* were a component of Union Minière's strategy of stabilisation as the company ascertained who was fit for work. Hygiene was considered crucial to a stable workforce, as Jean-Luc Vellut wrote, "The individual had become a unit of production, a tool".[30]

The archival photographs employed by Baloji are embedded in the entwined traditions of photography and anthropology and the specific context in which they collide and coincide, that of Europe's colonial and industrial expansion and its concomitant encounter with otherness and labour.[31] Photography's purported veracity was deployed during the late nineteenth century by a variety of scientific endeavours seeking claims to objectivity. However, the photographs themselves challenge such claims as they evince ways of seeing, constructing and experiencing the world according to time-bound conventions and systems of thought exterior to the photographs. The archival photographs transposed to *Mémoire* are embedded in conceptions of the black body as a legible or classifiable object of study and a site of curiosity.[32] Arrayed for the camera, they parade their posed subjects as specimens or exemplars for scrutiny. But the convergence of photography and anthropology was afflicted by a sense of anxiety over what Deborah Poole has described as the "excessive detail" and "temporal contingencies" of photographs.[33] Standardised arrangements of photographic subjects, she argued, were circulated from the 1880s onwards in order to counter such excess and to subsume individuality to the type.[34] The men in the photographs deployed by Baloji exemplify this standardised system. Naked, formulaic and repetitive, the anonymous black male body appears captured and controlled by the camera.

However, the photographs themselves simultaneously convey an excess of visual detail to that which the mining photographer had set out to capture. Turning to *Untitled* 3, one of the men appears to cover his sex, conveying a sense of vulnerability or anxiety inadvertently captured by the camera. In *Untitled 1* [fig. 1.3], the group of men standing for the photograph gaze outwards, towards the camera and consequently the viewer. Their gazes constitute a subversive site of encounter to the autonomy of the photograph, as the men appear to acknowledge the existence of the photographer and the camera.[35] Time is evoked through the apparatus of the camera, as it is embedded in the advancements of technology. Similarly, the photograph's colour, or lack thereof, conveys associations of time. Monochrome is today evocative of technological obsolescence and veracity, operating as a site

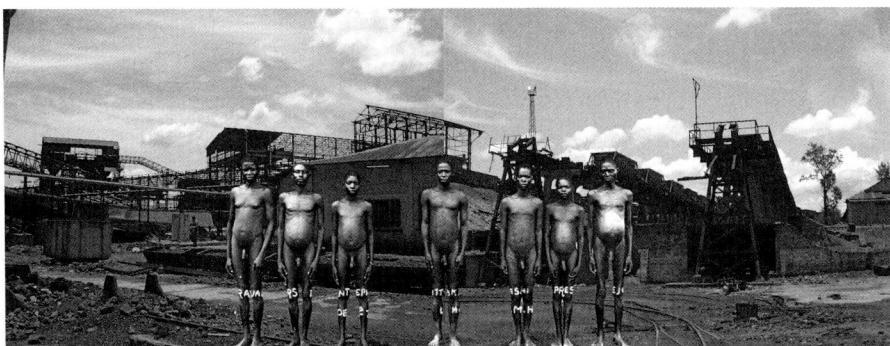

Figure 1.3: Sammy Baloji, *Untitled 1* from *Mémoire* series, 2006. Archival digital photograph on satin matte paper, 60 × 195.75 cm. © Sammy Baloji. Courtesy of Axis Gallery, New York.

of opposition to the colour overload of contemporary culture. Furthermore, the clarity and sharpness of the contemporary images of the sites contrast with the colonial photographs that appear softened, worn and sometimes even smudged. This collision enacts a temporal technological clash between a landscape preserved digitally and a scanned object of knowledge once circulated and exchanged as an analogue photographic print.

The anthropological set of conventions that permeate the archival photographs is concerned with types, groups and collective characteristics. The original black and white archival photograph from *Untitled 10* [fig. 1.4] appeared in a Union Minière report entitled "*Direction générale: rapport trimestriel (troisième trimestre 1925)*" that was sent back to Brussels [fig. 1.5]. The text accounts for the activity of the company in July, August and September of 1925, charting its overall administration, specific projects, surveys of the sites and their associations with other organisations in Lubumbashi. There are eight photographs that appear two-a-side at the end of the report, varying from shots of new recruits to the company's sites, specific equipment and the officers' library. The photograph from *Untitled 10* is second in the "*photographies*" section. Labelled with the glued text from a typewriter, it is titled "*Types d'indigènes Balovale*" ("Types of Balovale natives") and taken in one of the camps, showing thatched structures and a couple of figures in the background. Underneath the photograph are the cursive words "*Recrutements R. Miliamo*" ("Recruitments R. Milamo") scribbled in red. There is a section of the report called "Recruitment in the occupied territories" to which the photographs presumably correspond, as the text chronicles a successful expedition where Union Minière was able to enlist 211 workers. The writing goes on to typify the physical characteristics and comportment of the men: "good type, except for a few natives of Rwanda who were of a thin, weak and slender type".[36] In this context, the cloths that the men grasp onto are perhaps the clothes they were given for work on their ar-

Figure 1.4: Sammy Baloji, *Untitled 10* from *Mémoire* series, 2006. Archival digital photograph on satin matte paper, 60 × 178.56 cm. © Sammy Baloji. Courtesy of Axis Gallery, New York. (Plate 4, p. 197)

Figure 1.5: Photographs labelled "*Types d'indigènes des territoires occupés*" and "*Types d'indigènes Balovale*" in the Union Minière report, *Direction générale: rapport trimestriel (troisième trimestre 1925)*. Belgian National Archives 2–Joseph Cuvelier repository. Photo: Gabriella Nugent.

rival at the site. The photograph above the one transposed to *Untitled 10* captures a similar group of six men, labelled "*Types d'indigènes des territoires occupés*" ("Types of natives of the occupied territories"). There are two cooking containers on the ground, as if constructing a scene to convey the group's typical sustenance

In *Spectres of the Atlantic* (2005), Ian Baucom charts the use of the type as one of the central acts of violence in an Atlantic system of speculative capital, exemplified in the *Zong* atrocity, when, in 1781, the crew of this slave ship threw 133 captives overboard in order for Captain Luke Collingwood to claim their insured value. Drawing on Walter Benjamin's conception of allegory, Baucom explains the way in which the slave was abstracted to a commodity. Allegory, claims Baucom, "enacts the central logic of commodification by conferring on its subject matter an abstract signification analogous to the economic value that capital processes of exchange confer upon the commodity".[37] From the commodity, the slave is abstracted *again* to a type of interest bearing money.[38] By throwing the slaves overboard, Captain Collingwood was hastening their transformation into money, a value that had been determined through the typicalising mind of insurance.[39] Insurance is an enterprise through which the typical triumphs over the specific. The type is therefore, according to Baucom, "a refusal of the absolute, singular, individual, isolated lives of persons, events or things".[40] The logic of the typical seems to occur again through the traces of text written on the surface of the archival photographs. However, through Baloji's extractions, the once legible text is obfuscated. Letters appear on the group in *Untitled 3*. Naked group shots similar to *Untitled 3* are the only ones with writing on their surfaces. It is as if somebody had attempted to classify, categorise or study the Congolese men after the photographs were taken in order to judge who was in good enough shape to work. Doctors on the sites were asked to develop a sharp eye in order to reject medically unsuitable recruits.[41] They were looking for a certain type. The text, rendered illegible by Baloji, adds yet another layer to the series as the writing by the Union Minière official calls our attention to the surface of the original archival photographs.

Furthermore, the Congolese men montaged onto *Untitled 3* were once ordered to shed their clothing for the camera, involving an act which was likely profoundly shame-producing at the time.[42] For Congolese men and women, nakedness often conveys an experience of disempowerment. In rural central African society, an adult man stripped in public loses all respect, all status.[43] Under colonialism, African men were usually regarded as children who existed outside of time, and they were simultaneously treated as what Ch. Didier Gondola has termed "beasts of burden" in the expanding colonial economy.[44] Masculinity was eventually constructed for the Congolese according to a sliding scale devised by the Belgian colonial government where savagery and civilisation, tradition and modernity, "tribal" customs and European lifestyle constituted repulsive poles.[45] Unsuccessfully, they attempted to enforce this totality onto the Congolese. However, through such violence as well as that of the effects of subsuming people to typologies, the extracted figures from the archival photographs – situated as they are in a contemporary landscape as if plucked from history – came to occupy time in an extraordinary way. Black men and women had to confront what Toni Morrison called "'post-modern' problems", as in the alienating effects of capital and the shattering of the subject, already in the nineteenth century and earlier through the contexts of slavery and colonialism.[46] Drawing from Morrison, we may deduce that the group in *Untitled 3* encountered the concerns that we associate with post-modernism in the early twentieth century.

If time occurs in an exceptional way in the archival photographs, it also seems to travel. No photograph stands alone. Images exist simultaneously and offer a way to think through other photographs. The photographs in *Mémoire* accordingly speak to a wider archive of encounters with an oppressive state and its surveillance of labour. They are charged with semantic contamination through the visual economy of photography. *Mémoire* contracts these entanglements, as the photographs avoid any signifiers that give away a specific context. From *Untitled 3*, I am reminded of a comparable scene captured by Ernest Cole in apartheid South Africa of a group of miners subjected to a medical examination, arms extended and buttocks exposed.[47] The archival shot similarly evokes photographs of aboriginal slaves taken towards the end of the 1800s in Australia, the shakedowns of convicts in the Texas Department of Corrections as seen in Danny Lyon's series from the 1960s and the orders of colonial studio photography enforced across Africa.[48] In a single photograph are the traces of various others that preceded and succeeded it. They are connected through strains of colonial governance, enforced labour, subjection and the Atlantic economy, or, in other words, through "racial capitalism" as conceptualised by Cedric Robinson.[49] Racism and capitalism, according to Robinson, evolved from the old feudal order to produce a modern world system of racial capitalism dependent on slavery, violence, colonialism and genocide.[50] Racism was central to the development, organisation and expansion of a capitalist society as well as its social tenets.[51] Capital accumulates by producing and traversing through disparity, for example, capitalists in control of production/workers without subsistence or conquerors of land/the dispossessed.[52] These antinomies of accumulation entail disposability and a distinction between the "human" and the "less-than-human" that justify ongoing dispossession.[53] Racism enshrines the inequalities required by capitalism. *Untitled 3* accordingly extends from the early 1900s to a series of other times that evidence the same world order and are themselves available to viewers through the photograph.

The obvious conjunction of temporalities in the series is the convergence of the early twentieth-century colonial photographs with Baloji's own images of the contemporary sites. However, even the contemporary is more fragmented and splintered than conventional knowledge would assume. Turning again to *Untitled 3*, we notice that the background is comprised of two photos that construct the site from varying degrees of closeness. In the photograph on the left, the space is shown from a wider angle. We see the entirety of the constructed and cleared ground, as if it was taken from an elevation. Mountains wrap around the expansive scene. In comparison, the adjacent photograph appears condensed. Trees crowd in on the space, while the tarnished scraps of a railway transport system emerge. Up close, the once circular and working wheels are skewed and contorted and the train's colour corroded. Together, the two photographs construct the site, signifying the time of contemporary Lubumbashi onto which the colonial figures are transposed. Consequently, *Mémoire* shatters any sense of temporal coherence and wholeness, as even the so-called "present-day" emerges as a period occupied and shared by several times.

Mémoire appears to convey the experience of multiple temporalities, all of which occur concurrently alongside each other. Shaped by the complex experiences of Lubumbashi and the Congo in general, time occurs through the orders of the body, the contexts and collisions of colonialism and the concerns and conventions of anthropology and photography. Time is seized and grasped in colour and contemporary digitised culture, alongside the conflicting temporal connotations of analogue black and white. Time in *Mémoire* is entangled. The series captures the complexity of time in Lubumbashi.

Time and colonialism

David Van Reybrouck opens *Congo: The Epic History of a People* with an account of a 2008 visit to Étienne Nkasi, a Congolese man in Kinshasa. "*Je suis né en mille-huit cent quatre-vingt-deux*" ("I was born in 1882"), states Nkasi.[54] In disbelief, Van Reybrouck wrote: "Eighteen eighty-two? Dates are a relative thing in Congo. I have had informants tell me, when I asked how long ago something had happened: 'A long time ago, yes, a long, long time ago, at least six years, or no, wait, let's say: eighteen months ago'".[55] He observes: "My desire to provide a Congolese perspective would never be met with complete success: I myself am much too fond of dates".[56] In Van Reybrouck's account, a clash occurs between a standardised European clock and a local Congolese sense of time. There is a Belgian, "much too fond of dates", and a descriptor, "a long, long time ago", seemingly in conflict with Nkasi's own time world. Without wanting to conflate the cities of Kinshasa and Lubumbashi, Van Reybrouck's account offers a way to think about the alternative temporalities introduced by colonial rule. His confrontation with Nkasi around varying conceptions of time is embedded on the sites where *Mémoire* is set and suggested through the era of colonialism that the series invokes. For, the colonial government had attempted to conscript the Congolese to Western structures, one of which was time.[57] Nervousness, as articulated by Hunt writing on the two Congo states, could create an experience of extreme surveillance in terms of time; even colonial administrators were asked about "where they slept, for how long, how they used funds and speed in inspections".[58] Mines specifically were a site where autochthonous time was challenged and attacked, as employers like Union Minière were central to the spread of a standardised European clock.[59] This enforcement of "clock time" through the structures of labour has been explored by E.P. Thompson, Jean Comaroff and John L. Comaroff, Frederick Cooper and Giordano Nanni in various geographical contexts.[60] Money and time were explicitly equated.[61] The colonial government established the "time theory of value" in the Congo whereby work was assessed in terms of time; wages were calculated by the hour. Soon both employee and employer were supremely aware of hours per day and days per week of work for pay.[62]

In an essay on time and colonialism in Africa, Alamin Mazrui and Lupenga Mphande observed that greater rigidity and greater supervision at the place of work in mining economies necessarily led to the African mine worker being more conditioned by the capitalist clock than his equal in the agricultural sector.[63] There was a stringent European time schedule enforced onto the workers by Union Minière.[64] The archival photographs employed by Baloji in *Untitled 18* and *Untitled 29* were originally situated in a document entitled "*Travail rédigé en 1929*" that explores the activity of a Union Minière worker in 1929. The text was written by N.N. Genonceux, the wife of a colonial agent, and given to the Union Minière archive by her family in 1957. The chapter that chronicles a worker's typical day is structured through constant temporal signifiers. This obsession with time at Union Minière has been discussed by Hunt as the company attempted to control the time of workers' wives in order to alter African birth spacing customs, which were viewed by mine owners and officials as a kind of birth control.[65] Breastfeeding and weaning were scheduled in order to reduce birth intervals. Feeding older children above the age of one was also a company affair scheduled two to three times a day. The text in "*Travail rédigé en 1929*" exposes a similarly stringent structure. The workers comply with a standardised European clock: "It is two o'clock, "five o'clock", "six o'clock" and "six thirty".[66] Noise ceases after ten in the evening: "It's ten o'clock. No more noise can be heard".[67] The workers start their day at six: "The African is an early riser, he can get up perfectly at six in the morning".[68] A siren sounds every day at six thirty and, if the workers are slow to wake, the guards cry: "Get up, get up, it's time to wake up, don't be late!".[69] There is a second siren to signal that work is about to start and a third at seven o'clock, which is when the roll call is taken. The sounds of the gong signify the start of class for children and the availability of water. In the afternoon, a siren occasions the stopping of work for lunch in the cafeteria. The gongs, sirens and calls of the guards that splintered the air of Lubumbashi convey a time world in a state of shift, of shattering sounds that appear to conscript the spins of the earth. They are the aural components of colonialism's violence that effected, according to Frantz Fanon, a cultural obliteration, charting a transformation in space and time.[70]

However, the figures transplanted from the archival photographs attest to something else. At the very least they testify to a continued existence or occupancy of the land. Grounded in the space that constructs *Mémoire*, the worker's shoes in *Untitled 9* [fig. 1.6] stand aligned with the surface of the earth. His shadow is cast across the site, making him appear as physically there. In *Untitled 10* [fig. 1.4], the group's soles are exposed to the warmth of the ground and the coarse textures of jagged stones. More than just being *there*, the archival figures appear in Baloji's series as active occupiers of the landscape, tending to the site, still working the land. Men dig, equipped with shovels; their waists submerged in the earth [fig. 1.7]. In an interview, Baloji stated: "For Congolese people, the dead are not dead at all. They are still with us".[71] There exists an uncanny encounter set up in the series between the archival workers and the contemporary occupants of the space. Mazrui and Mphande characterised the way in which the dead continued to exist and affect the living as evidence of a certain kind of temporality.[72] Drawing from John Mbiti, they contended that prior to the imposition of the capitalist clock, there was more of an orientation toward concrete activities and events already experienced.[73] Like the ancillary figures in the contemporary landscape, "their past was inextricably connected with their present".[74] The primary orientation of time was towards the world of ancestors.[75]

In *Mémoire*, the archival workers are extracted, cropped and severed from one time, that of colonial and analogue black and white technologies, and enter another, the context of colour and contemporary culture. In *Untitled 10* [fig. 1.4], the light dirt ground clashes with the space of the compound in the early twentieth century, captured in shades of grey; cloths from the same era catch the sun of the contemporary landscape. The time across the sites seems oriented towards the early twentieth century, which appears in the series as entangled with the contemporary.

Figure 1.6: Sammy Baloji, *Untitled 9* from *Mémoire* series, 2006. Archival digital photograph on satin matte paper, 60 × 159 cm. © Sammy Baloji. Courtesy of Axis Gallery, New York. (Plate 5, p. 198)

Figure 1.7: Sammy Baloji, *Untitled 8* from *Mémoire* series, 2006. Archival digital photograph on satin matte paper, 60 × 160.18 cm. © Sammy Baloji. Courtesy of Axis Gallery, New York. (Plate 6, p. 199)

This orientation stands in opposition to the temporality that capitalism enforced, as in, according to Mazrui and Mphande, the spread of a time world whereby "man is always moving 'forward' toward the future".[76] The capitalist clock entered spaces where a smaller degree of emphasis had existed on what was to come or on endless tomorrows.[77] Newell S. Booth Jr. extrapolated on Mbiti to argue that social and economic activities created "time" and that, in this sense, "the future" was empty container defined by the absence of events and was therefore "unreal".[78] The archival figures in the landscape could therefore be seen as a continuation of an alternative time world to that of capitalism.[79]

Holding on

Muscles are tensed in *Untitled 10* [fig. 1.4]. The men's foreheads are wrinkled, and their jaws are clenched. Nostrils expand while lips are pressed together; the men's taut skin stretches over their chests. In *Untitled 3* [fig. 1.1], the group's buttocks are clenched as dimples appear on either side of their cheeks. This same sense of tension is seen again in *Untitled 9* [fig. 1.6] where a single worker stands erect for the camera. In each of the photographs, the men's arms are stiffly suspended alongside their sides. Far from expressions of ease or comfort, these are shots enacted through orders. "The native's muscles are always tensed", Fanon observed.[80] He continued: "You can't say that he is terrorised or even apprehensive. He is in fact ready at a moment's notice to exchange the role of the quarry for that of the hunter".[81] Drawing from Fanon, Darieck Scott has explored the trope of "muscular tension" to articulate the experience of the colonised.[82] Muscular tension, according to Scott, offers a space from which to think about other forms of possibility as in "the potential of transformation in however limited, constrained or attenuated a configuration".[83] It is about an effective capability, an opposition expressed through what Scott called "a refusal to give defeat any final acceptance, a refusal to acquiesce to it".[84] Such contractions suggest a "reservoir of resistance" to the coloniser's acts of subjugation.[85] Drawing from the resistance chronicled by Johannes Fabian in his study on a workers' movement against colonial rule in Katanga, Higginson wrote, "the African workers in Katanga were not simply a blank page upon which successive phases of industrial expansion and social engineering could impose themselves".[86]

In the document "*Travail rédigé en 1929*", where the archival photographs from *Untitled 18* and *Untitled 29* were originally situated, there is a chapter entitled "*stabilisation*" that chronicles the company's attempt at stabilisation in the 1920s. The text contains several accounts of various workers who visited their villages and chose to return to Union Minière; there were even some who enlisted others from their villages for work. They are accordingly stabilised as suggested in the often-cited phrase, "*Il est stabilisé*" ("he is stabilised"). The chapter champions examples of stabilisation that set workers up as family men with wives and children. The subtext is an exemplary colonisation that occurs as the workers actively choose Union Minière, "*l'équipe sanitaire*" ("the health team") and "*le lit*" ("the bed") over the contexts from which they originate. There is an ease conveyed in the writings that implies the process of stabilisation transpired effortlessly, and yet the archival photographs employed by Baloji suggest a sense of tension. We could speculate, that in the men's clenched jaws, stiffened arms and contracted thighs, there exist other temporalities onto which they grasp.

Historical repetition

The video component of *Mémoire* opens with white text against a black screen: "*Mémoire* is the story of politicians and the working-classes; of broken promises; of those in power and the work of those who are governed. It is also the story of a body that moves among the ruins of what was once the economic heart of the DR Congo". This text gives way to clips of a smokestack that emits white wispy clouds and shots of the site's dilapidated structures. The voice of Lumumba speaking on 30 June 1960, as part of the ceremony marking Congolese independence, plays over the scene. In the speech, Lumumba claims the Congo for its people and encourages them to engage in a struggle that will lead to prosperity and greatness, social justice and fair worker compensation. His optimistic words are juxtaposed with contemporary shots of men, known as *creuseurs*, searching the site for scraps to sell [fig. 1.8].

Following the sample from Lumumba's speech, the video plays clips of streaming water on site and active machinery after which the voice of Joseph Kasa-Vubu – "First President of DR Congo (1960–1964)" – takes over. Rather than document the dates of speeches on screen, Baloji transcribes the dates when the country's postcolonial leaders entered and served in public office. In his speech, Kasa-Vubu advocates that Congolese men work with enthusiasm for the cause of a "great, strong and single nation". As these words end, the camera cuts to the topless figure of Linyekula, holding an empty wooden frame and a broken doll's head, a recurring prop in his performances. Linyekula appears in three separate dance events in the video. His body begins to rhythmically writhe and contort. He crouches down to

Figure 1.8: Sammy Baloji, video still from *Mémoire*, 2006. © Sammy Baloji. Courtesy of Axis Gallery, New York. (Plate 7, p. 200)

Figure 1.9: Sammy Baloji, video still from *Mémoire*, 2006. © Sammy Baloji. Courtesy of Axis Gallery, New York. (Plate 7, p. 200)

Figure 1.10: Sammy Baloji, video still from *Mémoire*, 2006. © Sammy Baloji. Courtesy of Axis Gallery, New York. (Plate 7, p. 200)

pick up a sheet of paper accompanied by the sounds of static and feedback [fig. 1.9]. The soundtrack reaches a crescendo with the shout: "*Vive l'indépendance!*" ("long live independence!") [fig. 1.10]. This proclamation is swiftly consumed by the sounds of a car crash and intoned twice more over the wreckage. Derek Gregory has described the "postcolonial" as part of an "optical shift" in a teleological historical narrative based on "lazy separations between past, present and future".[87] He contends that the strength of the term has been in seeking to account for different colonialisms at different times, arguing that the capacities that inhere within the colonial past are routinely reaffirmed and reactivated in the postcolonial present.[88] Hence, the arbitrary temporal marker of independence and the car crash in the video, which suggest that the extractive economy that defined Leopold's Free State endures long after the official end of colonialism. Indeed, the photomontage series visually connects present-day Congo with the history of plunder that started with Leopold II.

In the video, several clips evidence various assets carried off screen. The camera zooms in on streaming water as its sprays cascade beyond the edges of the shot. This shot is succeeded by stones dragged away from the camera [fig. 1.11]. Hacked with various axes, they are separated and withdrawn from view, while a mining train subsequently traverses the site, its weighted and filled containers exit the screen [fig. 1.12]. The concept of "extractivism" seems an apt way to describe these clips.[89] Minerals and oil as well as other goods are exported from the Global South, and these extractions enable the development and prosperity of the Global North. Extractivism distorts the allocation of wealth and the structure of local economies, which are excluded from the gains arising through global economic growth and technological advancements. This system of accumulation was exem-

Figure 1.11: Sammy Baloji, video still from *Mémoire*, 2006. © Sammy Baloji. Courtesy of Axis Gallery, New York.

Figure 1.12: Sammy Baloji, video still from *Mémoire*, 2006. © Sammy Baloji. Courtesy of Axis Gallery, York. (Plate 7, p. 200)

plified in Leopold's Free State. Rubber and ivory, as observed by Antwerp-based shipping clerk E.D. Morel in the 1890s, arrived on ships loaded with wealth from the colony while the ones leaving Belgium for the Congo carried only guns, chains, ordnance and explosives.[90] The value of goods arriving from the colony was several times that of the goods leaving Europe. This same sense of exploitation is suggested in the video through an absence of salaried labour for the contemporary men on the site and simultaneously a world that depends on minerals from the Congo. In terms of the latter, the sounds of static and feedback that accompany Linyekula are evocative of early dial-up connection and static. Delinda Collier has written about the way Africa is excluded or ostracised from accounts of digital media.[91] However, the sonic evocations in *Mémoire* call our attention to the source of the West's celebratory global village, as in the phenomenon of the entire world becoming more interconnected through media technologies. Dependent on electronic devices, the global village championed by Marshall McLuhan is today conceived through the Congo's cobalt and coltan, a large portion of which is supplied by *creuseurs*.

After Linyekula's appearance and the car crash of independence, the screen goes black and the video returns to footage of the mining complex accompanied by the archival soundtrack of Mobutu Sese Seko, "Second Present of the Republic of Zaire (1965–1997)", and Laurent-Désiré Kabila, "Third President of DR Congo (1997–2000)", interspersed with a second appearance by Linyekula inside a dented and rusted conduit [fig. 1.13]. As the video nears its end, Linyekula is seen again in an open space surrounded by the site's structures [fig. 1.14]. The recurring warning 'tsss' sound of snake is heard as Linyekula springs across the site with arms outstretched in a series of arabesque movements. The voice of Mulumba Lu-

Figure 1.13: Sammy Baloji, video still from *Mémoire*, 2006. © Sammy Baloji. Courtesy of Axis Gallery, New York. (Plate 7, p. 200)

Figure 1.14: Sammy Baloji, video still from *Mémoire*, 2006. © Sammy Baloji. Courtesy of Axis Gallery, New York. (Plate 7, p. 200)

koji, "First President of the Sovereign National Conference (1990)", plays over the scene, stating:

> We owe it to ourselves, as we owe it to our ancestors as well as to our children, to be able to discuss at length, to talk about the past and the future of our country without indulgence but also without emotion and with no gratuitous violence, even if it is merely verbal. Given that those of our brothers and sisters who today find themselves in another place were also almost all of them, previously in positions of power at a time not necessarily that long ago, we could legitimately permit ourselves to show that they shared, to different degrees admittedly, responsibility for the general degradation into which we have fallen today.

Linyekula then turns away from the camera and walks toward the shadows, disappearing from view. The video subsequently loops and tells the exact same story over again.

The techniques of video deployed by Baloji enable an awareness around variations within the production, experience and tactility of time.[92] As previously discussed in terms of the photomontage series, the world is comprised of multiple temporalities. Time is a cultural construction, and the video component of *Mémoire* emphasises several experiences of it. Baloji's video plays with the repetition of history, eschewing the expectations connected to the passage of time. The speeches echo much of the same sentiment around a successful state and its people coming together. In listing the dates each politician served in office, Baloji evokes a temporal slice of the past that shaped the present or, rather, as evoked in the sheet of paper picked up and dropped by Linyekula, the failed promises of bureaucracy. The video creates a parallel between the speeches and the dancing body of Linyekula, both of which disappear without leaving any physical trace in the landscape. History repeats itself in an upending cycle, and the viewer is subjected to circular time as the artist constructs it. For, the video plays on loop without any beginning or end, and its circularity disrupts a linear reading of time, alluding to the artificiality of historical demarcations suggested by each politician's time in office. Whenever a viewer starts to watch the video is the start of the experience for them, which only ends when they walk away from it. Moreover, through Linyekula's appearances, there is sense of temporality as experienced and produced by the body. In comparison to the linear march forward, Linyekula often stays glued to one spot. He creates a series of extended circles with his body, echoing the video's looped circular time. His movements vary in speed, sometimes slowing down or speeding up the pace of a scene. His body rewrites history against the backdrop of the dilapidated mining sites, complicating conceptions of temporal progress.

In addition to this circular time, Linyekula simultaneously alludes to another time: the struggles of everyday survival. In his second appearance, Linyekula is situated in a cramped conduit [fig. 1.13]. His circular and controlled actions conform to the size of the space, adjusting to its constraints. Linyekula stands on one leg, wobbling, and then switches to the other, evoking a sense of precarity. Beneath him is a red bicycle lying on its side, reminding us of the ones ridden by the men who congregate on the site [fig. 1.15]. Improvisation as a style of dance is often linked by theorists to survival.[93] Indeed, Linyekula describes it as "a state of living, surviving in a hostile world".[94] Improvisation suggests something created spontaneously with-

Figure 1.15: Sammy Baloji, video still from *Mémoire*, 2006. © Sammy Baloji. Courtesy of Axis Gallery, New York.

out preparation, and its temporality is one of existing solely in the present moment. The *creuseurs* captured on the sites can only live day-to-day without the certainty of salaried work or the predictability of job security.

Responding to these conditions of crisis, the people of Lubumbashi coined the neologism, "*criseurs*", to refer to those so impoverished that they are unable to make ends meet.[95] As detailed by Georges Mulumbwa Mutambwa and Pierre Petit, the struggle against adversity has led to the creation of a lexicon around the courage and energy associated with everyday life. "*Choquer*" or "*ku-choquer*" from the French "*choc*" ("shock" or "hit") is a verb that emerged in Lubumbashi in the early 1990s to describe a person determined to go out every morning and search for work that will allow him to earn enough to feed his family upon returning home in the evening.[96] I write "him" as the deindustrialisation of the city has led to changes in gender and age relations, since many heads of households, typically male, lost their central role in the economic activities of the family.[97] The attention given to the everyday struggles of *creuseurs* in the video challenges the theoretical frameworks often deployed to comprehend the postcolonial state, specifically Mbembe's "necropolitics" which develops Giorgio Agamben's discourse of the *homo sacer* or "bare life". The victims of these concepts, or "the living dead" apropos Mbembe, are typically condemned to a state of passivity.[98] However, as described by Mutambwa and Petit, the man who "*choque*" ("shocks") is anything but passive; he is "*kasakasa*" (Lingala for "busy", "restless", "enterprising"), "*dare*" ("in a hurry", from the French "*daredare*", "double quick") and "*yuluyulu*" ("standing up, since he has no time to sit down").[99] This vocabulary suggests an alternative temporality that is sped up and a time frame too short in which to make enough money. Evoking Linyekula's movements, these men can improvise, one way or another, and obtain a "*contrat*" ("contract"), as in work for a day.[100] Their experience of time therefore always occurs in the short-term, until the end of the day. Mutambwa and Petit describe a situation in which parents often put off going home because they have not yet earned enough to buy the necessities for a meagre meal at the night markets.[101] This evening meal, often the only one of the day, takes place so late that it is called "*karibu na kesho*" ("close to tomorrow"), emphasising the lack of time to accommodate the temporal markers of each day.[102] The video component of *Mémoire* captures an alternative experience of time in the postcolony, one defined by the precarity of crisis.

What is shared across each of the archival speeches is a hope placed in the future. Throughout the video, there is a constant sense that the future could be different, both in terms of past futures never realised and the juxtaposition of these words with contemporary images that evidence their non-arrival, but also an undetermined future. In Linyekula's third appearance, he dances with arms outstretched and open, moving between the sunlight and shadows, while the voice of Lukoji speaks of taking responsibility for the past as a way to move forward [fig. 1.14]. This investment in the future is at once a historical repetition evidenced in the speeches themselves, but also a way to end a cycle of broken promises. The sense of possibility created by Linyekula's topless moving body opens up another set of questions. Collier has described a parallel between the two copper belts of Belgian and British colonial rule: the economies of extraction and the consumption of the black body.[103] She takes up Belgian colonisers' description of Lubumbashi as the "lung" of the empire due to both its economic significance and distance from the capital city of Kinshasa, adding, "the lung being an apt metaphor for the life force taken in extraction economies".[104] In its opening up of an undetermined future, the video asks if Lubumbashi can escape the terms of its creation, another loop or cycle if you will, as a city of extraction in which black bodies are consumed by global extractive economies.

To end this chapter on the possibility of an undetermined future is to return to the photomontage series and the imposition of a temporality in which one is always moving forward toward the future. To consider *Mémoire* as a whole, the photomontage series and video turn our attention to the competing time worlds introduced by Belgian colonialism, but also the ones that result from the forces of neocolonialism and global extractive economies in Lubumbashi.[105] The works explore these experiences through African miners in the early twentieth century and their contemporary equivalent in the *creuseurs* who search the same sites for scraps to sell today. By connecting images and voices of the past and present, Baloji charts a history of plunder that begins with King Leopold II and continues through present-day Congo. Much aligned with postcolonial theory and its promise to destabilise a Western world order, *Mémoire* seems to ask if emancipation, or an undetermined future, can be found in shedding light on the colonial past and its enduring effects in the present.

Figure 2.1: Michèle Magema, video stills from *Oyé Oyé*, 2002.
© ADAGP, Paris and DACS, London 2021. (Plate 8, p. 201-202)

Figure 2.2.: Michèle Magema, video stills from *Oyé Oyé*, 2002.
© ADAGP, Paris and DACS, London 2021. (Plate 8, p. 201-202)

Figure 2.3: Michèle Magema, video stills from *Oyé Oyé*, 2002.
© ADAGP, Paris and DACS, London 2021. (Plate 8, p. 201-202)

CHAPTER 2

The Maintenance of Mobutu's Zaire

Michèle Magema's *Oyé Oyé*

Oyé Oyé, a double screen video installation created by Michèle Magema, opens with the rhythmic gusto of Axel Mbouze's "Papa Mobutu", a song played in dedication to President Mobutu Sese Seko on state-controlled radio stations across the Congo, known then as Zaire. The chorus sounds over black and white archival clips of Congolese women on one screen and, on the other, a contemporary colour video of the artist [fig. 2.1–2.3]. Young girls in white, long-sleeve shirts, thigh-length skirts and Mary Jane shoes are succeeded by a series of women dressed in textiles that commemorate the state. Raffia skirts vibrate and shake with the coordinated gyrations of a group of young women who jump back and forth; their tied bandeau tops are visible from all angles. Flags are waved in tight coordination by the women in the crowd. The camera captures a close-up of one woman's circling textile-clad stomach and, as it zooms out, we see that she comprises a group dressed in the same vine covered textiles who perform a song for Mobutu. Hairstyles, slick and elaborate, are captured in their celebratory variety.

Produced in 2002, with a looped run time of around 4 minutes and 30 seconds, *Oyé Oyé* creates a confrontation between two screens facing each other. One screen, as we have seen, streams archival footage of the Mobutu era edited and combined by Magema. These clips, which vary from women performing in state-sponsored singing and dancing events to shots of Mobutu, are taken from Thierry Michel's documentary film *Mobutu, roi du Zaïre* (1999). Michel had acquired the footage from television broadcasts, and these clips are transformed by Magema in *Oyé Oyé* from colour to black and white. Magema also edited in a series of backward cuts so that the same actions repeat themselves several times over. The other screen comprises a contemporary colour video of Magema marching against a white background. Beheaded by the shot, Magema's torso is visible as she wears a blue thigh-length dress with a diagonal white band across it, a recreation of the compulsory school uniform from the artist's early childhood in Zaire. Her strides vary in speed and enthusiasm, and she stops every time Mobutu appears on the other screen [fig. 2.2]. Born in Kinshasa in 1977, Magema emigrated as a child to Paris, France in 1984. Her reference system brings together her immersion in both these worlds. *Oyé Oyé* emerges from her family's experience of Zaire from which they fled as a result of her father's support for ABAKO, the opposition party to Mobutu.[1] In the video, Magema turns to a gendered experience of the country, capturing the ways in which women in particular endured the policies issued by Mobutu. In doing so, she attends to the gendered experience of an oppressive postcolonial state, a trajectory with origins that exceed Mobutu's Zaire.[2] For, Zaire saw an accumulation of changes that had transformed the structures of gender in the country since the era of Belgian colonialism.

In her 1970 study on women's role in economic development, the Danish economist Ester Boserup cited the example of precolonial Congo to demonstrate female farming systems as an economic structure in Africa.[3] Labour in precolonial Congo was divided by gender, and women were in charge of agriculture and food production. Men assisted only with the felling of trees, they cleared the land for cultivation, while women sowed, looked after and gathered the crops. This control of agriculture offered women various advantages and status: they cultivated land and disposed of the crops as they wished, and in certain cases, they were able to inherit land and transfer it on to their children. Matrilineal and patrilineal systems both allowed women access to agricultural production and gave them control over any surplus generated. Women therefore had a source of earnings and were viewed as an economic asset to their community. Trade, like agriculture, was also controlled by women, although it lacked the same weight in the economy due to substandard transport and communication and various disruptions caused by the extension of the slave trade and a series of wars.[4] Limitations did exist on what tasks women were able to execute in certain areas of the Congo, for example, amongst the Bashi of eastern Congo, women were prohibited from owning cattle.[5] Nonetheless, women in precolonial Congo had a certain degree of autonomy and the ability to engage in economic activity and to control their own earnings.[6] On account of their contributions to agriculture, women's status in precolonial Congo was to a certain extent elevated compared to that of their European counterparts from the same time.[7]

The societal status of women was wholly transformed through the economic and social structures of colonialism. As discussed in this book's introduction, Belgian colonialism can be divided into two phases, one which prioritised extraction, the legacies of which endure in the second, and another which sought to transform the Congolese into citizens of empire, and we should consider both of these threads in the construction of gender. Motivation for earning combined with the values of Belgian colonisers disrupted divisions of labour in the Congo. Amina Mama has argued that colonialism attacked women as colonial subjects and then again in gender specific ways.[8] Missionaries in the Congo enforced a type of conservatism starting towards the end of the nineteenth century, especially Belgians from Flanders, a stronghold of Catholicism. They attempted to alter existent culture, specifically the tenets that were in opposition to Christianity, such as polygamy and sex outside of heterosexual marriage. The institution of monogamy was of crucial concern. The Belgians attempted to establish a European structure of the family, "in which pious Christian women fulfilled the roles of wife and mother", obstructing the various systems of kinship that had previously existed.[9] The African wife was obliged to tend the hearth and rear a generation of African Christians; she would be subservient to her husband.[10] In order to achieve this arrangement, the colonial government attacked the traditional separation of labour in agriculture. The aim was to take women away from the fields on the grounds that they were overworked. Men, on the contrary, it was believed, were simply lazy.[11]

The Belgian administration established Western-type schools, and the economic sector gave eminence to conservative Western concepts of gender, even in agriculture where Congolese women had a clearly defined status. Norms were conveyed through schools, which led to stereotyped linkages in access to education and employment that were well-established by the early twentieth century.[12] Reforms in 1948 further exasperated these separations.[13] Home economics created the groundwork of girls' education. Male education emphasised agriculture, from the export and cultivation of crops and soils to the techniques deployed to operate various types of equipment.[14] They were accordingly equipped to work in commercial agriculture whilst women were ousted from a sphere in which they had once specialised. Boys were offered a series of employment-oriented programmes and secondary and tertiary education from which girls were excluded. The exclusion of women from agriculture was also achieved through the state's legal structures. Men were accountable for taxation and controlled the money.[15] The ability to own land and to bequeath it to their children was also taken away from women. In written law, women's dependence was codified, with stipulations that they required their husband's authorisation to work or to sign any legal documents. These legal and educational conditions combined to create an erosion in status for women, which was evidenced in perceptions of women's standing in society both by Belgian administrators and by Congolese men and women themselves.[16]

"Big men", women and *authenticité*

In *Oyé Oyé*, Magema halts her incessant marching whenever the song exclaims "Mobutu" and the opposite screen switches from the archival women to Mobutu. In one clip [fig. 2.2], he is captured in a throne-like seat wearing an *abacost*, an outfit based on Chairman Mao's own with a collar and cravat, covered in white diamond designs, and a leopard-skin toque, slightly tiled to one side. His characteristic thick square, black-rimmed eyeglasses oversee the events on the opposite side of the camera. Writing on the postcolony, Mbembe has maintained that the bodies of leaders, or their images, play a central role in articulating state authority.[17] Subsequent clips show Mobutu standing at a podium with multiple microphones [fig. 2.4]. He appears smug and satisfied, as if waiting for the applause of the crowd to die down. Another clip captures an animation played every evening on Zairian TV in which Mobutu emerges as an omniscient entity from the clouds [fig. 2.5].

After seizing control of the country in 1965, a cult of personality developed around Mobutu as the Zairian president. His political party, Mouvement Populaire de la Révolution (MPR), was legitimised as the single party of the state in an attempt to end the infighting that had characterised the Congo crisis, a period of political upheaval and conflict following independence from Belgium.[18] In 1967, the Manifeste de la N'sele laid down the objectives of the government which included the policy of *authenticité*. The "*recours à l'authenticité*" ("recourse to authenticity") attempted to erase the vestiges of colonialism that lingered in the country. Rather than a regressive, conservative development, the project was envisioned as deploying a rich cultural heritage in the creation of a new Zairian identity.[19] Mobutu aspired to join together "authentic" Congolese culture with global standards of modernisation and progress. In 1971, Mobutu changed the Republic of Congo to

Figure 2.4: Michèle Magema, video stills from *Oyé Oyé*, 2002.
© ADAGP, Paris and DACS, London 2021.

Zaire. Names across the country were transformed from French, or their colonial titles, to more "African" ones, for example, Joseph-Désiré Mobutu became Mobutu Sese Seko Kuku Ngbendu Wa Za Banga, while Léopoldville was called Kinshasa and Katanga as Shaba.[20] Western clothing was also prohibited. Men could only wear an *abacost* – the term came from the phrase "*à bas le costume*" ("down with the suit") – while women's clothing was confined to the *pagne*, a wrap-around long dress. Hairstyles were governed by Mobutu's *authenticité* campaign, as the state outlawed straightening, "conking" and extensions, which were deemed "un-African".

In 1974, the MPR established "Mobutism" as the official ideology of Zaire, which was seen as the logical culmination of all concepts that had been developed by the state. Mobutism encompassed and glorified the thoughts and visions of Mobutu, the self-proclaimed *père de la nation*.[21] The language of family was employed to describe Mobutu's command over the country's citizens, echoing Mbembe's description of the postcolony in which "an intimate tyranny links the ruler with the ruled".[22] The vision of the omnipotent state cumulated in the 1974 constitution that claimed the will of the MPR as absolute; Mobutu presided over all areas of government.[23] The state was monolithic, and "deviationism" was a constitutional crime.[24] While the video suggests Mobutu's authority, as experienced by Magema's own family who left Zaire for France, it is worth observing that the state vanished by the early 1990s.[25] Mobutu looted the commons to such an extent that Zaire fell apart, and it was easy for Kabila to overthrow Mobutu's government when the time arrived.[26] However, over the course of the 1960s and 1970s, Mobutu welded together the territory of the Congo through absolutism.[27]

The persona of Mobutu came to encapsulate the quintessential postcolonial "big man". In *Paths in the Rainforest* (1990), Jan Vansina argued for the existence of an equatorial tradition in Congo Basin that spanned more than four thousand

Figure 2.5: Michèle Magema, video stills from *Oyé Oyé*, 2002.
© ADAGP, Paris and DACS, London 2021.

years.[28] According to Vansina, this tradition was characterised by a system of social organisation overseen by local "big men" who gained legitimacy by attracting and keeping followers through the distribution of wealth and the control of perceptions about their leadership. The status of big men endured over the course of the colonial era and thereafter. As evidenced in *Oyé Oyé*, Mobutu adopted the aesthetic of authority associated with strongmen, from leopard skin, a symbol of chieftaincy in many parts of Africa including precolonial Congo, to the worshipping crowds and the control yielded over Magema's actions on the other screen.[29] Mbembe has argued that postcolonial subjects embody the authoritarian epistemology of their government to the extent that they reproduce it themselves.[30] As Bob White has observed, there was a desire for the status of a chief in Mobutu's Zaire from which women were largely excluded.[31] Men in Zaire were treated as absolute chiefs who governed through their superiority, will and wit and who alone provided for the community, while women were supposed to rear children and to offer education in the values of the community.[32]

With Mobutu as *le père de la nation*, women were confined to the archetype of *la maman zaïroise*. There were two figurations of femininity in Mobutu's Zaire, as Francille Rusan Wilson has observed: "The ideal woman is a mother and housekeeper firmly under the authority of her husband, kinsmen and ultimately the president himself".[33] Motherhood as the sole function of women was stressed by the state. In 1975, the Zairian government changed International Women's Year (IWY) to International Mama's Year.[34] The "authentic" woman stayed away from clubs, alcohol and the cinema. Morality was the charge of women in Zaire: all of its shortcomings were blamed on women due to their having turned away from "authentic" actions towards the temptation of Western concepts. The only option for women if they transgressed these thresholds was that of the "whore" or *femmes libres*, the corrupted city woman who shatters traditions.[35] This dichotomy of the "Madonna" and the "whore" is embedded in an extensive Western genealogy and, in contrast to Mobutu's campaign of *authenticité*, it is typical of nineteenth-century France as expressed in the opposition, "*courtisane ou ménagère*" ("prostitute or housewife").[36] In 1846, French political philosopher Pierre-Joseph Proudhon suggested that women had only two possible roles in society: that of housewife (*ménagère*) or prostitute (*courtisane*). Far from repudiating this dictum, many of Proudhon's heirs in the French labour movement continued to cite it as a definitive statement about women's position in French society. Ironically, Mobutu's project of *authenticité* adopts European constructions of gender in order to project an "authentic" African femininity.

These contradictions were inherent to the construction of *authenticité*. The apparatus of *authenticité* staged traditional culture in a way that tended to obscure the country's transnationalism and shared concepts of governance such as socialism.[37] The Zairian architects of *authenticité* were likely shaped by the Belgian Franciscan Placide Tempels's *La philosophie bantoue* (1945), which was embedded in a long tradition of Western thinking on culture and the self, as well as the writings of Vansina who attempted to define the worldview and traditions of Congolese people as a coherent philosophical outlook.[38] Each offered powerful support for the concept of a common Zairian tradition that was adapted to the advantage of the state. Even the *abacost* was derived from Chairman Mao and was, alongside the *pagnes*, likely produced in Europe and exported to Zaire. The very inception of *authenticité*, seemingly an inward-looking political and cultural policy, was drawn from encounters with elsewhere.

The archival clips and song cited in *Oyé Oyé* evoke a specific component of Mobutu's *authenticité* project. In the early 1970s, the government launched a cultural policy entitled *l'animation politique et culturelle*, a system of state-sponsored singing and dancing based on the elaborate political dance spectacles that Mobutu had seen during visits to China and North Korea.[39] *Animation politique* combined the aesthetics of folklore with the spectacle of popular dance music whose lyrics praised Mobutu and the one-party state.[40] Life in Zaire was saturated by *animation politique*, captivating local audiences and dominating state-controlled channels of communication. In a study devoted specifically to this subject, Gazungil Sang'Amin Kapalanga wrote:

> *Animation politique* penetrated the rhythm of parties, work, and leisure... [and] located in the subconscious of the [Zairian] people, it ultimately created certain reflexes and attitudes in relation to situations that people experience every day: we hum the melody of an *animation politique* song while working, we go to parties with the songs and dances of *animation politique*, in front of a radio or television, the whole family sings and dances with the *animateur*, the funeral procession coming from or going to the cemetery shakes with the rhythm of *animation politique* in a hearse that becomes a space of play and a musical instrument that is played by any number of hands.[41]

From the start of the programme in the early 1970s until the end of the 1980s, tens of thousands of Zairians were involved in the organisation and execution of *animation politique*, which occupied over one third of total screen time on television.[42] An-

imation politique was a way to express loyalty to Mobutu and wholehearted support for the Zairian government, but many Zairians saw *animation politique* as a type of submission to and oppression by a corrupt government. In *Oyé Oyé*, Magema explores the specific experience of women in this context, employing the contemporary video as a critical gloss on the edited archival footage.

Men and women both performed in *animation* troupes, but the voices of women have been largely overlooked by scholars.[43] Lisa Gilman's study on performing women in Malawi is one of the only studies to examine gender, statehood and embodied performance.[44] More recently, Lesley Nicole Braun and Yolanda Covington-Ward have turned to women's experiences in Zaire's *animation* troupes.[45] Both Braun and Covington-Ward conducted interviews with ex-performers who were recruited as young women. Many emphasised the significance of coercion in their recruitment.[46] Youth who were jobless and out of school were targeted by the state, as were single women who had one or two children. They had to stop whatever work they were doing and heed the call to perform across the country, without any pay offered as compensation.[47] Gender effected the likelihood of enlistment as boys, in the 1970s and even today, were disproportionately more likely than girls to be enrolled in either primary or secondary school and more likely to find employment.[48] Girls and young women were structurally disadvantaged and more likely to be targeted as the "idle" subset of the population who were to situate their bodies in service of the state.

The sexual exploitation of young women in the Mobutu era extended to *animation* troupes whose services were often offered to visiting statesmen.[49] Through these encounters, Covington-Ward argued that women in Zaire were expected to sacrifice themselves for the country over and over again.[50] She advances the construction of citizenship as gendered since its origins in ancient Greece, where citizenship was based on the exclusion of women, and argues that women's experience in the *animation* troupes was an example of what she calls "gendered embodied citizenship" as in "the everyday imposition of coercive states on women's bodies in ways that differ from the expected activities of male citizens".[51] However, almost fifteen years before Braun and Covington-Ward, Magema turned to the young girls and women involved in the *animation* performances. In *Oyé Oyé*, she adopted television broadcasts of the women's performances from Michel's *Mobutu, roi du Zaïre* and edited them together to play on loop, as if stretched to abstraction in a way that sheds a light on Congolese women's labour. The video offers a consideration onto the complexity of the women's participation in these state spectacles, as well as the endurance of colonial ideology long after independence.

Mobutu, roi du Zaïre

Released in 1999, Michel's *Mobutu, roi du Zaïre* turned to the Congo after colonialism. The documentary film debuted at the same time as the re-emergence of colonial memories in Belgium. *Mobutu, roi du Zaïre* examined Mobutu's thirty-two years of dictatorship in the Congo through interviews with witnesses, external actors and experts alongside archival footage, photographs and a contemporary commentary. The film is comprised of three parts: it opens with "*La conquête du pouvoir*" ("The conquest of power") that centres on the years of 1960 to 1969; the second act, "*Le maître du jeu*" ("The master of the game"), covers 1970 to 1990 and the third act, "*La fin d'un règne*" ("The end of a reign"), travels from 1990 to 1997. The documentary is itself a collation of archival footage drawn from various television and radio stations, including Belgarchive, Radio Télévision Belge de la Communauté Française and Vlaamse Radio- en Televisieomroeporganisatie in Belgium; Radio Télévision Nationale Congolaise in the Congo; France 2 and TF1 in France; Télévision Suisse Romande in Switzerland; ITN Archive and Associated Press Television News in the United Kingdom and NBC in the United States.

The song that was adopted by Magema for *Oyé Oyé* – Axel Mbouze's "Papa Mobutu" – starts each episode of *Mobutu, roi du Zaïre*, while the archival broadcast clips of the women play during the documentary's opening credits. They also serve to separate witness accounts and aid changes in subject. Here, their original colours are evident: the women wear vibrant green textiles, the same colour as the country's flag that was introduced when it was renamed Zaire in 1971. The textiles are emblazoned with a picture of Mobutu and his wife Bobi Ladawa dressed in white against a background of a red heart. In the clip of Mobutu, he wears a grey *abacost* with white diamond shapes. His neckerchief is styled in the colours of the country, yellow, red and green, and these colours are reproduced in the raffia-style skirts worn by the group of dancing women. After the opening credits in *Mobutu, roi du Zaïre*, a man screams to the crowd, "*Mobutu, oyé!*", which the crowd confirms with the call "*oyé!*". He shouts to the crowd again, "*Maman Présidente, oyé!*", to which they answer in agreement "*oyé!*". This phrase, as adopted by the title of Magema's video, was ubiquitous in the Mobutu era, frequently heard as "*Mobutu Oyé*", as in "Long Live Mobutu".

In *Oyé Oyé*, Magema transforms the archival footage from its world of vivid colour to black and white. Gone are the vibrant greens and the gold leopard skin that characterise the era of *authenticité*. In doing so, Magema exploits a specific set of connotations associated with black and white. Monochrome on screen evokes early cinema, a world that precedes the existence of colour, calling up silent actors and old Hollywood. Newsreel footage of historic events is similarly evoked, from Hindenburg and the Depression to World War II. The archival clips are grainy, as if inflected by the process of being reproduced for *Mobutu, roi du Zaïre* and then again for Magema's video. There is a certain anachronism associated with the deployment of black and white in the video as it suggests a separation from the contemporary. Moments in the country's history are levelled to an invocation of a bygone age. However, there are only fifteen or so years that separate the video of Magema on the opposite screen from some of the archival footage. Her employment of black and white speaks to Mobutu's campaign of *authenticité*, which attempted to take Zaire back in time to supposedly traditional "African" values. Monochrome simultaneously conveys an opposition to the contemporary and the supposed changes entailed by the course of time. The "archival" women in the footage are denied a contemporary colour existence, as they were in the tenets of the *authenticité*. They are trapped in a colourless world.

In Michel's *Mobutu, roi du Zaïre,* men alone offer the witness accounts, contemporary commentary and expertise. These contributions include Larry Devlin, the CIA station chief in 1960s Congo; Sakombi Inongo, the Minister of Information in Mobutu's government; Alfred Cahen, the Belgian Ambassador to Zaire and Aubert Mukendi, the Congolese mathematician, amongst others. There is a short section where the various commentators speak about Mobutu's wives, Marie-Antoinette and Bobi Ladawa. Women function as peripheral adjuncts and background material in the documentary. They are charged with the task of opening each episode and easing transitions from one subject to another. Men in *Mobutu, roi du Zaïre* are constructed as the sole actors and agents in the country, ranging from King Leopold II and King Baudouin of Belgium to Lumumba and Mobutu and, again, as the contemporary voices that guide the viewer through history. They provoke and effect the country's course of events and simultaneously advance the structure of the documentary itself. Narratives around the Congo similarly construct the country through a series of male political figures, take the title of Georges Nzongola-Ntalaja's book, *The Congo from Leopold to Kabila: A People's History*, or Leo Zeilig's *Lumumba: Africa's Lost Leader*.[52] As Anne McClintock has observed, in the drama of the state, men stand for progressive agents of time, forward-looking and embodying a principle of discontinuity, while women are the atavistic and authentic conveyors of tradition, backward-looking and organic.[53] However, Magema challenges the exclusion of women from historical and political narratives. As we shall see, she extracts the clips of the women from *Mobutu, roi du Zaïre* in order to construct an alternative feminised account of the country's past and present.

Decapitation

Beheaded by the top edge of the screen, Magema's torso is the focal point of the contemporary video in which her Zarian school uniform takes centre stage. Her suggestion of execution and decapitation is echoed in the archival clips on the other screen. Heads were cut off by the various television camera crews from whom Michel and subsequently Magema adopted the clips. Hips covered in layers of vine embellished textile are captured gyrating by the camera [fig. 2.6]. Slowly, the camera ascends, videoing the torsos of the other women on stage. In the 1981 article "Castration or Decapitation?", Hélène Cixous, whose writings Magema encountered as a student in Paris, described the way women suffer from a "decapitation anxiety".[54] There were several examples of women's decapitation already existent in Cixious and Magema's own French culture. Headlessness was often the state of women in surrealism, for example, the Paris-based artists, Max Ernst's collage book *La Femme 100 têtes* (1929) or Man Ray's photograph from the same year of a headless body wrapped in plastic. Heads, for the surrealists, were the vessels in which the dreams of men were contained, while women were reduced to anonymous body parts.[55]

To illustrate decapitation anxiety, Cixous turned to "a little Chinese story" taken from General Sun Tse's *The Art of War* in which the Emperor of China challenged the General to train the imperial wives to wheel and march, just like male soldiers.[56] At first, the women refused to obey "the language of the drumbeat", as they fell about laughing rather than taking the exercise seriously, submitting, in Cixous's words, "feminine disorder".[57] Sun Tse immediately beheaded the two wives who were captains, and, thereafter, the other wives obeyed the code – they were transformed into automatons. The women's supposed gain in this exchange is their eventual ability to be perfect soldiers, which is of very little profit to them, suggesting rather an obedience and sub-

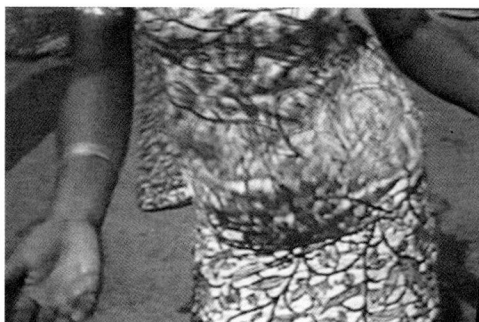

Figure 2.6: Michèle Magema, video stills from *Oyé Oyé*, 2002.
© ADAGP, Paris and DACS, London 2021. (Plate 8, p. 201-202)

ordination. Nothing has actually been given to the women, who are automatons threatened by death. Not only is the feminine silenced by a masculine code, "the language of the drumbeat", but, as Cixous asserts, a phallocentric culture "beheads" women by silencing their experience. To be silent, to lack subjectivity, is to be decapitated.

In Zaire, Mobutu's government enacted strategies that attempted to silence women and, in *Oyé Oyé*, it is Mobutu's head that is captured close-up several times and whose voice waits to be amplified by multiple microphones. Independence in the Congo saw the spread of women's organisations from 1960 to 1965.[58] The majority of women in Kinshasa belonged to some sort of organisation after 1960, and these organisations were increasingly feminist, nationalist and interethnic. Most organisations were started by women with little education and the groups were compromised of women speaking vernacular languages as opposed to French. These groups also organised for various political causes through 1965. However, they were suppressed by the MPR as soon as Mobutu took control of the country. Women's groups were prohibited, and, subsequently, a couple of women's organisations were created by the MPR, which were closely overseen by the government. Women therefore had to conform to groups created by the government, which lacked the same criticality as the ones constructed previously.

In *Oyé Oyé*, Magema's arms systematically swing back and forth in coordination with her strides. One two, one two – the artist's tempo is consistent, she obeys "the language of the drumbeat" so to speak. On the other screen, the historical women and young girls succinctly execute their actions as subscribed by the state's campaigns. Individuals concede to the structure of the group: the young girls stride obediently in the street cavalcade and their shoes stay within the thick white bands that mark the street [fig. 2.1]. The girls' scarves are wrapped with care, their collars lay flat and their socks sit just above the ankle. They each grasp onto the left side

Figure 2.7: Michèle Magema, video stills from *Oyé Oyé*, 2002.
© ADAGP, Paris and DACS, London 2021. (Plate 8, p. 201-202)

of their skirts and swing their right arm as they advance ahead. The women in the raffia skirts turn, spring and clap several times in tight coordination [fig. 2.7]. The group dressed in the vine-ornamented textiles shake their fingers and walk over to the opposite side of the stage where they start the same choreography all over again [fig. 2.8]. Practised weeks in advance, these are succinct yet subtle actions that are learned together and executed for the event, like the wives of the king in the story detailed by Cixous.[59] The women's lack of autonomy as they concede to the structures of the group is emphasised across the two screens that comprise *Oyé Oyé*. Magema's actions are in dialogue with the women and young girls on the other screen as she stalls whenever Mobutu appears. The contemporary video is seen in connection with the archival screen so that we are encouraged to conceive of the decapitated Magema as tied to the clusters of past women. Though separated, she is allied with the group. Furthermore, the way in which we engage with the archival video operates through the structure of the group. The camera often scans the various *animation* events. Moving from one woman to another, we are compelled to conjecture on the actions of a woman already seen through that of others on whom the camera swiftly turns. The women across the two screens create a whole that shifts together.

This compliance and lack of subjectivity is simultaneously suggested through clothing. Interestingly, the set-up of the video evokes the aesthetic language of portraiture as Magema is isolated against a white background. Portraiture conventionally expresses the autonomous subjecthood of its sitter and a sense of self conveyed through props and an engagement with the camera. In contrast, Magema's school uniform suggests a submissive compliance echoed in the archival clips through the state-sanctioned textiles worn by the women. The blue and white of the school uniform was used by the Zairian government to identify children in public space, again emphasising the way in which the individual is subsumed by the logic of the

Figure 2.8: Michèle Magema, video stills from *Oyé Oyé*, 2002.
© ADAGP, Paris and DACS, London 2021. (Plate 8, p. 201-202)

group. Writing on the intersections between independence, nationalism and gender, Elleke Boehmer has observed that the figure of the woman in the drama of the state is typically conveyed as generic.[60] Women are interchangeable in a way that suggests decapitation as their singularity is sacrificed, while men, on the contrary, are often individualised, for example, a John Bull, an Uncle Sam or a Saleem Sinai.[61] Exemplifying the apogee of masculine individuation, Mobutu appears framed by the edges of the screen. He is seen in complete specificity, as emphasised in his signature leopard skin, a costume prohibited to the subjects of Zaire.

However, Magema simultaneously provides a space for thinking about bodily opposition to the coercive structures of Mobutism. There is an antagonism set up between the two screens as Magema's torso confronts Mobutu. The contemporary video of the artist offers a critical gloss on, or disruption of, the archival footage. Magema's strides occur at various speeds, from the assiduously slow to the swift and expeditious, and they are at times over-exaggerated. Returning to Cixous, the women's laughter is described as disruptive to the masculine regimental order. In the same way that the women had laughed at the General's commands, Magema's strides parody the expectations of the state and a submission to its order. In doing so, Magema suggests the existence of an opposition to coercive structures while they are simultaneously obeyed in a superficial way. Though she complies with a dress code, as an adult, the Zairian school uniform is at once too short on Magema in terms of the Western outfits banned by Mobutu. However, Cixous contends that the women who obey the orders of the General lose their heads: "if they don't actually lose their heads by the sword, *they only keep them on the condition that they lose them* – lose them, that is, to complete silence, into automatons".[62] But Magema makes a case against the complete automation of the women in the archival footage who comply with the orders of the state. While they may seem to experience a decapitation of sorts through their obedience, apropos Cixous, Magema opens up the possibility that their minds remained free, even as they complied with an outward performance of submission.

Independence for whom?

The various groups of women in *Oyé Oyé* embody the philosophies of the state. Images of Mobutu and Bobi Ladawa, as previously observed, appear on their textiles. Raffia skirts are worn in complicity with the government's prohibition of Western clothing. Bandeau tops are constructed from "African" style textiles and adorned with a triangle of the country's flag that shakes as the women twirl. There is a crowd of women who wave flags steadily from side to side, while the group dressed in vine-ornamented textiles commemorate the state through a series of celebratory hairdos exemplified by stacked curls and standing spikes. The women in *Oyé Oyé* come, in effect, to stand in for the country, whose ideology is played out on their bodies. This phenomenon of women being representative of a body politic is echoed in Magema's dress where the sash is evocative the country's current flag, suggesting the endurance of this conflation.

To take up the phrase coined in the eponymously titled 1983 collection of essays edited by Eric Hobsbawm and Terence Ranger, Mobutu's Zaire operated in terms of an "invention of tradition" as in "a process of formalisation and ritualisation, characterised by reference to the past, if only by imposing repetition" – a repetition that is emphasised by the women who perform folklore-inspired dances on loop in the video.[63] An "authentic" Congolese culture was promoted in terms of cuisine, clothing and language, while a flag, anthem and currency were all established to define the emergent state. Isidore Ndaywel è Nziem has referred to Hobsbawm and Ranger's concept of "invention" when discussing Mobutu's seizure of power and subsequent administration.[64] The term was again taken up by Johan Lagae and Kim De Raedt to describe Mobutu's *"recours à l'authenticité"*.[65] However, there is a gendered component tied to the "invention of tradition" that is overlooked in these accounts. For example, Gilman linked the establishment of tradition in the emergent Malawian state with women's performances.[66] Women were gendered in such a way that they were closely associated with African or "traditional" cultures.[67] In *Oyé Oyé*, Magema makes visible the central role of women in the invention of Zairian tradition.

Hobsbawm and Ranger's conception of an "invention of tradition" is intimately related to the creation of modern nation states as developed by Benedict Anderson.[68] His "imagined communities" entail a shared experience of tradition. While Anderson has described print capitalism as the origins of communality, McClintock argues that this system of community was accessible only to a small literate elite.[69] Alternatively, Magema's video turns our attention to the performances staged by women dressed in "traditional" outfits and textiles depicting Mobutu, which proliferated across Zaire. They were an experience witnessed in arenas and watched everyday on television and, in this sense, these women were incredibly visible.[70] Nationalisms, as McClintock contends, are created through state-conscripted spectacles, taking shape through visual organisation, and these spectacles in Zaire were largely the purview of women.[71] The groups of women culled by Magema from *Mobutu, roi du Zaïre* conjure a sense of collectivity that was in keeping with Zaire's campaign of *authenticité* that is here repurposed and recontextualised. Specific hairstyles, textiles and choreography were once mobilised to construct an imagined community.

While the emergent Zairian state depended on these performances for its creation and its claim to authority through tradition, it simultaneously oppressed women. The

Zairian propaganda outlets supplied many contradictions around women.⁷² Speaking at the conclusion of a symposium on women in Zaire on 20 May 1975, Mobutu proclaimed that his takeover of the government in 1965 had liberated the women of Zaire: "November 24, 1965 was not only the date that marked the beginning of our total independence... but equally the start of the liberation of women in all forms".⁷³ However, just seven years later in another speech given at the third conference of the MPR:

> We want to recognise in the Zairian mother the rights that give her the quality of equal partner to men. But it remains understood that... there will always be in each family one boss... the boss... is he who wears the pants. Our female citizens must also understand that, accepting it with a smile and a revolutionary submission.⁷⁴

Women or *les mamans zaïroises* were submitted to the authority of Mobutu as *le pere de la nation* and then again to their husbands. The symbolic idealisation of motherhood in Zaire achieved very little for actual women, as it further entrenched men's authority, for example, a woman's engagement with the state was only achieved indirectly through a male head of household on whose identity card she appeared.⁷⁵ Male privilege was accordingly enshrined by the state as it sought to gain control over women who had been empowered through anticolonial struggles, such as the various woman's organisations that were shut down in Zaire.

Feminist scholars have long challenged the liberation of women in postcolonial nation states. In an essay entitled "How Could Things Fall Apart For Whom They Were Not Together?" (1994), Florence Stratton confronts the underlying assumptions of Chinua Achebe's *Things Fall Apart* (1958) from a feminist perspective. She writes that "things could not fall apart for African women because they never had been and never would be together".⁷⁶ The various celebrations of the state after colonialism's end share the same set of tensions. Postcolonial states did very little to change the subordinated status of women and the circumstance of their everyday existences. Even a leader as gender aware as Samora Machel of Mozambique enforced the sexual division of labour by calling solely on women to clean up the streets of Maputo after independence celebrations.⁷⁷ Boehmer has argued that "Mother Africa may have been declared free, but the mothers of Africa remained manifestly oppressed".⁷⁸ My reading of *Oyé Oyé* is in keeping with Boehmer's critique. The women in the video, rather than being "set free", appear to be caught in the same repetitive circles of activity. As the video cuts backwards, the women in the bandeau tops and raffia skirts clap for a second and then again for a third time. There is a "stuckness" exhibited in these actions, and the video itself as it plays on loop, that challenges the transformation and liberation evoked by the rhetoric accompanying the newly independent state and its apologists. The video, edited by Magema, streams the same clips again and again as if enacting the static state of affairs in a country that endlessly depended on women for its symbolic creation and yet from which they were simultaneously excluded.

Loss interlude

Briefly shifting away from *Oyé Oyé*, I want to turn again to Baloji's *Mémoire* to consider its gendered assumptions. Out of the thirty photomontages that comprise the series, there are only two that transpose archival photographs of women onto the contemporary sites. In *Untitled 7* [fig. 2.9], seven bare-breasted women wrapped in fraying, striped textiles stand with two children for the camera. One of the children is blurred ever so slightly, suggesting a reluctance to stay still. The women's brows are significantly tensed, as they appear solemn with downcast eyes. In *Untitled 6* [fig. 2.10], an-

Figure 2.9: Sammy Baloji, *Untitled 7* from *Memoire* series, 2006. Archival digital photograph on satin matte paper, 60 × 191.79 cm. (Plate 9, p. 203)

Figure 2.10: Sammy Baloji, *Untitled 6* from *Memoire* series, 2006. Archival digital photograph on satin matte paper, 60 × 170 cm. (Plate 10, p. 204)

other group of eight women stand closely together, their arms touch and occasionally wrap around each other, while the background shows a slagheap constructed from two contemporary photographs. Legs wrap around the sides of some of the women in the group, calling our attention to the small children carried on their backs.

As I discussed in the first chapter, conceptions of "loss" traditionally construct the way in which Baloji's series is viewed. The dilapidated contemporary background now replaces the once successful sites where many Congolese men were employed. As previously mentioned, Jewsiewicki has argued that *Mémoire* expresses the feelings of loss experienced by Congolese youth due to the closure of the sites.[79] Modernity, according to Jewsiewicki, was achieved through the salaried work offered by Union Minière, as their employees were able to access the economy and take advantage of its services through their wages.[80] He wrote: "Deprived of an active workforce, the industrial landscape is haunted by its ghost" – the ghost of the *kazi*, as in the Swahili word for salaried work. The series, Jewsiewicki alleges, grieves for the wages that the sites once offered. While I have argued that this overwhelming sense of loss and grief is not all that is pictured in *Mémoire*, I want to turn now to a specific erasure that seems to characterise both the series and its critical reception. In the various accounts of *Mémoire*, the perceived suffering is centred on the impoverished contemporary context and the assumption of the contrasting wealth that colonial times once offered. Men are exclusively constructed as the objects of our sympathy and the victims of the state. But I would like to argue that there is another site of grief represented by the women from the archival photographs. Theirs is the labour that was doubly displaced in the country's transition to a colonial state and then again by the gender politics of decolonisation that denied women access to a new modernity.

The civilising apparatus of colonialism obstructed women's access to and control of the land, and this change is exemplified in the structures of Union Minière. Men were the ones enlisted to serve the colonial economy. While the company had previously excluded women from the sites, marriage was employed as a strategy in 1933 to compel workers to stay in their employment. Union Minière enforced men's authority over women through their system of allowances, in which, for example, any stipends were given to men, who were accountable for the conduct of their wives and children.[81] Furthermore, Union Minière emphasised "freeing the woman from her village chores": if a woman's work was lightened, she was also deprived of a certain amount of economic autonomy, "an effective strategy for domesticating the woman".[82] In 1959, a company pamphlet stressed that the man is "the head of his household" and that "it is the husband who rules, not the wife".[83] And yet the colonial economy simultaneously depended on the work of the women. In 1928, Union Minière set up a series of *zones maraichères* ("gardening areas") around the compounds, and, by 1933, the workers' wives were expected to supplement the weekly food allowances provided by the employers.[84] Many women also ended up selling cooked food, alcohol or drinks or sewed and knitted to augment their family's wages.[85] The success of the colonial economic system was contingent on this support, as the wages given to the workers were too small to support a family. The wage conditions were therefore only viable through the so-called subsistence sector, which directly subsidised the colonial economy.[86]

The representation of the women in *Mémoire* seems to complicate the temporal orientation of photography. In *Camera Lucida* (1981), Barthes wrote, "the name of Photography's *noeme* will therefore be: 'that-has-been'".[87] Mourning the loss of his mother, Barthes saw the photograph as constitutive of "that-has-been". He continued: "For the *noeme* 'That-has-been' was possible only on the day when a scientific circumstance (the discovery that silver halogens were sensitive to light) made it possible to recover and print directly the luminous rays emitted by a variously lighted object".[88] The tense of "that-has-been" is created by the photograph. However, I want to suggest that this tense of "that-has-been" occurs *before* the colonial photograph. The women in the archival photographs employed by Baloji had already experienced a series of changes that led to their appearance before the camera, such as the erasure of female-led agriculture and their construction as wives. These changes exemplify a situation "that-had-been" prior to the arrival of colonialism, and they are the photograph's condition of possibility: the women arrive at Union Minière as the wives of the employees on whom they are dependent for earnings and the photograph is accordingly captured. Loss had already occurred, predating the photograph. Writing on a photograph of the young Lewis Payne who was hanged in Washington in 1865 for his involvement in the conspiracy to assassinate President Abraham Lincoln, Barthes argued: "But the *punctum* is: *he is going to die*".[89] He continued: "I shudder, like Winnicott's psychotic patient, *over a catastrophe which has already occurred*. Whether or not the subject is already dead, every photograph is this catastrophe".[90] However, in the colonial photographs, a casualty has already occurred. The colonial catastrophe, which attempted to subordinate women, is the source of the photographs.

The casualty encountered through the women in *Mémoire* seemingly continues over to the present-day. In 2015, the exhibition *Beauté Congo 1926–2015: Congo Kitoko* was staged in Paris at the Cartier Foundation. Lauded by the catalogue as the largest display of twentieth-century Congolese art ever, the exhibition was comprised of vivid large-scale oil paintings as well as sculpture and photography. However, from the forty-one artists exhibited, there was only one woman who was cited as the wife of the early twentieth-century artist Albert Lubaki. Notably, Magema was excluded from the exhibition. The French curator André Magnin was confronted several times about the absence of women artists in *Beauté Congo*. In an article from the *New York Times*, Magnin said, "I'm sure they exist... Unfortunately I haven't met them".[91] To *Jeune Afrique*, Magnin explained: "As for women, I have not had the chance to meet a woman artist in Congo in thirty years".[92] Based in France, Magema's exclusion from *Beauté Congo* is even more significant given her geographical proximity. The absence of women is further emphasised by the artwork that Magnin chose to exhibit, several of which conveyed titillating and eroticised women. Breasts and exaggerated behinds occupied the space. Masculinist assumptions evaded the exhibition, as Magnin seems to imbibe the gendered terms of the postcolonial moment as well as the culture of European modernity. The significance of women's exclusion in *Beauté Congo* is perhaps beyond comprehension for the curator. Magnin also overlooked the ongoing efforts in the Congo to spotlight women artists, for example, in 2014, Robinah Nansubuga curated the exhibition *Women Without Borders* in Kinshasa, showing the works of women artists from Central and East Africa. Magnin's gender blindness means that he skips over the origins of women's exclusion and the historical separations of labour established by Belgian colonialism and perpetuated long beyond the decolonial moment.

The grief that I perceive to be thematised in *Mémoire* is charted in *Oyé Oyé* across Mobutu's Zaire and is again constitutive of Magema's own contemporary experience as a woman artist. The apparatus of colonialism seized the control of agriculture from Congolese women who were excluded from wage-earning employment. Independence did little to change the situation of women. In *Oyé Oyé*, the archival clips are changed by the artist from their vivid colours to a greyscale world in which the women appear to be trapped. There is a constant sense of cuts in the video, from the white stripe that severs Magema's torso on the one screen to the fragmentation of the Congolese women on the other. Taking on the colonial view of agriculture, Zaire further excluded women from the economy. They were confined to a series of archetypes who had to perform for, and arguably construct, a state from which they are excluded. *Oyè Oyé* challenges the violent and systematic erasure of Congolese women.

Maintenance

In Michel's *Mobutu, roi du Zaïre*, the archival clips of the women open the various episodes. They gently introduce the viewer to the oppressive, corrupt and violent world of Mobutu's Zaire. The Congolese women are employed as a background for Michel's opening comments and the title of the documentary film. Throughout *Mobutu, roi du Zaïre*, the women serve to ease the transitions from one segment to another. For example, the group in the vine textiles aid a change in subject as considered by Alfred Cahen, the Belgian ambassador to Zaire, and Hugues LeClercq, the Belgian president's economic advisor. The two commentators speak on Zaire's wealth in copper and Mobutu's investment in the construction of Inga dams, two hydroelectric dams connected to Inga Falls on the Congo River, in the 1970s and 1980s. After the women's appearance, the subject of discussion shifts to Mobutu's authoritarianism and the concept of Mobutism as relayed by Cahen. Functioning as decorative cyphers, the women offer solace from the weighty topics explored by Cahen and LeClercq. In the segment with LeClercq, the one-time economic advisor is seated in an office with a window through which we see the overcast Belgian winter weather. On the windowsill and a stand nearby, there are three African sculptures, all of which portray the female form with breasts exaggerated in conical shapes. Like the women in the archival clips, they too comprise the background as they set the scene for the advisor's expertise on the Congo.

However, in *Oyé Oyé*, there is a shift that occurs: the women from the archival clips do not just operate as background material or connective tropes but are spotlighted and highlighted by Magema. They are thus brought into visibility and, as I will argue, so is their labour. In the absence of the vivid colours from the original clips in Michel's *Mobutu, roi du Zaïre*, our attention centres on the actions of the women who perform on loop. Their activity is emphasised in the video through the cuts that skip backwards so that the same steps are shown several times over. Hands are expressive, swinging in the street cavalcade and extending in an open-ended gesture from the group with Mobutu and Bobi Ladawa emblazoned on their textiles. Hands clap and clap again and wave flags, they twinkle and welcome Mobutu in the shot of the crowd captured from a speeding car [fig. 2.11]. Hands wrinkled from age turn towards the sky [fig. 2.6], while the camera subsequently shifts to others in the group who clap and shake their fingers [fig. 2.8].

Figure 2.11: Michèle Magema, video stills from *Oyé Oyé*, 2002.
© ADAGP, Paris and DACS, London 2021.

Figure 2.12: Michèle Magema, video stills from *Oyé Oyé*, 2002.
© ADAGP, Paris and DACS, London 2021.

Dance is foregrounded in the video as an endless labour performed for the state. Moreover, the actions of the women start to exceed the space of the choreographic. Hands are evocative of the labour in general assigned to women in Mobutu's Zaire, the ones charged to cooking, cleaning and care, that service the wage earner. The occasional, aesthetic and visible labour of the women captured in the archival clips prompts a consideration of the less visible everyday domestic labour charged to these same hands ever since the transformations in structures of gender enforced by the colonial government.

Motherhood seems equally central to the video. In the shot of the crowd from the car, the men and women amalgamate to one shifting expanse. The only visible whole is a child dressed in white elevated above the crowd [fig. 2.12]. Maternity was the sole character of women stressed in official statements from the government. This characteristic is emphasised in the clips chosen by Magema and their employment in *Mobutu, roi du Zaïre* as tools for solace. Care, love and affection as well as childrearing are accordingly charged to the work of Congolese women. Hips are central in the video as if to emphasise women's capacity for childbirth. The camera stalls on the textiles that adorn a woman's torso [fig. 2.6]. These textiles are gathered and layered, creating a sense of generativity, while their vine ornamentation simultaneously speaks to a kind of fecundity. Hips serve as a centre of gravity from which all their other actions originate. Movement seems to extend upwards through the body, as the hips of the women dressed in the raffia skirts dictate when they rotate and clap. The group with Mobutu and Bobi Ladawa emblazoned on their textiles swing side to side; their own textiles are the carriers of other Zairians.

Through these repetitive and automaton-like actions, the video engages the extensive tradition of women's labour that constitutes the background of everyday operations in Zaire. The steady onslaught of labour ascribed to women has been described by the American artist Mierle Laderman Ukeles in the "Manifesto for Maintenance Art" (1969). She wrote:

> ...clean your desk, wash the dishes, clean the floor, wash your clothes, wash your toes, change the baby's diaper, finish the report, correct the typos, mend the fence, keep the customer happy, throw out the stinking garbage, watch out don't put things in your nose, what shall I wear, I have no sox, pay your bills, don't litter, save string, wash your hair, change the sheets, go to the store, I'm out of perfume, say it again – he doesn't understand, seal it again – it leaks, go to work, this art is dusty, clear the table, call him again, flush the toilet, stay young.[93]

Though speaking from another geographical and cultural context, Ukeles's words echo in Mobutu's Zaire. Guided by the tenets of Christianity, the colonial education system siphoned off women's work to the household. Maintenance comprises, as Lisa Baraitser wrote, "the durational practices that keep 'things' going: objects, selves, systems, hopes, ideals, networks, communities, relationships, institutions".[94] The notion of "maintenance" offers a lens through which to engage with the concealed exertions of women in Zaire. To the series of chores described by Ukeles, we could add in the context of Zaire the *animation* performances that construct the state. From clip to clip, the women in the video commemorate Zaire, and, through their various coiffures, textiles and coordinated actions, they aid in the construction of the country. They are charged as the carriers of *authenticité*, as Zaire's existence, which is consolidated through *animation politique*, is contingent on them. On a more physical level, the survival of Zaire depended on the women's capacity for childbirth.[95] The acts of sex and care for offspring continued the social and symbolic conditions of the Zairian state.

* * *

Maintenance is described by Baraitser as "the durational practices that keep 'things' going", and, with this definition in mind, I wish to explore another aspect of women's labour. In *Oyé Oyé*, the women's textiles tell a story themselves. Images of Mobutu and Bobi Ladawa, as we have already seen, are emblazoned on their chests, spines and thighs. The women offer a series of angles from which to view the couple who appear as if they are dressed in wedding attire. With puffed sleeves and a clinched waist, Bobi Ladawa's mermaid style gown is synonymous with 1980s fashion, while Mobutu is seen in a white suit and his signature leopard skin. The

Congolese women relay a story of a ceremony entwined with the state. Finding love again after the death of his first wife Marie-Antoinette in 1977, as the official state account would construct, Mobutu married Bobi Ladawa on 1 May 1980 on the eve of a visit by Pope John Paul II.[96] Mid-stride, the couple advance hand in hand: Mobutu walks ahead while one of Bobi Ladawa's arms swings forward. This depiction could be seen as an analogy to the country's advancements and its state of togetherness.

With the privilege of hindsight, as when the video was produced by Magema in 2002, the textiles could also be seen to transmit a story of the state and its collapse. Retrospectively, the women's textiles communicate the abandonment of the country's citizens, the same ones that waved flags side to side and twisted, twirled and clapped in the service of the state. In the early 2000s, political discourse in the Congo relied heavily on the image of Mobutu as a foil to responsible leadership and civic duty.[97] Mobutu and Bobi Ladawa expropriated the wealth of Zaire. Resources and profits were once again siphoned off to the elite. The couple's togetherness comes to stand in for their shared corruption of the state and its assets, a togetherness that cumulated in exile to Morocco in 1997 and led to their separation as Mobutu died that same year while Bobi Ladawa absconded to Europe.

There are other accounts that come to our attention through the women. The textiles themselves engage a specific tradition in the Congo. Though the ones seen in the video were likely produced in a textile factory abroad, they are embedded in the cultural heritage of Zaire. Indeed, Mobutu's government promoted Kuba culture in the creation of Zairian identity.[98] In the seventeenth century, the Bushoong settled in the Kasai region. Under the guidance of their kings, these settlers established the Kuba Kingdom whose thriving economy was based on the cultivation of the raffia palm, which comprises the skirts worn by the women in *Oyé Oyé* [fig. 2.7]. The Kuba treated the raffia palm in order to create textiles. The creation of skirts started with a coarse cloth made from raffia fibre and woven by men on simple wood looms. Beaten to a smooth linen, the skirts were worked on collectively by the women in the group who subsequently added their unique repertoire of embroidered appliqué, patchwork and cut pile designs of largely geometric designs. These textiles were worn by royalty for ceremonial events. The embellishment executed by Kuba women is evoked in the ornamentation on the Zairian textiles. The vines create a series of jagged shapes, while there is an engagement with colour and layering in the textiles that project Mobutu and Bobi Ladawa. Dressed in white, the couple is emphasised against an opaque background, which is surrounded by a series of geometric shapes. This sense of weaving and embroidery is echoed in the contemporary video for which Magema recreated the Zairian school uniform she sported as a child. In *Oyé Oyé*, Magema's own ancestry in Zaire is engaged, and, in this sense, she continues a tradition of which she is comprised. We could conceive of the textile-clad women in *Oyé Oyé* as well as Magema as performing the labour of ancestry and tradition.

Maintenance involves the transmission of cultural practices and their concomitant emotional and physical labour. This evocation of tradition is evocative of a photograph of Pauline Opango, the wife of Lumumba, printed in the American weekly *Time* magazine on 24 February 1961 and subsequently reworked by South African artist Marlene Dumas. In 1982, Dumas deployed the photograph of Opango in the collage *Three Women and I* and again three decades later in two separate paintings entitled *The Widow* (2013) [fig. 2.13]. The photograph captures Opango after Lumumba's assassination [fig. 2.14]. Bare-breasted and shoeless, Opango led a ritual of mourning through the streets of Léopoldville. In doing so, she protested, as Tamar Garb has argued, against the Belgians and their culpability in Lumumba's assassination as well as the circumstance in which she had found herself as an African woman.[99]

Lumumba had attempted to circumscribe Opango to the tenets of the *évolué* class. The *évolués*, as described by V.Y. Mudimbe, were Africans from various ethnic and cultural backgrounds, seen to be "making the transition from ethnic customs to the new culture" and to have taken on European sartorial and social codes.[100] Acutely aware of appearance, the *évolués* were clean cut and had a "European" sense of style. Their visual signifiers were the suit, tie and derby, and they expected their wives to wear the female equivalent. In 1948, the Belgian administration offered a solution to the *évolué*'s aspirations, the *carte de mérite civique*. Any man who was educated, who had sworn off polygamy and sorcery and had embraced Western ways was eligible to apply for this identity. Through the certificate, the *évolué* was supposedly given access to European spaces. However, its advantages were considered, by aspirant Congolese, to be small, and, therefore, in 1952, the *carte d'immatriculation* was offered, which in theory equalised the *évolué* to the European, though far from it in actuality. Stringent conditions were created for obtaining such a card. During the application process, an inspector was allowed to pay surprise visits to the family home to see whether they lived in a truly "civilised" style. Lumumba obtained the *carte d'immatriculation* in 1954 after an original attempt two years earlier.

As can be deduced, the *évolué* was always a man, women only qualified as wives.[101] The gap between the genders was sizeable. Men were educated and worked for an employer, while women were uneducated, jobless and lacked the same French language skills that their husbands had acquired.[102] The wives of the

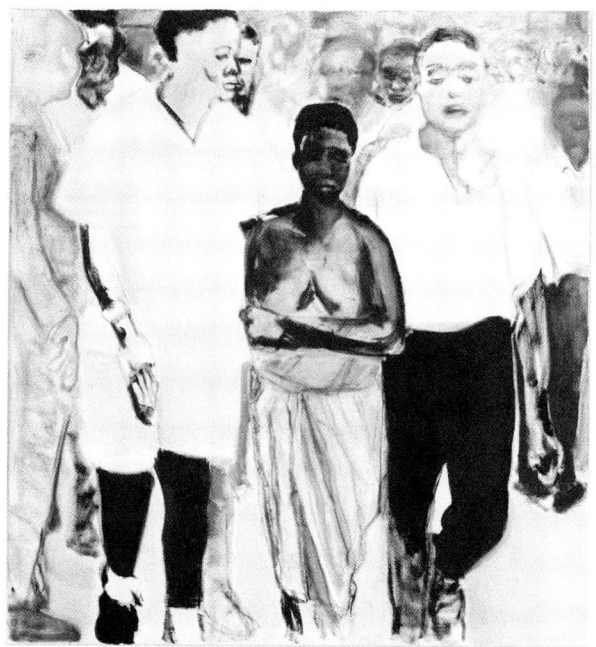

Figure 2.13: Marlene Dumas, *The Widow*, 2013. Oil on canvas, 150 × 140 cm. Collection Defares. © Marlene Dumas. Photo: Peter Cox. (Plate 11, p. 205)

Figure 2.14: Photograph of Pauline Opango in *Time* magazine (24 February 1961).

évolué men were blamed for any of their shortcomings. As the child of an *évolué* family described: "I often heard my father tell my mother: 'You, you're the real Negress, you know! The white people don't live like that!'".[103] The *évolués* often attended events alone as they were embarrassed that their wives lacked the French necessary to be able to converse with Europeans. As discussed by Hunt, the wives of *évolués* attended the activities of a *foyer social* which were established by the Belgians to create a small cadre of elite Congolese wives.[104] By joining the city's *foyer social*, Congolese women were able to learn household skills. Motherhood classes were offered, as were various contests and ceremonies that attempted to encourage women to adopt a European lifestyle. House visits were also established to check for cleanliness and propriety and to evaluate the women's achievement in emulating what was taught in the classroom. Ultimately, women felt left behind in the status typical of the *évolué* class. Independence did little to change the preoccupation with the *évolué*. An article from *Time* entitled "How to Appear Évolué" (25 September 1964) chronicles Kantangese men's desire to appear *évolué* in the eyes of visiting Africans and Europeans. However, according to the article, their wives hinder such attempts: "At a formal affair, she usually sits immobile, responding to conversational gambits with an agonised *oui* or *non*, counting the minutes until she can return to her manioc masher".[105] Returning to the photograph, the absence of Opango's typical clothes was emphasised in the caption from *Time*: "Gone were the Paris frocks".[106] This split in the gendered experience of the country is echoed in the colours of Dumas's *The Widow* where Opango appears oversaturated in shades of blue and black compared to the white shirts and bleached skin of the two men who accompany her. This saturation could be seen in terms of the customs and traditions that Opango sustains in comparison to her whitewashed and unencumbered companions.

Women are traditionally associated with a static sense of time and tradition, while men are seen to create change and charge ahead. For Opango, an act of sadness and commemoration can be argued to be emblematic of a sign of opposition against the Belgian state. The photograph conveys the continuation of traditions and their significances in the contemporary world as they take on other connotations over time. If we are to conceive of the women in *Oyé Oyé* as sustaining ancestry, these are equally traditions that shift and transform: from the Kuba skirts to the wrappings of Zairian textiles. Far from static, these traditions are adapted and changed, and, as suggested by the video, these processes are performed by women.

Endurance

In *Oyé Oyé*, there is a comparison created between the figure of Mobutu, who is always pictured as stationary, either seated or standing, and the women who perform in the *animation* troupes. One can rest, while the others cannot. The labour that is thematised in *Oyé Oyé* is emphasised in the mechanisms of video, specifically the function of the loop, which evokes a Sisyphean task without end in which the women are endlessly bound to the same set of actions. They swing from side to side and spring and clap across the stage. The women's endless activity is echoed in the circular structure and rhythm of the video's soundtrack, i.e., Axel Mbouze's "Papa Mobutu". We could even think of Magama's video itself as a kind of laborious task that sews together a series of clips. Her own work is visible as she sources the clips from the background of *Mobutu, roi du Zaïre* and edits in a series of cuts. The laboriousness that is thematised in the video is emphasised in its creation.

The politics of women's labour has been the subject of extensive feminist scholarship and critique. I want to consider Magema's *Oyé Oyé* in light of this discourse and the way in which filmic or cinematic practices have given visibility to labour that is so often cast to the background. Scholars have long debated if work or labour is a filmable subject, as it seems to depart from cinema's constitution as a site of leisure, enjoyment and spectacle.[107] One of the first real motion pictures ever made, Louis and Auguste Lumière's *Workers Leaving the Lumière Factory in Lyon* (1895), shows, as its title suggests, approximately one hundred workers at a factory for photographic goods leaving through two gates. Based on this origin story, it has been argued that films are set in the area of life where work has been left behind.[108] Others have speculated that cinema abstracts labour, leading to the aestheticization of gesture and its entry into the world of entertainment.[109] However, since its inception, African cinema has given visibility to the subject of racialised and gendered labour often rendered invisible in everyday life. Senegalese director Ousmane Sembene's first feature length film *Black Girl* (1966) chronicles the arrival of Diouana, a young Senegalese woman, to France and her descent into depression and ultimately suicide. Thinking that she was employed to take care of the family's three children, they are completely absent, and her tasks are reduced only to cooking and cleaning. We watch as Diouana scrubs the bathtub, prepares the meals, cleans the kitchen, vacuums the apartment and does the laundry. Monumentalised on screen, Diouana's actions take on the status of an event through the cinematic. The labour of women has been similarly foregrounded by arthouse films that emerged out of second-wave feminism. In Belgian filmmaker Chantal Akerman's 201-minute film, *Jeanne Dielman, 23 quai du Commerce, 1080 Bruxelles* (1975), we witness Jeanne, a widow in a working-class commercial zone of Brussels, over the course of the three days. In comparison to Sembene's *Black Girl*, the chores completed in *Jeanne Dielman* are captured in extreme detail. Akerman shows the way in which the protagonist cooks a wiener schnitzel, from the laying out of flour and the plate with the egg yolk to the breading of each veal cutlet and the clean-up afterwards. Akerman opted for the actual experience of time as it is lived rather than the sped-up tempo of cinema. Long takes expose the veritable time it takes the actor to complete a task. If cinema plays with duration, video turns to the loop to convey this same sense of endurance.

Similarly aligned with second-wave feminism, Berwick Street Film Collective's *Nightcleaners* (1975) captures the endless nature of the labour often ascribed to women that exceeds the end of the contractual workday. The British documentary film centres on a campaign to unionise the women who cleaned office blocks at night and who were being victimised and underpaid. One of the women describes the tasks that await them when their cleaning shifts end:

> ...prepare the children for school, take them to school... and back, get my tidying up done, washing up, shopping, preparing what's to be made for dinner... and after coming home, getting dinner, feeding them, get them ready for bed and then finish getting ready myself to come back to work.

Magema extends our consideration of this gendered labour beyond Europe and North America to Mobutu's Zaire, a context in which women's liberation has been treated as secondary to the concerns of colonialism, independence and neocolonialism. *Oyé Oyé* conveys the same endurance as the other works discussed and, in doing so, it connects the Zairian women's labour to a larger feminist history and social and political movement. Like much feminist work, Magema's *Oyé Oyé* expands the lexicon of the political to include strategies of maintenance and endurance typically excluded from grand accounts of historical revolution. Over the course of the following sections, I will explore the ways in which these strategies offer a counter to seismic revolutionary change. Maintenance, I suggest, offers other ways through which we could envision Mbembe's construction of the postcolony.

Detail

In *Discipline and Punish* (1977), Michel Foucault claims that, "Discipline is a political anatomy of detail".[110] He continues: "The meticulousness of the regulations, the fussiness of the inspections, the supervision of the smallest fragment of life and of the body will soon provide... an economic or technical rationality for this mystical calculus of the infinitesimal and the infinite".[111] As we have seen in terms of clothing and choreography, the women in the archival video are submitted to the orders of detail. The control of the small and the trivial in the everyday creates a state of total surveillance. From young to old, the women are watched over by Mobutu. His omnipresence is evoked in the clip of the clouds from which he descended every evening on television. However, the two screens in Magema's *Oyé Oyé* simultaneously complicate the effectiveness of the state in terms of both its surveillance and oppression.

The details of the details seem to challenge the complete order suggested by Foucault.[112] As previously discussed, the contemporary video of Magema offers a sense of parody onto the government's orders, and, through the coupling of the two screens, we are encouraged to view the archival footage of the women against the grain or through another perspective. Magema's exaggerations turn our attention to the slip-ups that occur in the *animation* performances. In the street cavalcade of white shirts and Mary Janes, there is a young girl to the right of the central figure who appears downcast [fig. 2.1]. Her arm seems weighted and yielding as she occasionally offers a weak swing. Her skirt is similarly deflated compared to the tent-like structures of the other girls. Meanwhile, in the group with Mobutu and Bobi Ladawa emblazoned on their chests, the woman on the left accidently extends the wrong arm [fig. 2.15]. Her thoughts are suddenly visible as she sees the other women and transfers the handkerchief-like offering to the correct side. Her arm then extends in coordination with the others. In the group with the bandeau tops and raffia skirts, one of the women on the right-hand side lags behind the others [fig. 2.7]. She forgets to clap and quickly shuffles to catch up with the group. In the absence of Mobutu's eyes, Magema's strides are overexaggerated, from the wide angle of their

Figure 2.15: Michèle Magema, video stills from *Oyé Oyé*, 2002.
© ADAGP, Paris and DACS, London 2021.

swings to changes in speed that vary from the sedate to the satirically swift. These actions create a crack in the absoluteness of the state apparatus as they suggest the tensions that exist within it.

In demarcating the characteristics of the postcolony, Mbembe offered a case study on "political derision" in Togo. He explored the ways in which citizens developed techniques of separating words or phrases from their conventional significances and employed them to other ends.[113] In Togo, the ruling political party, Reassemblement du Peuple Togolais (RPT), claimed to control the whole of public and social life, orienting it towards what were decreed communal goals and exclaiming the oneness of the citizens. However, there endured considerable disparity between the state's projections of itself and the way people played with and exploited these projections – and they did so within the arenas where they were gathered to confirm state legitimacy. These strategies, according to Mbembe, operated as avenues of escape from the *commandement* of the state. When the Togolese were called upon to exclaim the RPT's slogans, many would travesty the expressions meant to glorify the state. With a simple tonal shift, one expression could take on many significances, as Mbembe wrote: "Under cover, therefore, of official slogans, people sang about the sudden erection of the 'enormous' and 'rigid' presidential phallus, of how it remained in this position and of its contact with 'vaginal fluids'".[114] This example conveys a concurrent obedience and disobedience of state orders, and it connects to my earlier contention that the women in the archival footage perform like automatons and yet avoid decapitation, as they offer an outward display of submission while keeping their own mind.

Furthermore, the Togolese party acronym, RPT, was associated with "the sound of faecal matter dropping into a septic tank" or "the sound of a fart emitted by quivering buttocks", which "can only smell disgusting".[115] Mbembe asserted that the same obsession with orifices, odours and genital organs occurs in the writings and speech of other sub-Saharan countries.[116] The Congolese author Sony Labou Tansi described "the strong, thick, delivering thighs" and "the essential, bewitching arse" of women in the context of "the tropicalities of His Excellency".[117] The societal contexts and vocabulary cited by Mbembe and Tansi suggest a public and political space dominated by men. Moreover, the various aggressions of the state are simultaneously echoed in subversions of it, for example, through virile erections. This gendered conception of space is depicted in Guy Tillim's photographic series *Congo Democratic*, which examined the lead up to the Congo's first general election in more than 40 years in July 2006. In the series, Tillim captured the civil disorder spurred by Étienne Tshisikedi's call for a boycott of the elections, as well as the rivalry between two candidates, Jean-Pierre Bemba and

Figure 2.16: Guy Tillim, *A traditional dancer and crowd salute Jean-Pierre Bemba as he walks to a rally from the airport, Kinshasa, 2006* from the series *Congo Democratic*, 2006. Archival pigment ink on 300g cotton paper, 91 × 133 cm. © Guy Tillim. Courtesy of Stevenson, Amsterdam/ Cape Town / Johannesburg. (Plate 12, p. 206)

President Joseph Kabila, who had assumed the presidency when his father was assassinated in 2001. Men dressed in caps and sunglasses scream and shove each other in the crowds [fig. 2.16]. Heads shaved and styled in crew cuts are seen from various angles. Men charge the spaces captured in the series, from the streets of Kinshasa to its stadium. They are the candidates in the election [fig. 2.17] and the ones commemorated by the statues in the city – a victorious Lumumba soars above the crowd in one of the photographs from Tillim's series. The only woman who takes centre stage in *Congo Democratic* is, as Tillim's caption states, "a traditional dancer" who wears a headdress, orange face paint, a bikini of the same colour and a leopard print skirt. She is elevated above the crowd in a wooden watchtower-like structure adorned with palm leaves. As previously discussed, she comes to embody the state and its traditions, as an elevated site of values.

In a critique of Mbembe, Bennetta Jules-Rosette argues: "From Nigerian market women to Congolese *cambistes* (street bankers), African women have occupied creative spaces from which they have influenced the course of history. Mbembe avoids any systematic discussion of gender as an aspect of selfhood or subjectivity".[118] She describes the way in which Mbembe privileges "dominant ideologies, institutions, and public instruments of power" over "private sources of resistance".[119] By con-

Figure 2.17: Guy Tillim, *Lumumbiste Party supporters prepare for a meeting, pinning up pictures of Patrice Lumumba and their leader Antoine Gizenga, who was a deputy to Lumumba after the first elections in 1960*, 2006 from the series *Congo Democratic*, 2006. Archival pigment ink on 300g cotton paper, 91 × 133 cm.
© Guy Tillim. Courtesy of Stevenson, Amsterdam/ Cape Town / Johannesburg. (Plate 13, p. 207)

trast, the actions that I explore in *Oyé Oyé*, the details of details so to speak, are small and subtle gestures that serve to trouble the absoluteness of the state. These various details suggest the effects of something wearing off, leaking or lagging over time, of coordinated actions extended to exhaustion or perhaps even boredom. For example, the woman who extends the wrong arm from the others in the group looks weary [fig. 2.15]. Her eyes are closed as she shifts from side to side, as if her mind had travelled elsewhere over the course of several seconds. Maintenance, as Ukeles wrote, "is a drag... it takes all the fucking time".[120] Drawing from Ukeles, the actions that I cite in the video emerge as small subversions in the steady onslaught of women's work. This kind of lapse is echoed in the accounts of Lumumba and Pauline Opango. Opango recalled the situation when Lumumba was attempting to acquire official *évolué* status from the colonial state, as she explained: "My husband and my sister had to teach me everything. Lumumba had asked me to hide myself, each time I saw him arriving, in the bedroom where he would come and find me to judge my appearance".[121] Apparently, Opango was absent on the day of Lumumba's greatest triumph, 30 June 1960, because "her hair was a mess!".[122] Maintenance disrupted creates a sense of chaos in the operations of the everyday.

Mbembe is often explicitly scathing of what Jules-Rossette called "African feminisms" or "womanisms".[123] For him, "the philosophical poverty of these discourses is notorious, and several isolated attempts to correct this shortcoming have not succeeded".[124] But, Mbembe has failed to notice the space of the everyday so often occupied by women. Returning to the video, the subtle changes enacted by the women and young girls stand in contrast with the contexts described by Mbembe. They are small in scale and subject, and their subtlety is emphasised even more when construed against totalising accounts of action and change.[125] The details of the details captured in the video are perhaps a site where subjectivity and other types of temporality or existences can be (re-)claimed.

Life-work

Life seems to evade *Oyé Oyé*, from the endless activity shown on the archival screen to Magema's own exaggerated march. The women engage in a challenge of endurance. There is the occasional sense of tiredness or lag and yet the performance continues as the women's capacity and capaciousness are exponential. This sense of vivacity evades women both young and old, as they sustain the same actions on loop. Moreover, *Oyé Oyé* is suggestive of the women's capacity for childbirth and the care offered to children. Hips are a seat of gravity, and their energy, which continues even as the women tire, is echoed in the vine textiles worn by the group. The source of the entwined vines' growth is obscured, as they spread endlessly across the garment; theirs is a tenacious expansion.

Death is consistently written across constructions of "Africa" through coups, wars and states on the verge of collapse as if it were a cloak that shrouds the entire continent. And yet this orientation overlooks the complexity of the everyday and the way in which these events are actually experienced. In Mobutu's Zaire, the care of children was assigned solely as a task of women. And though the video did not set out to convey the labour of mothers, the small child lifted above the crowd in *Oyé Oyé* speaks to a maternal tactility. Hands convey the way in which the child is embraced, tended to and looked after. Nurtured and well-fed, the child's little round stomach emerges from its spotless white shirt. The clothes of the young girls in the street cavalcade are similarly laundered. The unseen care of women sustains the children in the video, while the adults suggest other generations of carers that saw them through their own young age.

In this context, it is worthwhile to consider the French-Senegalese director Alain Gomis's film *Félicité* (2017), which was set in the capital city of Kinshasa. The film centres on a woman called Félicité scratching together a living as a bar singer and single mother. Gomis's film is the only cinematic production to my knowledge that considers the contemporary labour of single Congolese women in the context of childcare.[126] In doing so, it extends the women's labour that we have seen in *Oyé Oyé* to a present cinematic moment. In *Félicitié*, the protagonist's teenage son Samo is gravely wounded in a serious car accident. Gomis captures Félicité as she travels to various companions and acquaintances in Kinshasa asking for loans or cash that she is owed in order to pay for Samo's surgery. She confronts a proprietor who refuses to pay her and only does so when she returns with a bribed police officer. She takes the same police officer to confront a female friend. These scenes are constructed by Gomis through a sense of speed, from the cinematography to the sometimes-violent encounters that transpire. The camera captures Félicité and others in a series of close-ups that engage the emotions of the scene, from expressions of anger to Félicité's strength and sense of obligation. These encounters are interspersed with shots of Félicité caring for Samo. She confronts Samo's father to assist with the payment, calmly stating, "it's your child". He screams and physically shoves Félicité away from the apartment. This violence is seen again in the wealthy neighbourhood of Gombe where she is physically removed for trespassing. Her braids slip out of a ponytail as she is pulled across the carpet screaming. In a review of *Félicité* for the British newspaper, *The Observer*, film critic Wendy Ide wrote, "At times, it seems that violence is not just near the surface, it *is* the surface of life in Kinshasa".[127] However, *Félicité* captures the embodied, corporeal and emotive experience of what is to love and care for someone in a context so often defined by violence, as suggested by the women in *Oyé Oyé*.

To consider the time and space surrounding violent events is to consider the exertions and efforts that attempt to obstruct its course, for example, the care given to the child that soars above the crowd in *Oyé Oyé*. The events after violence are illustrated by Félicité's care for Samo as she washes his wounds and feeds him by the spoonful. These physical acts of care are often overlooked in narrative and cinematic accounts of Africa. Due to the gendered division of labour, such actions are shouldered by women. Necropolitics, as in the creation of death-worlds and its conflation with the postcolony discussed in the first chapter, is accordingly complicated through these efforts. Far from an eschewal of violence, my analysis is a call to look on the other side of it for the labour of women and the way in which they sustain survival and complicate constructions of the Congo.

Un recours

Loss appears central to Magema's video, from the women's autonomy and subjectivity to their exclusion from the state. However, if Mobutu's Zaire was defined through a *"recours à l'authenticité"*, as in the resumption of traditional African values that had been attacked by colonialism, then *Oyé Oyé* attempts its own *recours* of sorts. Throughout the video, there is a recouping of women's labour erased in the various accounts of the country. Through the two opposite screens, Magema confronts Mobutu with her own person and body, while, recovered from the background of Michel's representation of Mobutu's Zaire, the archival clips speak to the occluded, everyday operations of women that sustain the state. The *animation politique* enacted by the women created the imaginary of the country, as their textiles, coiffures and choreography enacted its tenets. Hands simultaneously speak to the endless tasks and chores so often cast to the background, while the women's torsos engage the work of childbirth and care, the capacity that allows for the reproduction of the state. For *Oyé Oyé* turns to the transmission of ancestry and change through women. Their endurance is echoed through the apparatus of video, which plays on loop.

Taking cognisance of the work of Congolese women offers a way in which to complicate the constructions of space and time that emerge from the experience of colonialism and are routinely seen as defined solely through violence. Maintenance and endurance open up other terms of engagement. The small details of the everyday captured in the video stand in contrast to totalising accounts of action and change. By turning away from grand gestures, we are able to engage with the minute actions that often occur on either side of gunshots, coups and aggression. Hands caress, tend, sustain and lift children above the crowd. They trespass onto the scene of the state's gaze. This is the endurance of social life lived alongside the visible surface of violence

CHAPTER 3

The Image of Lumumba

Georges Senga's *Une vie après la mort*

In 2012, Georges Senga collaborated with Kayembe Kilobo, an elderly schoolteacher in Lubumbashi whose clothing, lifestyle and opinions had been self-consciously styled on Patrice Émery Lumumba since the 1950s. Senga was taught by Kayembe in primary school, twenty or so years before the series was completed. Born on 6 January 1935, Kayembe's obsession with Lumumba started in adolescence. On its origins, Kayembe explained: "I was a fan of the politician from the first hour... This was the beginning of a great adventure for me".[1] His recollection of these years goes back, he alleges, to a moment in Congo Brazzaville when Fulbert Youlou, a laicised clergyman who led the country's campaign for emancipation, confronted President Charles De Gaulle. De Gaulle claimed, according to Kayembe, "Independence is granted to the one who wants it".[2] In September 1958, a referendum was held on independence in the French Congo, and, as per Kayembe, on the other side of the Congo River, Lumumba seized the same opportunity to strive for the colony's emancipation, becoming the first democratically elected prime minister of the newly independent state. For *Une vie après la mort*, Senga worked with his old schoolmaster, Kayembe, to a create a series of fourteen photographic diptychs centred around the figure of Lumumba.

Born in 1983, Senga grew up in Lubumbashi, the city on whose outskirts Lumumba was assassinated on 17 January 1961. The artist had learned about Lumumba in school. However, Senga could only recall studying the country's first elected prime minister in the years after he had taken Kayembe's class.[3] Lumumba was murdered directly by the Belgian government and Congolese rebels with the indirect help of the United States and United Nations. In the context of the Cold War, he was perceived as a threat to the United States and its Western allies who wanted to control the country's mineral resources. Uranium, as obtained in Katanga, was crucial to the construction of atomic bombs. As we saw in the second chapter, Mobutu seized control of country in 1965 and created an authoritarian one-party state that plundered the Congo. As a result, Lumumba is often spoken about in mythic terms. There is a sense that the young statesman could have delivered the aspirations of the independent state for which many yearned. Nzongola-Ntalaja wrote that Lumumba's assassination was "a stumbling block to the ideals of national unity, economic independence and pan-African solidarity" as well as "a shattering blow to the hopes of millions of Congolese for freedom and material prosperity".[4] The assassination opened up a state of speculation around Lumumba that acted as the original prompt for the series. As Senga explained:

> The original idea was to make a fiction about Lumumba's life after 1961, while posing a question. What would become of Patrice Lumumba if he had survived his fate? Would he have become a rich and corrupt man watching the Congo transform itself with this spirit of injustice; or would he have been a rich man through what he tried to do for Congo in fighting for independence? A modest man who would have continued to defend rights in the absence of rights?[5]

These same concerns were shared by Emmanuel Gerard and Bruce Kuklick in *Death in the Congo: Murdering Patrice Lumumba* (2015), as they wondered:

> Few African politicians who actually wielded power for any length of time in the twentieth century have escaped the stain of corruption, accusations of neo-colonialism, the taint of warmongering or the label of ineffectiveness. Had Lumumba survived, would he be regarded as a Mobutu?[6]

However, Senga changed the direction of the series after speaking with Kayembe. *Une vie apres la mort* accordingly turns to three entangled worlds, that of Lumumba, Kayembe as well as the artist himself. In the photographic diptychs, Senga explores the effect that Lumumba had on Kayembe. The left side of the diptych is dedicated to Lumumba, whose story starts with Kayembe's own personal archive shared with Senga. The artist scanned a historical article and leaflet on Lumumba collected by Kayembe [fig. 3.1; fig. 3.2]. Published in *Le Stanleyvillois: Quotidien Independent de la Province Orientale* on 2 November 1959, the article claims "*L'INDEPENDANCE AVEC OU SANS LUMUMBA*" ("INDEPENDENCE WITH OR WITHOUT LUMUMBA"), while the commemorative leaflet asserts "*Vive le libérateur! Vive le Congo libre!*" ("Long live the liberator! Long live free Congo!") with a photograph of Lumumba above the text. The right-hand side of the diptych is dedicated to photographs of Kayembe. The article on Lumumba from *Le Stanleyvillois,* for example, is coupled with an old black and white headshot of Kayembe that opens

Figure 3.1: Georges Senga, *Une vie après la mort*, 2012. Inkjet on Baryta paper, 170 × 60 cm. Courtesy of the artist. (Plate 14, p. 208)

Figure 3.2: Georges Senga, *Une vie après la mort*, 2012. Inkjet on Baryta paper, 170 × 60 cm. Courtesy of the artist. (Plate 15, p. 209)

Figure 3.3: Guy Tillim, *High school, Lubumbashi, DR Congo* from the series *Avenue Patrice Lumumba*, 2008. Digital print on paper, 91.5 × 131.5 cm. © Guy Tillim. Courtesy of Stevenson, Amsterdam/ Cape Town / Johannesburg.

the series, while the subsequent diptych juxtaposes a commemorative leaflet with a flyer for the teacher's candidature in local government from 1989 photographed by Senga. Thereafter, the story of Lumumba is told through the recycling of old press photographs. Images of the young Lumumba were sourced online from a variety of websites; they were downloaded by Senga and edited for the series. These historical press images are coupled with contemporary colour photographs of Kayembe pictured by Senga around Lubumbashi.

Recent artistic engagement with Lumumba extends beyond Senga's series alone, and, when *Une vie après la mort* premiered at the third edition of the Biennale de Lubumbashi curated by Elvira Dyangani Ose in 2013, it was shown alongside two other projects that centred around Lumumba. These were South African photographer Guy Tillim's series *Avenue Patrice Lumumba* (2008) and Belgian artist Sven Augustijnen's filmic essay *Spectres* (2011). For *Avenue Patrice Lumumba*, Tillim travelled across western, central and southern Africa to photograph the decaying legacy of colonial modernity [fig. 3.3]. He captured streets, squares and buildings named after Lumumba who was revered as a liberator of independent Africa. Meanwhile, in its Congolese debut, Augustijnen's *Spectres* attempted to shed light on the assassination of Lumumba through an exploration of colonial guilt.[7] The work centres on Jacques Brassinne de La Buissière, a French-speaking Belgian who was 82 years old at the time of filming and had been a colonial official when Lumumba was killed in 1961. Noteworthy is Brassinne's denial of Belgian complicity in the assassination of Lumumba. Alternatively, in *Une vie après la mort*, Senga turns to local on the ground experiences, and, more specifically, the ways in which they complicate official state accounts.[8] Discussions around Lumumba, apropos Nzongola-Ntalaja and Gerard and Kuklick, have occupied the tense of "what-could-have-been". However, as Senga asks, "Beyond fantasy, what is left?".[9] His series, as I will argue, shifts our attention to what it was like to live alongside the young statesman and to experience these historic events. This chapter weaves together visual and material culture surrounding Lumumba, exploring the transmission and circulation of photographs and the ways in which these images were absorbed and deployed by audiences at the time. It simultaneously considers their afterlives in Congolese popular painting, cinema and again in Senga's series. For, *Une vie après la mort* explores the legacy of Lumumba in Lubumbashi through the figure of Kayembe.

Kayembe and Lumumba

In the diptych that opens the series, Senga, who was given access to Kayembe's personal archive, deployed a slightly damaged photograph of the then young man who wears a shirt with clearly defined lapels [fig. 3.1]. His bespectacled eyes stare toward the camera. His short hair cut is evocative of Lumumba's own style. Kayembe had adopted Lumumba's appearance in adolescence in the 1950s, copied from some of the many photographs that circulated at the time.[10] He was regarded as a look-a-like of Lumumba and was even called "Lumumba" by colleagues.[11] As evidenced in this pseudonym, there was a certain strangeness to Kayembe's act of assimilation, though Lumumba was already a trendsetter amongst the Congolese. He had set the trend of beards and encouraged all Congolese to keep their beards until the colony was liberated from the Belgians.[12] Beards, in the 1960s and 1970s, were a global signifier of anti-imperialist, *tiers-mondiste* opposition. Beatniks in America sported beards and goatees in the 1950s, but Lumumba seems to have started this specific "look" on the Congolese scene. However, Kayembe's adoption of Lumumba's appearance predated the specific trend for taking on the guise of the young statesman that surged after the assassination. This enactment was far from an anomaly in the 1960s. Pedro Monaville has explored how the attachment of young Congolese men to the memory of the assassinated Lumumba was expressed stylistically. Informants often spoke to Monaville about their experience of adopting Lumumba's hairstyle, goatee and glasses in the 1960s.¹³ In this same era, many young Congolese attempted to expand their sources of support and access to the world through letter writing.¹⁴ Standard headshots were often included in their envelopes to addresses overseas, and, as observed by Monaville, these photographs suggested associations with Lumumba and, of course, the *évolué* of which Lumumba was the exemplar.

As discussed in the second chapter, the *évolues* were Africans from various ethnic and cultural backgrounds seen to have taken on European sartorial and social codes. Acutely aware of appearance, they were clean cut and had a "European" sense of style. Their visual signifiers were that of the suit, tie and derby. The Belgian administration offered *évolues* an official status, first through the *carte de mérite civique* in 1948 and then through the *carte d'immatriculation* in 1952. Lumumba obtained the *carte d'immatriculation* in 1954 after an original attempt two years earlier. Though adopted by Lumumba, it is worth stating that the term *évolué* itself was ambiguous. Belgians and other white colonials in the Belgian Congo employed the term to refer to "any Congolese whom they deemed to have ideas above his station".¹⁵ The *évolué* was also a subject of debate as a site of self- and group-creation for Congolese men writing in *La Voix du Congolais*, a journal in which many photographs of the self-conscious *évolué* circulated.¹⁶ There was a vagueness and ambivalence to the concept of the *évolué*, as it was created according to a European archetype and implied a sense of shame thrust onto the Congolese. However, the category gained its fullest adoption by educated Congolese men who sought to engage in an exchange with the colonial administration and each other.

The explicit adoption of Lumumba's appearance by Congolese youth as well as Kayembe seems specific to the country. And while the guises adopted by youth in the 1960s operated as fashion trends, Kayembe's adoption carries its own set of connotations. Interviewees in Monaville's 2013 text considered the way they had adopted the appearance of Lumumba in the 1960s, soon after the assassination.¹⁷ Their assumption of this costume is an event in their lifetime associated with a specific era, an act that they once adopted, tried on and eventually abandoned. However, the embodied practice of Kayembe as relayed in *Une vie après la mort* tells of an extended commitment. The elderly schoolteacher's embodiment of Lumumba endures from adolescence through to Senga's contemporary photographs. In the series, an advertisement for Kayembe's candidature in local government from the year of 1989 shows a photograph of the schoolteacher [fig. 3.2], which, as we have seen, is coupled with the leaflet owned by Kayembe that exclaims Lumumba as *"le libérateur!"*. The design of Kayembe's own layout of self-endorsement clearly evokes the other side of the diptych in its arrangement of the photograph and text. This photograph appears to convey Kayembe's adoption of an *abacost* – gone were the suits and ties of the *évolué*. As we saw in the second chapter, the term "*abacost*" was another Mobutuist expression that came from the slogan, "*à bas le costume*" ("down with the suit").[18] The "authentic" Zairian was perceived as the complete opposite of the *évolué*.[19] However, the traces of Lumumba's guise linger in Kayembe's handkerchief, glasses and hairstyle as well as the design of the layout. These allusions to the deceased leader suggest a small act of resistance to Mobutu's *authenticité* project, as Kayembe stated: "My style, my hair and my nickname could also get me killed".[20] Kayembe's style endured through the era of Mobutu onwards. In 2013, when Senga photographed the elderly schoolteacher for the series, Kayembe was still dressed in the same suits. He remained committed to the guise adopted in adolescence. Furthermore, Kayembe sustains the tenets espoused by Lumumba. Masculinity as constructed by the *évolué* class continues to be expressed in the contemporary photographs. Kayembe is an educator and an elected counsellor. The traits associated with the father of the liberated Congolese state transfer to that of the schoolmaster.

The example of Kayembe illustrates how styles of dress and fashion have been used as oppositional strategies in the Congo. Established in the 1950s, the Kinshasa youth culture who worshipped Buffalo Bill adopted a dress code that consisted of scarves, jeans and turned up collars in an evocation of the Far West.[21] Mocking the impeccable *évolués*, the Bills emerged in defiance of colonial culture.[22] Through the peripatetic cowboy silhouette, the Bills exemplified an "emancipatory figure, representing the spirit of the coming independence".[23] Resistance in Mobutu's Zaire was alternatively shown through suits and ascots. While in Europe the tie operated as a symbol of bourgeois values and oppression, in the Congo, it was a statement of opposition and a desire for freedom. As Van Reybrouck observed, some people would even wear a tie just to sit in the living room.[24] Youth in particular protested against Mobutu's regime of *authenticité* with clothes, as they dressed in extremely flamboyant and European-branded outfits, christening themselves as "*la Sape*" as in "*La société des ambianceurs et personnes d'elégantes*" ("The society for tastemakers and elegant people").[25]

The old articles and leaflets included in the series attest to the course of time over which Kayembe continues to embody the appearance of his hero Lumumba. Papers are compromised by the tropical climate: an orange crease appears in the centre of the crinkled article from *Le Stanleyvillois*, attesting to the way in which it was stored away [fig. 3.1]. The other side of the diptych is equally worn and aged. The edges on the photograph of the young Kayembe are tattered as the gloss appears to tear away from the layer of white card and one corner curves from wear. The leaflet that celebrates Lumumba with the words "*Vive le libérateur! / Vive le Congo libre!*" [fig. 3.2], shows several creases and stains. White scratches appear across the photograph of Lumumba. Faded, torn and wrinkled, the leaflet for Kayembe's

Figure 3.4: Santu Mofokeng, *The Black Photo Album / Look at Me: 1890-1950*, 1997. © Santu Mofokeng. Courtesy of Lunetta Bartz, MAKER, Johannesburg.

candidature curls toward the camera. Lines suggest where the paper was folded, and a tear appears in one corner. Senga photographed and scanned these objects owned by Kayembe, maintaining their worn appearance in a time when he could have easily cleaned them up using Photoshop. Historicity is foregrounded as Senga eschews the compulsion to conceal signs of wear and age. Instead, the artist saves their temporal signifiers. A precedent for Senga is Santu Mofokeng's *The Black Photo Album / Look at Me: 1890-1950* (1997) [fig. 3.4].[26] Mofokeng collected, reworked and scanned damaged photographs of urban black working and middle-class families in South Africa commissioned between 1890-1950. One effect of the photographs' signs of age and wear and tear, as Jennifer Bajorek has argued, is the attention given to "the deeply historical nature of the images" and consequently "their subjects' capacity for historical experience".[27] Bajorek interprets the damaged photographs in Mofokeng's work as a challenge to the colonial archive that attempted to convey African subjects as outside of time. Denied a sense of coevalness, Africans were believed to occupy an earlier stage in development following a teleological construction of time.[28] However, the aging evoked on the surface of the photographs calls our attention to the historical experience of their subjects. In the case of *Une vie après la mort*, the signs of wear and tear on the archival items and their juxtaposition with the contemporary colour photographs attest to the time-bound endurance of Kayembe's embodiment. Perhaps there are others who donned suits like Kayembe, for example, the African émigrés in Europe who continued to style themselves in suits and abide by the social distinctions of class.[29] Nevertheless, what is specific to Kayembe's embodiment is the conscious commitment to Lumumba for more than 60 years.

Photographs in circulation

Through the slightly damaged photograph of the young Kayembe, we can trace the development of photography across the Congo. In the early twentieth century, there emerged amateur and professional African photographers in the country thanks to the growing availability of the camera. These "while-you-wait" photographers travelled through villages to city centres and even opened studios, the likely context in which Kayembe was photographed.[30] In 1931, the Belgian colonial magazine *L'Illustration Congolaise* reported that "*les civilises*", i.e. urban, Western-educated Congolese, were all eager to acquire photographs of themselves.[31] The accessibility of photography was taken advantage of by Congolese workers who stayed only for a limited time in the city and subsequently travelled back to their villages. Men turned to photography in order to capture themselves as modern and elegant and as a success in the colonial world.[32] Photography also enabled the assimilation of one's self to a traditional cultural hero.[33] Heroes in Luba culture, an ethno-linguistic group in south-central DR Congo that comprised a precolonial kingdom, were often shown alongside objects with which they were associated.[34] A salaried worker followed the same self-construction by taking photographs with objects that characterised their occupation. To take a photograph with a bicycle, for example, or wearing glasses engages the same kind of self-construction that was suggested in the earlier tradition of calling oneself "*Kapitula*" ("shorts", at one time the distinctive dress of Africans working for Europeans), "*Belegi*" ("Belgian") or "*Usungu*" (from *muzungu*, "white").[35] Mechanically produced and acquired as a commodity, the photograph situated the subject in the colonial world with which they could engage through their salary.[36] This experience of photography in the colonial era has been described by Manthia Diawara: "To go before... [the camera's] lens is to pass the test of modernity, to be transformed as an urbane subject even if one has no power in the market or at the train station".[37] These photographs created a sense of a connection with the city in the twentieth century and yet were simultaneously tied to local and older aesthetic traditions.

The self-construction entailed in photography was embraced by the *évolué* class. This was of course a characteristic of studio photography in general; selves were staged in photographs all over the world from the nineteenth century onwards. However, *Une vie après la mort* calls our attention to the ways in which photography was specifically engaged by the *évolués*. The slightly damaged headshot of Kayembe is evocative of the photographs that young men appended to letters that were sent abroad. Both suggest associations with Lumumba as the *évolué par excellence* and, in doing so, they convey an image of Europeanised masculinity. The photographs seem to visually authenticate the *évolué* without the stringent conditions set up by the Belgians. When the Belgians left the Congo in 1960 so did their systems of examination that granted the *carte d'immatriculation* to authorised *évolués*. Thus, we could argue that photography too operated as a strategy of legitimation. Hunt has suggested that the *évolué* was premised on "colonial mimicry" in the sense developed by Homi K. Bhabha to explain how members of a colonised society knowingly imitate and take on the culture of the colonisers.[38] As Hunt wrote: "the word *évolué* was always a misnomer in Belgian colonial discourse, for civilisation could never be reached by nonwhites".[39] Mimicry, for Bhabha, was associated with a kind of ambivalence, summed up in the phrase "almost the same, *but not quite*" as in a reformed, recognisable Other who is still a subject of difference.[40] There is a clear sense of separation that is always maintained. The colonised subject is "almost

Figure 3.5: Georges Senga, *Une vie après la mort*, 2012. Inkjet on Baryta paper, 170 × 60 cm. Courtesy of the artist. (Plate 16, p. 210)

the same" as the coloniser yet never "quite" fits in with the systems that govern them both. However, for the young Congolese, the coloniser was supplanted by the *évolué* as the figure that they wanted to emulate. No longer defined by a sense of ambivalence, the exemplar of the *évolué* was embraced as an achievable guise that, arguably, existed to be photographed.

Furthermore, the photographs in Senga's series speak to the customs of the *évolué* class. In one of the diptychs, the photograph of Kayembe in the leaflet for the schoolteacher's candidature in local government is cut out and glued to another sheet of white paper decorated with a red and green border [fig. 3.5]. Interior decoration was promoted by the colonial administration in the 1950s.[41] Previously, the walls were drawn with objects and figures and occasionally decorated with clippings from journals or catalogues thrown away by Europeans. Wedding photographs and snapshots started to be displayed on walls in the 1940s and 1950s. These wall adornments were captured by the photographic wing of the governmental agency, InforCongo, established after World War II to testify to the advancements in the Belgian Congo for a local and worldwide audience. For these photographers, the *évolué* was a strategic subject. The agency employed several Congolese photographers, such as Joseph Makula, whose oeuvre is largely dedicated to the *évolués*, a group to which Makula also belonged. In Makula's *The Living Room of a Congolese Family in Matete* (1950–1960) [fig. 3.6], there are two couples and several children in the comfortable space of a living room decorated with various kinds of wall adornments. Windows are absent in many of the photographs, and, in Makula's shot, the outside world appears tamed as a snakeskin sits on the wall. Nature was separated from the everyday world by the Belgians. In

Figure 3.6: Joseph Makula/Congopresse, *Life in Léopoldville under Belgian Rule. The Living Room of a Congolese Family in Matete*, 1950–1960. Photo, 18/16.8 × 24.4/23.3 cm. Courtesy of Liberas, Ghent.

1925, Belgium's King Albert I established the Virunga National Park (erstwhile Albert National Park) in eastern Congo where wildlife was suddenly engaged as spectacle.[42] The living room captured by Makula shows vistas of the colony displayed on the walls as well as several sculptural objects situated on an armoire. The Congolese are surrounded by a certain "civilised" window onto the environment that they shared with the Belgians, through artefacts and photographs hung on the walls. They appear to be from the colony and yet simultaneously separated from it through these *objets d'art*.

If commissioned photographs and wall adornments constitute two threads of photography engaged in the series, the third appears to exist in the black and white archival photographs that circulated in the mass media at the time.[43] The artist, Senga, is part of a generation that grew up in the aftermath of colonialism and the era of Lumumba, and, as previously mentioned, their memory of this time is always already mediated through literature, images and representations.[44] Senga was acquainted with Lumumba through photographs rather than the lived events themselves. The colony's struggle for emancipation and the subsequent Congo crisis yielded endless photographs of Lumumba that travelled around the world, and these photographs were often tied to texts that were largely biased against the young statesman. In an article from *Time* magazine on the May 1960 elections, Lumumba was called "the tall, goateed radical".[45] Within Belgium, Lumumba was seen as the embodiment of "Congolese impertinence, immaturity and savagery".[46] He was portrayed as an "unstable, nationalistic radical".[47] Instability was also the subject on the cover of *The Daily Mirror* from the United Kingdom on the 6 September 1960: "LUMUMBA 'SACKED' RIDDLE: Congo drama of 'I am still Premier' broadcast". The text is coupled with an often reproduced photographic portrait of the young Lumumba, seen again in Senga's series [fig. 3.5]. In a study of the Belgian newspaper *La Libre Belgique*, Christine Masuy observed that "media representations of Lumumba became increasingly demoniacal over time".[48] Much of the coverage centred on Lumumba's physical attributes – "choppy" French, white and broad teeth, and goatee – to convey the prime minister in solely adverse terms.[49]

The now-famous speech delivered by Lumumba at the ceremony marking Congolese independence, part of which is sampled in Baloji's *Mémoire*, galvanised the tone of the coverage. At the ceremony, the Belgian King Baudouin applauded the work of his countrymen during the colonial period as well as his great-granduncle King Leopold II. President Kasa-Vubu subsequently offered a conciliatory address. However, Lumumba seized the opportunity to emphasise the bitter experience of the colonised. He attested to years of oppression and slavery enforced by the Belgians and the struggle won by the Congolese for emancipation. He described the lack of wages, the lands spoiled through legislation that favoured the colonial government and the taunts endured "morning, noon and night": "Who can forget that a black was addressed in the familiar form, not because he was a friend, certainly, but because the polite form of address was to be used only for whites?".[50] *La Libre Belqigue* referred to the speech as "*un affront au Roi et à la Belgique*" and sharply chastised "*l'insolence*" of this upstart African.[51] Lumumba was attacked for having the audacity to criticise the Belgians who had offered the "gift" of independence with "grace" and "dignity".[52] He was conveyed as a devil across Europe and referred to as "*le sale nègre*".[53]

Photographs of Lumumba circulated widely in the mass media due to the context of the Cold War against which the Congo crisis occurred, and it is again through this international lens that Lumumba is often analysed in histories of the Congo.[54] In *Congo: The Epic History of a People*, Van Reybrouck offers a wrenching account of the conspiracy against Lumumba that entailed the Belgians, the CIA, white mercenaries and Western-backed secessionists in Katanga and southern Kasai. He goes on to describe Lumumba as a false messiah who lacked the ability to or-

Figure 3.7: Georges Senga, *Une vie après la mort*, 2012. Inkjet on Baryta paper, 170 × 60 cm. Courtesy of the artist. (Plate 17, p. 211)

ganise the Congolese. He acknowledges that the Congolese army was led by bigoted commanders from the colonial Force Publique, but criticises Lumumba's attempt to Africanise its leadership as "sympathetic but disastrous".[55] Van Reybrouck characterises Lumumba's telegram to the Soviets after going to the United Nations and the Americans for assistance in the wake of Katanga's secession as "understandable but frighteningly frivolous".[56] He even offers an anecdote from when Lumumba had asked a CIA officer to send over *une femme blonde* ("a blonde woman"), the significance of which is sidestepped. As illustrated by Van Reybrouck, Monaville has noted a trend of historical judgement in accounts of Lumumba.[57] He observes that there is a tendency for writers to parade as advocates, judges and prosecutors of his deeds and misdeeds.[58] As early as 1961 and 1963, Fanon and Jean-Paul Sartre reflected on the steps that Lumumba could have taken to avoid his fate, while, in a book published in 1990, Jean-Claude Willame listed all of Lumumba's political mistakes.[59] The significance of Senga's series is in its departure from these written accounts. The juxtaposition of the two sets of photographs turns away from the world context central to other analyses, situating Lumumba in Lubumbashi. Senga explores the significance of Lumumba to Kayembe and, in turn, to other Congolese, whose agency is often overlooked in these histories. Lumumba was an *évolué* lifted onto the world stage. His charisma echoes across the series [fig. 3.7], and it this charisma that convinced Kayembe to adopt the guise of the young *évolué* in the 1950s followed by other youth in the 1960s. The series takes away the compulsion to assess or judge Lumumba's actions.

Furthermore, the photographs of Kayembe come to weigh on those of Lumumba; there is an exchange across the two sides of the diptych. Like Kayembe, Lumumba was vested in the same sense of self-construction. In *Une vie après la mort*, Senga

Figure 3.8: Georges Senga, *Une vie après la mort*, 2012. Inkjet on Baryta paper, 170 × 60 cm. Courtesy of the artist. (Plate 18, p. 212)

created a diptych with an old photograph of the Congolese cabinet, dressed in the typical suits of the *évolué* class, standing outside the Palais de la Nation in Kinshasa after Lumumba was sworn-in as prime minister [fig. 3.8]. Briefcases are carried by some of the cabinet while others wear sunglasses. Dressed in a bowtie, Lumumba is set apart from the sea of ties. This adoption of suits and ties was seen by the Congolese themselves as a transgressive act when compared to the way they were treated by the colonial government. There is a sense of the personal and intimate created in the juxtaposition with Kayembe, as if the structure of the diptych calls attention to Lumumba's own self-construction. We are prompted to reflect on the fact that Lumumba too sought out suits to wear, that the young statesman turned to clothes in the same way as Kayembe was to do. He was aware of the weight that appearance and photographs carried.[60] It could be argued that the series is charged with a masculine reproduction that travels from Lumumba to Kayembe. However, when people in the Congo remember Lumumba, the image they have is that of a martyr rather than a big man in the style of Mobutu.[61] Moreover, Senga's series seems invested in breaking down an aesthetic of authority to a series of choices and an act of self-construction as exemplified in the case of Kayembe. Masculinity is constructed through a sense of fragility, as prompted by Lumumba's short life and Kayembe's elderly age. There is an awareness of the vulnerability of death and its certainty for all. The everyday experiences of an elderly schoolteacher serve to ground Lumumba who is often spoken about in mythic terms. In actuality, Lumumba was an ordinary man who styled an appearance and aspired to greatness, who led the charge for the country's emancipation and who confronted a series of actors that attempted to take control of the Congo, and, in the course of doing so, there may have been errors, but these are not the concern of Senga's series or, indeed, Kayembe's act of homage.

The assassination

The diptych that ends Senga's series deploys a photograph from the final time that Lumumba was ever captured on camera, Friday, 2 December 1960 [fig. 3.9]. Handcuffed and tousled in appearance, Lumumba is pictured surrounded by guards. His white short-sleeved shirt appears wrinkled and open, a far cry from the composure and the suits of the young statesman seen in the other photographs included in Senga's series. His signature glasses and charismatic smile are gone. This is one of the only times that Lumumba appears to turn away from the camera. The photograph borrowed by Senga is from a collection of images taken when Lumumba arrived shortly after 5 p.m. at Ndjili, Kinshasa's airport, and again later that day at Binza paratroop camp. He had been arrested on the orders of Mobutu, then in command of the army, while attempting to escape from his residence in Kinshasa to Kisangani, his political stronghold. Dozens of people were waiting on the tarmac at Ndjili. From there, Lumumba was transferred in the back of a lorry alongside two associates, Maurice Mpolo and Joseph Okito, to the Binza paratroop camp and again paraded for the press. Images and newsreel footage of the punishment inflicted on Lumumba at the airport and the Binza camp were disseminated around the world. The crowds were told to taunt the young statesman who was forced to eat a transcript of a recent statement in which he declared that he was the head of the country's legitimate government. The following day, 3 December 1960, the US Ambassador to the Congo, Clare Hayes Timberlake, sent Secretary of State Christian Herter a telegram asking him to stop these photographs from being disseminated as they would have an "atomic bomb" effect.[62] On this same day, Lumumba was sent with Mpolo and Okito to Campy Hardy in Thysville (today Mbanza-Ngungu) where they were detained. On 17 January 1961, the group was transferred to Lubumbashi. They were driven to its outskirts and executed by a firing squad. In an attempt to cover up the assassination, their bodies were exhumed from shallow graves, dismembered and dissolved in sulfuric acid, allegedly supplied by Union Minière.[63]

The succession of events chronicled here that led to the assassination was only made known in 1999 with the publication of Ludo De Witte's study, *The Assassination of Lumumba*, which acknowledged the complicity of both the Belgian and American governments.[64] According to De Witte, the last stage of the operation was personally controlled and led by the Belgians. Directly after the events in the Congo, there was speculation as to what had happened to Lumumba. His death was announced three weeks after it had occurred over Katangan radio on 13 February 1961.[65] The broadcast alleged that Lumumba was killed by enraged bush villagers three days after escaping from Kolatey prison farm. The circumstance that led

Figure 3.9: Georges Senga, *Une vie après la mort*, 2012. Inkjet on Baryta paper, 170 × 60 cm. Courtesy of the artist. (Plate 19, p. 213)

to the arrest photographs, one of which is deployed by Senga, and the assassination thereafter created a mythology around Lumumba.[66]

If the arrest photograph reworked by Senga captures the final time that Lumumba was ever seen by the camera, the events thereafter are frequently envisioned by Congolese popular painting. There is little research around photography's entanglements with other arts across the continent.[67] Mediums are often treated as separate fields of enquiry. The tradition of Congolese popular painting emerged in Lubumbashi and Kinshasa in the 1960s and 1970s. Thousands of paintings (many of them narrative or popular retellings of history) were produced by self-taught or apprenticed artists and sold to a local audience. Clients were after subjects with a wide appeal, showing scenes of which they were already aware.[68] These paintings were hung in people's homes where they acted as prompts for conversation alongside other forms of interior decoration, such as photographs and magazine illustrations.[69]

Exemplary of this trend is the Lubumbashi-born painter Tshibumba Kanda-Matulu, who had conceived of a project of painting the entire history of Zaire. In 1973, when the anthropologist Johannes Fabian befriended Tshibumba, the artist had yet to find the economic means to make the comprehensive series, as local customers only purchased one or two works.[70] Fabian accordingly sponsored the series of one hundred paintings, and, while working on the project and in subsequent years, several expatriate colleagues acquired shorter versions of it.[71] In one of the works from the series, *Calvaire d'Afrique* (c. 1970–73), Tshibumba rendered Lumumba's transfer to Lubumbashi on 17 January 1961 after having been imprisoned at Camp Hardy in Thysville since December. There is a control tower as well as a Sabena aeroplane in the background while a smokestack suggests the ongoing work of Union Minière. Lumumba's hands are tied behind his back with rope. He is accompanied by agents of the Sûreté and soldiers from the Katangese gendarmes. There are several versions of this exact same scene painted by Tshibumba in both colour and black and white [fig. 3.10]. In conversation with Fabian while working on the series, the artist explained:

> One in colour, the other not. It's like the photographs your wife took of me. She said she would photograph me in colour as well as in black and white. And that's how I did it, in colour and in black and white.[72]

Tshibumba's comment seems to convey the affinity of Congolese popular painting with photography. I would argue that popular painting, a post-photographic phenomenon, takes over from the camera in capturing Lumumba after the arrest.[73] For example, Tshibumba's *Calvaire d'Afrique* turns to an event that occurred after the final photographs were taken, the arrival of Lumumba in Lubumbashi. Notably, Lumumba is pictured by the artist in a white undershirt, as was the case in the global coverage around the arrest, suggesting the dishevelment seen in the photographs. This outfit represents a significant change for the statesman, who was typically clean-cut and dressed in suits.

In a photograph of the artist painting from 1973, Tshibumba appears acutely aware of photographic culture [fig. 3.11]. A black and white illustrated newspaper article is turned toward the camera, while in the background, there appears a collection of photographs, varying from passport photos to shots of Mobutu, tacked onto the wall.

Figure 3.10: Tshibumba Kanda-Matulu, *Calvaire d'Afrique*, c. 1970–73. Acrylic on flour sack, 38.89 × 72.39 cm. Virginia Museum of Fine Arts, Richmond. Eric and Jeanette-Lipman Fund. © Virginia Museum of Fine Arts. Photo: Travis Fullerton.

Figure 3.11: Etienne Bol, *Tshibumba Kanda-Matulu Painting*, 1973. Digital print on diasec mount, 35.24 × 52.07 cm. Virginia Museum of Fine Arts, Richmond. Gift of Etienne Bol. © Virginia Museum of Fine Arts. Photo: Sydney Collins.

Passport photographs were deployed to validate one's official identity as, since the start of the 1970s, the state had required its citizens to carry a photo identity card.[74] These passport photos were provided by clients who wanted to commission a painted portrait. Not only was a painting cheaper than a photographic enlargement, but it also offered artists the opportunity to enhance their subjects.[75] There is a clear exchange that occurs between photography and popular painting. Jewsiewicki went as far as to say that, in the 1970s, "an urban painter would 'photograph' with a paintbrush the face of his client".[76] Moreover, it is as if the black and white and coloured versions of Tshibumba's work attempted to enter the sphere of photography through which events in the country had been chronicled since the Congo atrocities captured by Seeley Harris in the early twentieth century. This emphasis on photography was continued by InforCongo as it attempted to counter prevailing conceptions of the colony. Images were similarly central to several journals and magazines started in the Belgian Congo. For example, *Nos Images*, the Congolese equivalent to *Life* magazine that circulated widely from 1948 onwards, was a predominantly visual publication filled with large format photographs spanning entire pages.[77] Bearing this in mind, painting perhaps provided a site for imaging what might have happened to Lumumba, whereas photography at this moment in the Congo was still largely tied to the idea of recording actual events.

Figure 3.12: Burozi, *Lumumba Arriving in Elisabethville*, c. 1970s. Oil on fabric, 32.39 × 57.15 cm.
Source: Bogumil Jewsiewicki, *A Congo Chronicle: Patrice Lumumba in Urban Art* (New York: Museum for African Art, 1999).

The entanglement of Congolese popular painting with photography is exemplified in the case of Lumumba. In *Lumumba Arriving in Elisabethville* (c. 1970s) [fig. 3.12], Burozi, the Likasi artist who had taught Tshibumba, turns to an earlier instance in the same event seen in *Calvaire d'Afrique*.[78] He renders Lumumba, Mpolo and Okito as they disembark in Lubumbashi from an aeroplane emblazoned with the words "AIR CONGO C-B" and a Belgian flag. The three men, each dressed in a white undershirt, descend the staircase led by a bespectacled Lumumba. Interestingly, Burozi chose to add three white male photographers dressed in black suits to the scene. Two appear on the right-hand side of the three captives, while another is shown at the top of the staircase. From the top of the stairs, the photographer angles the camera toward the viewer. The scene rendered by Burozi suggests the sea of cameras edited out of the many iconic photographs. The camera is similarly occluded in Senga's contemporary photographs of Kayembe. However, the arrival of Lumumba in Lubumbashi was actually characterised by a complete omission of photography as it occurred after the final arrest photographs were taken. Nonetheless, the painting speaks to the omnipresence of the camera around Lumumba who was, in turn, acutely aware of photography's significance to his life.

In addition to capturing Lumumba's arrival in Lubumbashi, the assassination itself was depicted by popular painting. Around 1970, Burozi executed a work entitled *Bodies of Lumumba, Mpolo and Okito* [fig. 3.13], which shows three corpses laid to rest in a woodland. The men are watched over by a solider with a gun. Painting

Figure 3.13: Burozi, *Bodies of Lumumba, Mpolo, and Okito*, c. 1970s. Oil on fabric, 38.74 × 49.53 cm.
Source: Bogumil Jewsiewicki, *A Congo Chronicle: Patrice Lumumba in Urban Art* (New York: The Museum for African Art, 1999).

is employed as a continuation of the photojournalism that comprised the era, and, in the case of Tshibumba, it even travels back in time to events that escaped the camera's eye, from the assassination of Msiri, the King of Katanga, by Leopold's army in 1891 to the strike at Union Minière in 1941. There is a collapse that occurs as the camera and canvas come to share in the same operation through their collation of an archive around Lumumba. Moreover, there is an attempt in the paintings that render Lumumba after the arrest to restore the young *évolué* from the tousled appearance seen in the photographs. In *Bodies of Lumumba, Mpolo and Okito*, as in the other paintings that depict the group's arrival in Lubumbashi, Lumumba appears without any wounds. The final collection of photographs is suddenly an object to ameliorate and surpass.

The tradition of Congolese popular painting is itself indebted to photographic culture, a thread often only acknowledged by existent scholarship (largely written by anthropologists) in a couple of sentences.[79] Newspaper photographs, as suggested in the image of Tshimbumba painting, were the sources for many of the artist's paintings based on Lumumba.[80] Tshibumba's turn to photography has also been observed by Erin Haney who argued of the paintings that "their compositions rely

Figure 3.14: Tshibumba Kanda-Matulu, *Discours du 4 janvier 1959, les martyrs de l'indépendance*, c. 1970–73. Acrylic on flour sack, 38.42 × 73.03 cm. Virginia Museum of Fine Arts, Richmond. Eric and Jeanette Lipman Fund. © Virginia Museum of Fine Arts. Photo: Travis Fullerton. (Plate 20, p. 214)

on the artist's sense of history", a statement which is left somewhat vague.[81] History in the Congo and the era of Lumumba, as argued above, is largely informed by the photographic. In *Discours du 4 janvier 1959, les martyrs de l'indépendance* (c. 1970-73) [fig. 3.14], a portrait of Lumumba is coupled with a history style painting of him leading the Congolese with the country's flag. The portrait is suggestive of the often circulated photograph of Lumumba deployed by Senga [fig. 3.5], as the highlights on his face summon the flash of the camera. Additionally, the juxtaposition of two images in one painting is evocative of an editorial layout that would set photographs side by side alongside text or even the double page spread characteristic of photo magazines like *Life*. Tshibumba's works were also annotated, similar to those of the Kinshasa-based Chéri Sambi who borrowed from the world of comics; the texts guided the audience on their engagement with the visual. These texts seem to operate in similar ways to the photographic caption, which accompanied the typical circulation of Lumumba's image, as suggested in the leaflet collected by Kayembe in the series.[82]

The omnipresence of photography continues even in paintings without an identifiable source photograph. In a painting by Tshibumba entitled *La mort historique de Lumumba, Mpolo et Okito* (c. 1970-73) [fig. 3.15], the body of Lumumba is shown lying on the grass alongside that of Mpolo and Okito.[83] The angle from which Lumumba is rendered creates the impression of a photographic sensibility as if Tshibumba had also laid on the ground to capture the scene. This same kind of

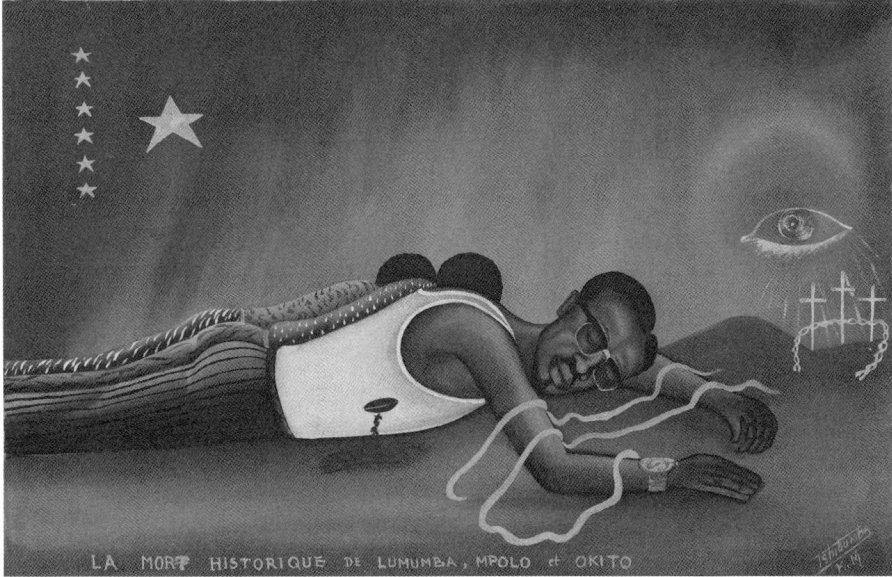

Figure 3.15: Tshibumba Kanda-Matulu, *La mort historique de Lumumba, Mpolo et Okito*, c. 1970–73. Acrylic on flour sack, 44.93 × 71.12 cm. Virginia Museum of Fine Arts, Richmond. Eric and Jeanette Lipman Fund. © Virginia Museum of Fine Arts. Photo: Travis Fullerton.

sensibility is observed by Haney in the work of Samba whose subjects often appear as if they were suddenly stopped mid-activity by the camera.[84] In both Tshibumba's *Calvaire d'Afrique* and Burozi's *Lumumba Arriving in Elisabethville*, Lumumba and the others in the group appear to advance toward an imaginary camera. They are painted in the style of a newsworthy snapshot, evoking documentary reportage and the technologies of modern history.

Congolese popular painting developed when photography was already a well-established tradition in the country; however, the existent photographic traditions in the Congo were already entwined with the conventions of Western painting.[85] In 1960, Lumumba's political party, Mouvement National Congolais-Lumumba, distributed a photograph of him dressed in his habitual suit and tie [fig. 3.16]. The same photograph is seen reproduced on a tattered black and white flyer created by the Lumumbiste Party in Tillim's 2006 series *Congo Democratic* [fig. 2.17] discussed in the second chapter. In the shot, Lumumba stands with a globe that turns Africa toward the camera, evoking the continent's purported ascendancy in this same era as the world is physically held by Lumumba. The significance of props had long been associated with painted portraiture. The addition of the globe extends all the way back to Hans Holbein in *The Ambassadors* (1533). In the 1970s, Burozi created both black and white and colour paintings entitled *Lumumba, Master of the*

Figure 3.16: Photographic print of Lumumba distributed by Mouvement National Congolais–Lumumba in 1960. Source: Bogumil Jewsiewicki, *A Congo Chronicle: Patrice Lumumba in Urban Art* (New York: The Museum for African Art, 1999).

Figure 3.17: Burozi (signed Tshibumba), *Lumumba, Master of the World*, c. 1970s. Oil on fabric, 45.72 × 31.75 cm. Source: Bogumil Jewsiewicki, *A Congo Chronicle: Patrice Lumumba in Urban Art* (New York: The Museum for African Art, 1999). (Plate 21, p. 215)

World based on interpretations of this photograph. In a black and white version, Lumumba appears against a white wall like the subject of a studio photograph. The colour version appends two red curtains on either side of Lumumba as if evocative of a theatre or even classical portrait painting in which drapes often provided a backdrop [fig. 3.17]. His shadow is cast to the left in both paintings, suggesting a light source beyond the edge of the work. Flat in effect, the black and white version of *Lumumba, Master of the World* evokes the softly faded edges of a well-worn photograph. Commercial studio photography as well as painterly conventions endure and are, above all, enmeshed in Congolese popular painting.

Photography appears to have had an effect on the conception of an artwork in Congolese popular painting. Tshibumba and Burozi produced several copies of the same work as evidenced in the various collections by which they were acquired.[86] Though obviously influenced by sales, we could speculate that the various versions of one work speak to the countless copies of the photograph, as already analysed by Walter Benjamin in 1935. Benjamin had proposed that photographs dissolved the aura of original works of visual art: "Every day the urge grows stronger to get hold of an object at very close range by way of its likeness, its reproduction".[87] Uniqueness and genius are shed by the reproducibility of photographs, which perhaps effected the employment of the signature in Congolese popular painting. Paintings were often signed, though these signatures carried less weight than they did in the West: they occasionally signified the artist or sometimes even the salesman or the client who had left the work to someone else.[88] These circumstances could perhaps be explained through an absence of a market for these paintings at the time. Now that a market has emerged, these signatures are of significance. Of course, Benjamin could not have predicted that photographs too would become subsumed into the authorial structures of the market – and counterintuitively into the fetishisation of the "original" in the sale of vintage prints.

In addition to photography, there were other sources from which artists borrowed that are illuminated through the case of Lumumba. In Tshibumba's *La mort historique de Lumumba, Mpolo et Okito*, three crosses appear in the background, as the artist stated: "I saw that Lumumba was like the Lord Jesus. He died the same way Jesus did: between two others. And he was tied up the way Jesus was. It was just the same".[89] Christian iconography was disseminated in the Kingdom of Kongo by the Portuguese as early as the fifteenth century. However, as Jewsiewicki contends, "Tshibumba and other popular painters did not invent the representation of Lumumba as Christ".[90] Black Francophone writers often portrayed Lumumba as Christ, which was then translated to the visual by Tshibumba and others.[91] There were also the comic books previously mentioned from which Samba worked. In this sense, Congolese popular painting is a tradition shaped in "the contact zone", as in the social spaces where cultures clash, often in contexts of asymmetrical power, such as colonialism.[92] The colonial era and its aftermath saw the appearance and intersection of various mediums that came to constitute Congolese popular painting. The case of Lumumba's image exemplifies the complex entanglements that comprised traditions and technologies of representation specific to the time and space in which it was developed.

Forgetting Lumumba

Turning again to the era of Mobutu, the leaflet for Kayembe's candidature in local government attests to Lumumba's continued existence in Zaire. Kayembe seems to embody Lumumba over the years in the shape of suits, ties and spectacles as well as opinions and lifestyle. The account conveyed in *Une vie après la mort* stands in contrast to scholarship on Lumumba that asserts that the era of Mobutu's Zaire entirely suppressed the assassinated leader's legacy. Writing in *A Congo Chronicle: Patrice Lumumba in Urban Art* (1999), Jewsiewicki asserted:

> Paintings of Lumumba appeared in Katanga in great numbers in response to particular political situations – for example just after Mobutu's coup d'état of 1965, when he was seeking the modicum of international legitimacy that he needed to allow him to hold a summit for the Organisation of African Unity. Mobutu was trying to pass himself off as Lumumba's political heir. As soon as the summit was over, however, he reduced Lumumba to nothing – an empty shell, as empty as the pedestal built in Kinshasa to receive the hero's statue. The historical Lumumba was quickly confined to the archives, his memory banished from political life and his image from public space, where the only political image permissible became that of Mobutu.[93]

Jewsiewicki contends that Lumumba was relegated to the archives after 1965. He suddenly vanished from any active trace in the everyday. However, the visual and material culture of popular painting that is the very subject of Jewsiewicki's analysis contradicts this claim. Nonetheless, Jewsiewicki ascribes to the standard postcolonial narrative developed out of the official rhetoric of Mobutu-era Congo that contends there was only a turn again to Lumumba in the 1990s after decades of amnesia.

It was in the context of a latter-day re-evaluation of Lumumba that Haitian filmmaker Raoul Peck produced the documentary film, *Lumumba, la mort du prophète* (1991). In *La mort du prophète*, Peck considers the events around the assassination through archival photographs and newsreel footage from the colonial and post-independence era, conversations with critics and supporters of Lumumba, videos and photographs from Peck's childhood years spent in the Congo and sequences captured in the streets of Brussels. Peck was prevented from travelling to the Congo by the Zairian government who expressed deep concerns around anything that would compromise Mobutu's stranglehold; we are consequently left with clips of the airport in Brussels. In the film, Peck addresses and criticises pervasive media representations of Lumumba. In order to counter dominant perceptions, his strategy was to juxtapose a calm and lucid Lumumba with a Belgian condemnation of his apparent wild volatility. A central concern of Peck's *La mort du prophète* is Mobutu's corporeal and symbolic eradication of Lumumba. To this end, the opening voice-over states: "His message has vanished, but his name remains. Should the prophet be brought back to life again? Should he be given the floor one last time? Or should the final traces of his memory disappear with the snow?".⁹⁴ The film explores the past and present consequences of historical and political neglect and erasure of Lumumba. The expression "My mother told me..." or "My mother tells..." a story is repeated several times over. Escaping the Duvalier government in Haiti, Peck's family moved to the Congo in 1961, and his mother worked in the mayoral offices in Kinshasa. However, Peck confessed to only a small awareness of Lumumba until working on *La mort du prophète* thanks to the success of the Mobutu cult.⁹⁵ It was Mobutu who was celebrated in the eyes of children, as Peck stated:

> He was a handsome guy and he used to talk almost every day on TV... We'd see him on Sunday when we would go to the cinema to see the local newsreels, and it was always him going here, there, going to some military campaign or jumping in parachutes. For us young kids he was a sort of Rambo-type figure.⁹⁶

Karen Bouwer accordingly wonders: "Had the Peck family lived in Lumumba's stronghold, Stanleyville (Kisangani today), would the young Peck have known so little about him?".⁹⁷

Literature on the visual culture surrounding Lumumba also started to emerge in the 1990s. In 1996, as previously discussed, Fabian published *Remembering the Present: Painting and Popular History in Zaire*. He had collaborated with the artist Tshibumba from 1973–74 to visually chronicle the events in the Congo, many of which centre on Lumumba. Representations of Lumumba across a wide array of culture outside of the Congo were explored in a 1997 volume edited by Pierre Halen and János Riesz entitled *Patrice Lumumba entre dieu et diable: Un héros africain dans ses images*. Biographies on Lumumba were also published around the same time. Jean-Marie Mutamba Makombo's "La destinée de Patrice Lumumba (1925–1961)" appeared in the edited collection, *A la redécouverte de Patrice Emery Lumumba*, in 1996, while Jean Omasombo Tshonda and Benoît Verhaegen's *Patrice Lumumba, jeunesse et apprentissage politique* was published in 1998. In 1999, Jewsiewicki staged the exhibition entitled *A Congo Chronicle: Patrice Lumumba in Urban Art* at the Museum for African Art in New York City.

In the Congo, the exclusion of Lumumba in the Mobutu era was overturned when Laurent-Désiré Kabila seized control of the country in 1997. In Kinshasa, a statue of Lumumba was erected in January 2002. It is said that Kabila senior visited *féticheurs* who granted the rebel leader the ability to conquer the capital city.⁹⁸ He was told to visit Lumumba's tomb and awaken the spirits. One of the clauses in this agreement with the dark world was to erect a statue for the deceased leader. Kabila was a self-proclaimed Lumumbaist. After his assassination in 2001, the government proceeded with the plans for the statue, evoking Kabila as the ancestor to Lumumba. As observed by De Boeck, the statue itself offers a strange palimpsestic portrayal of Lumumba who wears Mobutu's spectacles and carries Kabila's waistline.[99]

In 2000, Peck released a second eponymously titled film on Lumumba, which attempts to restore and foreground what he sees as a neglected history. For *Lumumba*, Peck chose to work in a more cinematic Hollywood style than he had done with *La mort du prophète*. Verisimilitude or the appearance of truth and the employment of synchronous sound is privileged. The events are linked by cause and effect and the story is character-led. Working against the supposed amnesia, Peck attempts to leave the audience with the sainthood of Lumumba intact. He stated: "I decided to return to Lumumba and set the record straight, 37 years after the fact, about a murder-cum-sacrifice. It's also a matter of transcending my own griefs, regrets and still-burning anger".[100] The screenplay starts in 1958 in Léopoldville after the Pan-African Conference in Accra and ends with the assassination. We witness the Round Table Conference in Brussels in January 1959 and the weeks after 30 June 1960, which were characterised by the collapse of the army and the secession of Katanga and Kasai, Lumumba's suspension by Kasa-Vubu, Mobutu's coup d'état, Lumumba's arrest and the violence that preceded the assassinations. Famous photographs were theatrically staged for the story. This recourse to photography takes up the same archive as deployed by Senga as well as that seen in Congolese popular painting. As Peck specified: "Familiar scenes from the photographs and newsreels have also had an emotional force for me. Their dramatic impact is intact".[101] The story of Lumumba as conveyed by Peck is based on photographs.[102] Images of the arrival at Ndjili airport and the subsequent torment are staged in *Lumumba*. To open the scene, Lumumba steps off an aeroplane and silently stares at a group of stationary journalists and photographers, as if the film is acknowledging the act's original shape in a still photograph. As already seen in Senga's series [fig. 3.9], Lumumba is led through crowds by the soldiers. He is grabbed by the head and fed a copy of a recent statement in which he declared that he was the head of the country's legitimate government. Through these scenes, the other side of the photographs are seen, the sea of cameras and exclamations. Memories of Lumumba are accordingly substantiated or even created through the photographs.

Repression is overturned in the various engagements with Lumumba in the 1990s. However, Kayembe's performance of self in the guise of Lumumba reveals something else. For one thing, it speaks to the tenacity of Lumumba's memory and image. Far from disappearing from view, Lumumba evidently endured in Lubumbashi over the course of sixty or so years. His legacy and image were enacted and embodied for the young Senga in the 1980s in the very same classrooms photographed in the series. It does not matter if Lumumba's name was not mentioned or his place in history was not imparted, the daily witnessing of a teacher who embodied his persona and appearance constitutes a form of remembrance. This powerful act may have even had a subliminal effect. For Kayembe was glimpsed on the streets of the city in the guise of Lumumba dressed in the suits of the *évolué*. Disappearance is eschewed in Kayembe's embodiment of Lumumba. This effect is further emphasised in Senga's treatment of the black and white archival photographs. The artist sources, edits and prints the archival images available online as if to assert their continued existence in the contemporary world. More than traces from a bygone era, they come to occupy the same time as the elderly Kayembe.

The claims of amnesia around Lumumba call for further scrutiny. Perhaps he was forgotten to some extent in the West, in Belgium and in Peck's own experience of the Congo. However, the total disappearance of his memory that is assumed seems false. This assumed amnesia presupposes a Western centre as well as the total control by the state of the everyday, a condition that was subtly subverted by Kayembe who lived and embodied the man. Personal memories across the Congo escaped the absolutism of the Zairian government. As we have seen, Lumumba was the subject of much Congolese popular painting in the 1970s. In an exchange with Tshibumba on *Grâce à MPR / Lumumba héros national* (1974), Fabian comments, "I see that you show Lumumba near that famous house. And here inside a window – or is it next to a window? – I see a man's face", to which the artist answers:

> It is Lumumba's face... Well it's a little trick I used. When you go to this house – you can do this tomorrow – you will find a portrait of Lumumba inside. Underneath there is an inscription: "A country needs it martyrs; I offer myself as the first". Lumumba himself said this.[103]

Drawing from this scene, we could assume that Lumumba endured as a subject of exchange in living rooms around Lubumbashi.[104]

As I mentioned at the start of this chapter, Senga's *Une vie après la mort* was exhibited at the Biennale de Lubumbashi in 2013, and its display was coordinated with Tillim's series *Avenue Patrice Lumumba*.[105] In Tillim's series, the apparent dilapidation of the pictured spaces seems to suggest the abandonment of Lumumba's memory and his vision for the Congo [fig. 3.3]. The Biennale also screened Augustijnen's filmic essay *Spectres*, which explores the suppression of colonial violence in the Belgian psyche as Brassinne denies Belgian complicity in Lumumba's assassination. Histories that had been forgotten were central to Dyangani Ose's curatorial strategy.[106] Lubumbashi lacks any official commemoration of Lumumba. The square in the city centre is dedicated to Moïse Tshombe, the president of the secessionist state of Katanga from 1960 to 1963 who was implicated in Lumumba's assassination, and includes a statue of him. Though Senga adopts the slick language of large-scale digital photography, *Une vie après la mort* is more aligned with Congolese popular painting in its engagement with the endurance of Lumumba on a local level. Karen Barber and Fabian have both defined popular arts in Africa as operating "behind the back" of the established authority.[107] They tell the stories of the people, an objective shared by Senga's series. Material culture and lived experience reveal an alternative account to the dominant postcolonial one premised on amnesia developed in the 1990s. Kayembe's performance is proof that Lumumba did not disappear from view or consciousness. For Lumumba continued to exist on walls, in crinkled photographs and old articles folded and stored away. He was to be found in the spectacles and suits worn by Congolese men for whom he remained a model, a mentor and an ancestor.

Then and now

In *Une vie après la mort*, Senga sets up a series of comparisons between the then and the now inherent to the still image. In one of the diptychs [fig. 3.18], he deploys a black and white photograph of the young Lumumba who stands in the back seat of a Cadillac convertible situated on the tarmac of Kinshasa's airport. The car is surrounded by a sizable crowd: there are the suits of the *évolués*, several army officers and a couple of women as well as the photographers themselves. A wing of an aeroplane emblazoned with a lofty "S" emerges from the background. The "S" stands for the Belgian airline, Societé Anonyme Belge d'Exploitation de la Navigation Aérienne (SABENA), which started travelling from Brussels to Kinshasa in the 1930s. This archival photograph is juxtaposed by Senga with a contemporary colour photograph of Kayembe standing with a bicycle in a dirt street. Pinstriped, the suit of the *évolué* endures, while the bicycle appears as a substitute for the convertible car. In another diptych [fig. 3.19], Senga reworked a photograph showing Lumumba alongside two cars. The archival photograph conveys the young Lumumba dressed in the customary suit, gazing toward the camera with a solemn expression. His papers and notebook are held tightly under one arm. This reworked photograph is coupled in the series with a shot of Kayembe captured again in a dirt street in Lubumbashi. A child walks by in the background, acknowledging the camera, and wheels a dusty tyre down the street. Dirt is visible on Kayembe's trousers

Figure 3.18: Georges Senga, *Une vie après la mort*, 2012. Inkjet on Baryta paper, 170 × 60 cm. Courtesy of the artist. (Plate 22, p. 216)

Figure 3.19: Georges Senga, *Une vie après la mort*, 2012. Inkjet on Baryta paper, 170 × 60 cm. Courtesy of the artist. (Plate 23, p. 217)

and shoes while the child's own appear similarly stained. All that is left of the cars seen on the other side of the diptych is one single old tyre carried by a child.

Here the contemporary photographs act as a critical gloss on the older ones of Lumumba. In her study on photography and decolonial political imagination in Francophone west Africa, Bajorek considers what it means to look at photographs of African politicians from the 1950s and 1960s today, arguing against "the lure of nostalgia or redemptive narratives".[108] She warns: "Decolonisation and liberation movements did not succeed on the terms that they set for themselves. Untold dreams were dashed".[109] The photographs of the young Lumumba deployed by Senga convey the aspirations of the liberated state, and yet the other side of the diptych – in which Kayembe suggests an elderly Lumumba – tells of an alternative outcome. The juxtapositions created by Senga offer a series of comparisons in which cars have been replaced by bikes. Bicycles were once an emblem of modernity in

Figure 3.20: Georges Senga, *Une vie après la mort*, 2012. Inkjet on Baryta paper, 170 × 60 cm. Courtesy of the artist. (Plate 24, p. 218)

the colony adopted by colonial officials and subsequently by the Congolese. They were "a symbolic marker of the middle class", a technology with which to cultivate an "*évolué*-style".[110] However, in the 1950s, cars were the coveted commodities amongst the elite Congolese. Thus, there is something anachronistic about Senga's contemporary colour photograph of Kayembe standing with an object that was already widespread in the 1930s when the photographs from the 1950s and 1960s capture cars and aeroplanes.

This type of anachronism is echoed in one of the other diptychs where a young Lumumba stands to address Congolese Parliament [fig. 3.20]. The archival shot is coupled by Senga with a contemporary colour photograph of Kayembe leaning against a fallen tree trunk in a vegetable garden where shrubs are cultivated. As described by Kayembe: "I turned to small-scale farming to pay for my children's education and bought a small bike as a means of transportation. It was a shame for me".[111] In addition to teaching, Kayembe assumed extra work through the small-scale agricultural endeavour captured in the series. His children's education costs exceeded the wages offered by the school. The case of Kayembe speaks more generally to the changes in the city that added to the toil of everyday life. In comparison to the bike, car ownership offers a lifeline to many who live in areas without public transport as they are able to travel beyond their locale for employment. Mobutu is widely viewed as having taken away the tomorrows that awaited the country after the assassination of Lumumba, as Peck remarks at the start of *La mort du prophète*, "The future has died with the prophet".[112]

In many ways, Senga's series serves as a reminder that independence did not occur on the terms set out by Lumumba. Matthias De Groof has argued that the figure of Lumumba endures across the arts because the need for decolonisation does as well.[113] However, Peck's assertion, that "the future has died with the prophet", shuts down a sense of the future in the Congo from the moment of Lumumba's assassination onwards. The structure of the diptych alternatively opens up this claim. Other futures transpired, though obviously not the one that Lumumba had envisioned, but outcomes that were very much so lived by people like Kayembe. Returning to Bajorek, in her discussion of old photographs, she dismisses nostalgia as a counteractive force, however I contend that nostalgia can act as a critical force in the present. Kayembe's embodiment suggests a kind of sentimental longing for Lumumba. Nostalgia in contemporary art has been explored by Paolo Magagnoli who challenges its dismissal by scholars.[114] Instead, Magagnoli argues that "the past can provide positive models of resistance to the status quo and show possibilities which are still valid in the present".[115] In the same vein, the old photographs of Lumumba are more than just static artefacts of the past. Their circulation online attests to the way in which they animate a present moment. Nostalgia is often derided as the opposite of history, or what is considered an objective and well-documented account of the past.[116] But, in turning to the time of Lumumba, Senga engages an alternative vision of the world, and a longing for it, one in which the young statesman had lived. Nostalgia in *Une vie après la mort* suggests a critique of the present and the continued need for decolonisation and transformative politics in the Congo.

Heroes

Narratives on independence movements across Africa often hinge on the actions of a singular leader. From Lumumba in the Congo to Léopold Sédar Senghor in Senegal and Kwame Nkrumah in Ghana, the tale through which emancipation was won travels through various statesmen. Senga's *Une vie après la mort* conveys events surrounding Congolese independence in an alternative way. The concept of heroism is rendered complicated as the series turns to the existences entangled with Lumumba's own. Devotion is simultaneously embraced and enacted through the case of Kayembe. The series engages the ordinary actions of a schoolteacher. Kayembe teaches the same group of students every day of the school week and cycles through the streets of Lubumbashi. Monumentality is abandoned, rather, the series foregrounds the existences that occurred alongside and in the wake of Lumumba's own. The photographs complicate a simple timeline of the country that cites the assassination of the hero and then moves onwards. For, Senga turns to the space surrounding these events and the gaps that complicate the standard narrative trajectory of the country. The photographs tell of the various Congolese people that looked towards the deceased leader and who championed the aspirations of the independent state. Some men dressed like Lumumba as the exemplary *évolué*, while others stored away memorabilia, articles and photographs. The series invokes the *évolués* who decorated their walls with photographs of Lumumba and the artists who produced paintings in commemoration of the events for the salons of a local audience. *Une vie après la mort* conveys the sociality of photographs, their circulation and visibility and the audiences that they encounter in their transmission. Senga captures the visual economy that centred on Lumumba and its effect on concurrent and asynchronous lived experiences, the outcomes of which are far from epic. *Une vie après la mort* is about a schoolteacher who had attempted to enact changes on the small scale in the classroom and through local government. In his series Senga emphasises the collective experience of events in the city of Lubumbashi through the case of Kayembe, a Congolese teacher dressed in European suits and known by his colleagues as "Lumumba".

CHAPTER 4

From Kinshasa to the Moon

Kongo Astronauts

In September 2013, a series of verbal accounts emerged in Kinshasa of an astronaut walking the streets of the city in a silver spacesuit constructed from discarded junk and electronic debris spray-painted silver and gold.[1] First sighted in Lingwala, a neighbourhood near the city centre, the astronaut, it is alleged, subsequently travelled through the streets of Kindele; Kimbanseke, where the prophet Simon Kimbangu had lived; Ngwaka, one of the city's toughest areas; Matonge, the site of the historic boxing event "Rumble in the Jungle" graced by Muhammad Ali and George Foreman in 1974, and finally Massina, also known as the People's Republic of China. This apparition was in fact a performance by Kongo Astronauts, an artist collective established in 2013.

As is often the case with performance art, I came across the work of Kongo Astronauts through documentation, specifically through photographs that someone had taken of what the collective termed their "urban landings" in Kinshasa in June and November 2013. Eléonore Hellio, one of the collective's co-founders, had arranged these photographs into a collage and uploaded them onto to their WordPress website. These collages were early attempt to disseminate their work, a dissemination which has been successful. The collective's work has been included in exhibitions and film festivals both nationally and internationally. As their website states, Kongo Astronauts' concerns vary from the "contemporary cyborg", "an attempt to resist psychic ghettos that subsume multiple postcolonial realities" and "the digital globalisation where the past, the future and the present collide".[2] Although their performances are designed for the streets and audiences of Kinshasa, the collective are simultaneously vested in the transmission and retransmission of their work through photographs, short films and collaborations. Shot by Hellio, their ongoing series of short films is entitled *Postcolonial Dilemna* [sic], while, more recently, they have started to produce their own photographic series, such as *Capital SCrashed.exe* (2021) [fig. 4.2]. Musicians offer one avenue of collaboration for the collective. In 2014, their image appeared in the music video for Kinshasa-based band Mbongwana Star's "Malukayi", travelling through the layered cityscape of

Figure 4.1: Baloji, still from music video for "Capture" (feat. Petite Noir and Muanza), 2015. Courtesy of Baloji and NOWNESS.

Figure 4.2: Kongo Astronauts, *Untitled [-6]* from *Capital SCrashed.exe* series, 2021. © Kongo Astronauts. Courtesy of Axis Gallery, New York. (Plate 25, p. 219)

Kinshasa. In 2015, they collaborated with the Belgian rapper of Congolese origin, Baloji (cousin to the artist Sammy Baloji) in the music video for "Capture" [fig. 4.1] where two astronauts search a warehouse for the toppled statue of Henry Morton Stanley, the explorer who had spent 1879–84 assisting King Leopold II claim a large area of the Congo. They collaborated again with Baloji in 2019 for the short film, *Zombies*, that was written, directed and produced by him.

The body of work created by Kongo Astronauts is grounded in Kinshasa, a megacity with an estimated population of fifteen million, and, although the Congo has immense natural resources, its citizens have limited access to basic commodities such as electricity and running water. The inhabitants of Kinshasa have become adept at navigating the vertigoes of an informal economy based on recycling. This same ethos shapes the spacesuits worn by the collective. Mineral extractions from Katanga endure as the bedrock through which contemporary digital technologies are created. Cobalt and coltan are shipped to China where they enter the production of electronic devices that are subsequently distributed and sold around the world. Finally, the objects themselves travel back to the Congo and other African countries as e-waste. It is cheaper for the West to export these discarded electronic devices than to recycle them, and they end up in Kinshasa's markets and scrap heaps. The collective construct their spacesuits from this e-waste, studded with discarded wires, circuit boards and smartphone parts. Like the spacesuits themselves, the collective's artwork connects stories and scales that are most often kept separate.

Kongofuturism

Media accounts typically associate Kongo Astronauts with Afrofuturism.[3] The term "Afrofuturism" was coined in 1993 by the American cultural critic Mark Dery through conversations with writer Alondra Nelson. Drawing from African American writers like Samuel R. Delany and Octavia E. Butler, Dery argued that African Americans were the actual "descendants of alien abductees": "they inhabit a sci-fi nightmare in which unseen but no less impassable force fields of intolerance frustrate their movements; official histories undo what has been done; and technology is too often brought to bear on black bodies".[4] Dery asks: "Can a community whose past has been deliberately rubbed out, and whose energies have subsequently been consumed by the search for legible traces of its history, imagine possible futures?".[5] In 2002, Nelson elaborated on the conversations she had had with Dery. One crucial aspect of Afrofuturism, she believed, was the digital divide and the way in which blackness gets constructed as oppositional to advanced technologies: the labour of black people is excluded as well as the historical truths of black participation in technological development.[6] Afrofuturism critiques contemporary crises experienced by black people often through re-examining historical events, correcting the problem of black erasure in the past by looking to an imaginary future. These objectives have been taken up by various African American artists since the 1990s. In 2004-5, Ellen Gallagher, for example, created a series of prints, entitled *DeLuxe*, using advertisements found in magazines from the 1930s to the 1970s aimed at African American consumers. Extracts of textual advertisements and images promoting a range of beauty products for women and men, including wigs and pomades, were cut and layered by Gallagher to create the effect of a collage. In one of the works, she appends yellow plasticine over the models' faces and heads, transforming the women into futuristic alien mock astronaut figures. In doing so, Gallagher collapses the past into the future and obsolescence into technology.

In its conception, Afrofuturism was largely the purview of African American voices. However, in a 2003 article, Kodwo Eshun declared Afrofuturism's currency in an African context as it serves to operate against endless projections of the continent's predicted dystopia.[7] On the occasion of the 2013 exhibition *The Shadows Took Shape* at The Studio Museum in Harlem, its co-curator Zoé Whitley suggested that the speculative and technological concerns of Afrofuturism proliferate beyond an African American context to address themes of alienation, anxiety, social acceptance, national belonging and personal identity worldwide.[8] Though Whitley soon admits we are perhaps left wanting for a more appropriate term.[9] Nonetheless, the exhibition joined together a series of artists from around the world by treating Afrofuturism as an aesthetic strategy to address race, displacement and difference using recognisable visual symbols.[10]

Since Dery's coinage of the term as a critical category and theoretical concept, Afrofuturism has operated as a spur to artistic practice. One manifestation of it might be captured in the turn to outer space. Several artists in various geographical contexts have aligned themselves with Afrofuturist cultural production through the figure of the astronaut. In the late 1990s, British-Nigerian artist Yinka Shonibare started to integrate the figure of the alien, a mainstay of science fiction, and subsequently the Apollo-mission-styled astronaut into his practice, both of which are clad in batik textiles, a material that signifies as "African" and yet is the product of global commodity exchange.[11] These works play with British colonial expansion, as well as themes of family and national belonging during a time in which postcolonial migrants in the United Kingdom were rhetorically being scapegoated for the nation's economic woes.[12] Alternatively, in an ongoing work entitled, *The Final Frontier* (c. 2008), the Canadian artist Camille Turner created a series of African Astronauts who have returned to earth after ten-thousand years to save the planet. These "Afronauts" are seen as descendants of the Dogon in Mali; their costumes are a blend of articles associated with the latter as well as space travel garb. Similarly drawing on Afrofuturist theory, the Spanish artist Cristina de Middel's series *The Afronauts* (2012) envisions an African space programme as previously attempted by Eduard Makuka Nkoloso in Zambia after the end of colonial rule in the 1960s. Like in the case of Shonibare, De Middel's astronauts, who wonder across a landscape of eroded spaceships and elephants, spacesuits made out of African textiles.

In a 2018 essay entitled "Afrofuturism: Ayashis' Amateki", South African writer Mohale Mashigo argued that Afrofuturism as developed out of slavery lacks the same kind of traction in Africa.[13] Race as it is experienced in the United States is crucial to its construction. According to Mashigo, Afrofuturism acts as an escape for those who find themselves in the minority and divorced from their African origins, so they envision a "black future" where they are the majority and are able to join their culture together with technology.[14] Drawing from a 1980s song by Mercy Pakela called "Ayashis' Amateki" about shoes that were too tight, Mashigo creates an analogy between Afrofuturism and the wrong size of "takkies", a term for trainers or sneakers in South Africa.[15] She suggests that it is wrong to take Afrofuturism in its entirety and to act as if it were "my size".[16] Instead, she argues for a project that predicts each country's own postcolonialism.[17] Mashigo advocates exploring what size takkies fit specific contexts in Africa and for these stories to address "Now" as well as "The Future".[18] Following Eshun and Whitley, there is a clear desire for projects that distort African dystopias. However, as observed by Mashigo, Afrofuturism is the wrong size. She calls for an expansion in the vocabulary around the way in which artistic projects are conceived rather than their conflation with the category of Afrofuturism.

What I would argue is characteristic of Kongo Astronauts and the other contemporary artists discussed in this chapter is an engagement with the time and aspirations associated with the end of colonialism and the emergent postcolonial state. As deployed by Kongo Astronauts, the figure of the astronaut evokes the era of the Space Age in the 1960s and 1970s, which, as I will demonstrate, was entangled with struggles for emancipation across Africa. Independence was supposed to yield a prosperous state that, for many, never arrived as they thought it would, whether dashed by corrupt politicians or predatory capitalism. Futures that slipped away create a space from which to contemplate "what might have been". Through the figure of the astronaut, the collective evokes a sense of optimism associated with the independent state that enables a critique of contemporary affairs. In comparison to Afrofuturist projects that link black people with advanced technologies and a prosthetically enhanced vision of the world, Kongo Astronauts cast doubt over the technologies themselves and their concomitant optimism. Rather than coining an alternate phrase to Afrofuturism, I suggest attending to the individual artworks themselves, even though one member of the collective describes their practice as "Kongofuturism".[19] There is an orientation in the artwork produced by Kongo Astronauts towards times already experienced, even the collective's title calls up the Kingdom of Kongo, the origins of which travel as far back as the fourteenth century. Moreover, the visual culture of Kongo was shaped through transnational encounters, a theme which I will similarly engage over the course of this chapter.[20]

Urban landings and postcolonial dilemmas

Kongo Astronauts was established by Eléonore Hellio and Michel Ekeba, but the team varies from between two and seven members. On the collective's website, Hellio writes that she "expands KA's fields of action through importable connections. Interspace and species communications, paranormal phenomena, dilettante cybernetics, cognitive dissent that shapes her video practice".[21] Meanwhile, Ekeba "embodies KA through an action that proceeds from states of consciousness, from urban *dérives* to collisions".[22] He creates "the spacesuits with old electronic circuits loaded with cobalt, copper and coltan, putting them into action, crossing the city, its streets, its roundabouts".[23] Hellio and Ekeba are joined by Bebson Elemba, a "composer, inventor of instruments, performer and instigator," and Danniel Toya, a builder of robots, who contributes to their films.[24] On occasion, Hellio and Ekeba, the two "co-pilots", are accompanied by other passengers, such as Amourabinto Lukoji, Chara Kalej, Cedrick Tamasala, Céline Banza and Rachel Nyangombe.

The performances staged by the collective are rarely announced, and they produce a sense of surprise amongst onlookers who witness them, giving this strange aberration a double take [fig. 4.3]. Dressed in a gold or silver spacesuit, with a matching helmet and boots, Ekeba wanders from one district to another in the Kinshasa megalopolis, appearing in bars, sometimes helping a passer-by cross the street or change a tire. He often counters accepted ways of occupying the city as demarcated by its layout, eschewing sidewalks to tread along the centre of a throughfare with cars on either side. Ekeba's intentions are opaque, and it is up to the spectators to deduce what they want to take from the collective's costumes and performances.

As previously mentioned, the collective is concerned with the urban *dérive*, a tactic developed by mid-twentieth century avant-garde collectives, the Lettrist International (LI) and subsequently the Situationist International (SI). In the three-channel digital video installation, *One.Two.Three* (2015) the Belgian artist Vincent Meessen explored the connections between the SI and the Congo. The SI developed a sustained interest in the Congo when the country started to appear in global press coverage in 1960.[25] Meessen's *One. Two. Three* centres around a protest song written by the Congolese Situationist Joseph M'Belolo Ya M'Piku in May 1968 that was discovered by the artist in the archives of the Belgian Situationist Raoul Vaneigem.[26] Scholarship on the SI often overlooks the participation of activists beyond Europe.[27] Working with M'Belolo and young singers in Kinshasa, Meessen developed a version of the song that was subsequently videoed in the Kinshasa club Un Deux Trois, the same space where OK Jazz orchestra led by Franco Luambo had played in the 1960s. Kongo Astronauts' engagement with

Figure 4.3: Kongo Astronauts, *Untitled [-3]* from *Capital SCrashed.exe* series, 2021. © Kongo Astronauts. Courtesy of Axis Gallery, New York. (Plate 26, p. 220)

the city speaks to an analogous set of concerns to the ones that were developed by the Paris-based collective the LI, the group that preceded the SI, in the 1950s. These strategies offer a paradigm through which to consider the activities of Kongo Astronauts.

One of the concerns central to the LI and subsequently the SI was that of "psychogeography" as in an exploration of everyday city environments that emphasised a sense of playfulness. Developed by the theorist and filmmaker, Guy Debord, in 1955, the term encouraged an alternative engagement with architecture and city space.[28] Central to Debord's thinking was a 1952 study by French sociologist Paul-Henry Chombart de Lauwe, which observed that "an urban neighbourhood is determined not only by geographical and economic factors, but also by the image that its inhabitants and those of other neighbourhoods have of it".[29] In order to illustrate "the narrowness of the real Paris in which each individual lives... within a geographical area whose radius is extremely small", Chombart de Lauwe diagrammed the activities of a student living in the sixteenth arrondissement over the course of a year.[30] Her itinerary delineated a small triangle from which she rarely ever deviated. DeBord extensively discussed and reprinted Chombart de Lauwe's diagram, commenting on the lack of variety and suggesting that occupants of the city were trapped in their own arrondissements, overlooking otherness and actuality, even when it is in close proximity. The circuits of everyday life discouraged exploration and enquiry and constructed obstacles. As Debord wrote:

> Others unthinkingly followed the paths learned once and for all, toward their work and their home, toward their predictable future. For them duty had already become a habit, and habit a duty. They did not see the insufficiency of their city. They thought natural the insufficiency of their life.[31]

In contrast, the strategy of the *dérive* proposed to venture through new urban environments, complicating the way in which arrondissements were conceived and allowing for an alternative experience of the city: "We wanted to get out of this conditioning, in search of different uses of the urban landscape, of new passions".[32] In a *dérive*, the participants were expected to explore the streets, observing the way in which their emotions changed according to the environment. Releasing "themselves to the solicitations of the site", the wanderers on the *dérive* escaped the totalisations of the eye and over-determined constructions of space.[33] The city and its arrondissements were conceived as social constructions through which the *dérive* operates and simultaneously disrupts.

In this book's first chapter, I discussed the way Mbembe's conception of "necropolitics" or "death worlds" is often conflated with that of the postcolony, as well as the oversights existent in scholarship preoccupied with claims of dystopia. We could extend this enquiry to conceptions of Kinshasa at stake in the work of Kongo Astronauts. De Boeck collaborated with the photographer Marie-Françoise Plissart to create the book, *Kinshasa: Tales of the Invisible City*, published in 2004. This study of the city emerged out of the country's tumultuous 1990s and early 2000s, an era that saw the First Congo War, the overthrow of President Mobutu Sese Seko by rebel leader Laurent-Désiré Kabila, the Second Congo War and the assassination of Kabila. In another conflation of Mbembe's "necropolitics" and "postcolony", De Boeck explored the omnipresence of death in Kinshasa. He claimed that the citizens of the Congo were "more dead than alive".[34] However, the playfulness of the performances staged by Kongo Astronauts engenders another vision of the city. As Donna Haraway has asserted, the joy of play breaks the rules in order to make something else happen.[35] This same strategy was deployed by Polish artist Pawel Althamer in the 1990s who, through the performed figure of the astronaut, attempted to see the world and more specifically the city of Bydgoszcz with a "fresh eye".[36] Alongside other Kinshasa-based artists, the collective appeared in the 94-minute documentary film *System K* (2019), or "System Kinshasa", by the French director Renaud Barret. Its title is a play on the French slang expression "Système D", as in *débrouille-toi!* ("fend for yourself"). Under Mobutu, the informal economy of Zaire was also re-

Figure 4.4: Mbongwana Star, still from music video for "Malukayi" (feat. Konono No. 1), 2015. Courtesy of Michel Winter.

ferred to as "Système D". While the Zairian constitution had only fourteen articles, Kinshasa's population added their own "Article 15": *débrouille-toi!*.[37] Describing the transformation enabled by the spacesuit, Ekeba states: "When I put my astronaut suit on, I disconnect myself from the system. I change dimension. I hover about the negativity of reality. I become the system that controls the world".[38]

In the collective's work, the figure of the astronaut operates as a kind of alien. To confront the astronaut on earth is to see it displaced from outer space as if it were dropping in from above. This extra-terrestrial element to the construction of the astronaut in the city prompts one to see the surrounding space again. In the music video for Mbongwana Star's "Malukayi", Kinshasa coalesces with that of a lunar landscape through the appearance of the astronaut [fig. 4.4]. Puddles outside of a club look like craters designed for exploration. The evening sky appears as though it belongs to another planet, while cars are transformed into space vehicles alongside the astronaut. No one goes anywhere and yet the astronaut takes Kinshasa seriously as outer space. In a performance from June 2013, the astronaut collected a sample of sand for a specimen container while children played in background, kicking up the same sand that the astronaut carefully inserted into a test tube. There is a sense of the absurd in the landings staged by the collective, as audiences are confronted by an astronaut dressed in a spacesuit comprised of recycled junk who is completely earth-bound. For, Kongo Astronauts create an alternative collective imagination around Kinshasa transmitted through speculation and gossip, or what is called *radio trottoir* as in sidewalk radio, the rumour mill of the city.

In addition to taking up the tactics developed by the LI and the SI, Kongo Astronauts adopt another technique associated with the historical avant-garde. Montage,

Figure 4.5: Kongo Astronauts, film still from *Postcolonial Dilemna #Track2*, 2012.
© Kongo Astronauts. Courtesy of Axis Gallery, New York.

the today commonplace aesthetic strategy of combination, juxtaposition and overlap, is deployed by the collective in their series of short films, *Postcolonial Dilemna*. The technique was largely developed by the Soviet avant-garde, specifically Sergei Eisenstein, in the 1920s. Eisenstein's style was guided by cultural currents that had emerged after the Russian Revolution in 1917. Film was to educate the workers and enforce the values of socialism; its study was supported by the state. Eisenstein's style developed from theatrical experiments. He believed traditional theatre encouraged viewers to engage too vicariously with fictional action, siphoning off their anarchic energies.[39] On the contrary, Eisenstein thought that theatre should be based on a "montage of attractions" which would take it back to its origins in spectacles and sights or circus entertainment – a set up that encouraged the audience's attention to travel across two or more simultaneous scenes. These strategies were exemplified in *Battleship Potemkin* (1925) where Eisenstein staged a brutal slaughter on the Odessa Steps. The camera centred in on characters who had trouble escaping the stairs. Eisenstein compelled the audience to watch in shock and captivation as terrible ends befell the citizens of Odessa: a sick child and a young woman with a baby carriage are shot by a solider. Images such as these kept the spectator's eyes cemented to the screen. Einstein conveyed this slaughter through separate fragmented shots joined together. Film, for Eisenstein, was intended to produce a series of shocks

Figure 4.6: Kongo Astronauts, film still from *Postcolonial Dilemna #Track3 (Unended)*, 2014.
© Kongo Astronauts. Courtesy of Axis Gallery, New York.

through visual conflict or discontinuity across shots, the goal of which was to create a jolt in the spectator's psyche and to keep the audience wide awake.[40] Illusionism was eschewed as a coherent screen space was constantly challenged.

These same effects are taken up by Kongo Astronauts in their series of short films. With a run time of 7 minutes and 38 seconds, *Postcolonial Dilemna #Track2* (2012) opens with the sounds of a storm coupled with black and white shots of a flashing lightbulb. The collective's films lack any sense of narration aimed at guiding the spectator, but there is a very clear sensation of violence. A woman is soaked by a torrent of water and she struggles to breathe through the icy downpour. Text in the language of administration streams across the edge of the screen: "Prepare and update security guidelines". A cat yowls and swiftly vanishes off screen. There are clips of a barge carrying ore [fig. 4.5], a close-up of an eyeball, the graphics of a video game whose gun shots echo across the screen and a hand that covers the sun. Another clip shows what looks like the lights of a city captured from an airplane at night, against which a one-sided telephone conversation ensues. The camera shifts to a wall of graffiti and circles back over a man's smile. We see a swampland and a town at sunrise or twilight. Inside an empty room, the camera surveys debris and abandoned electronic cables. These shots are coupled with the sounds of Skype.

The strategies of montage are continued in the collective's 6-minute and 31-second short film, *Postcolonial Dilemna #Track3 (Unended)* (2014). The work opens with a black and white clip of a homemade silver satellite surrounded by wisps of smoke.

Figure 4.7: Kongo Astronauts, film still from *Postcolonial Dilemna #Track3 (Unended)*, 2014. © Kongo Astronauts. Courtesy of Axis Gallery, New York.

The scene shifts to a termite invasion [fig. 4.6], and the escalating sounds of electronic music create an anxious atmosphere. The camera travels over barbed wire, while a single eye transposed onto the scene moves erratically. There is a lumino-sonic sculpture created by Bebson, a spinning wheel with flashing lights, that gives way to the astronaut seen through overlapping colours of red, purple and green. There is a shot of a monkey captured through a blood red filter, which is succeeded by soft gentle vocals as the astronaut walks through the jungle to Zonga Falls accompanied by sounds of static [fig. 4.7]. Here the city is replaced by a landscape of forest and waterfalls, but its apparent tranquillity and peacefulness is haunted by the violence of the earlier scene.

Finally, the collective's 14-minute and 8-second short film, *Postcolonial Dilemna #Track4 (Remix mix)* (2019), evokes the same anxious atmosphere as their other works. *#Track4* opens with a man hacking a shallow hole with a pickaxe and shovelling the dirt to one side [fig. 4.8]. His actions are coupled with a fast-paced drumbeat. The hole is superimposed with Ekeba's face, so that these actions appear as if they were happening to him, again connecting mining and the consumption of black bodies seen previously in Baloji's work. This obvious violence is broken up with the gentle movements of a man dappled in sunlight, as the soundtrack switches to a piece on piano. The music subsequently changes to a jolting electronic soundtrack and a disturbing cast of figures appear one after another, as if stalking each other on screen. There is an astronaut sitting in a control deck whose metal helmet has been punctured with holes, a character in a helmet straight out of Star

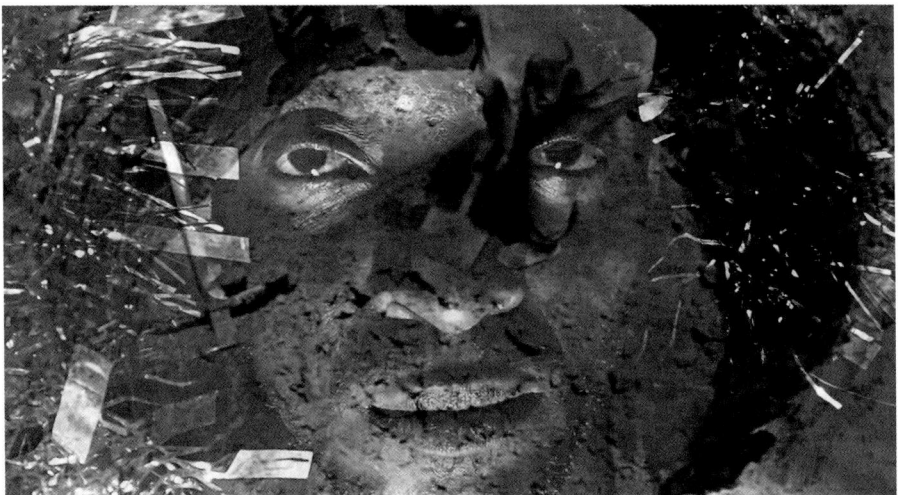

Figure 4.8: Kongo Astronauts, film still from *Postcolonial Dilemna #Track4 (Remix mix)*, 2019. © Kongo Astronauts. Courtesy of Axis Gallery, New York. (Plate 27, p. 221)

Figure 4.9: Kongo Astronauts, film still from *Postcolonial Dilemna #Track4 (Remix mix)*, 2019. © Kongo Astronauts. Courtesy of Axis Gallery, New York. (Plate 27, p. 221)

Wars who repeatedly strikes a sheet of metal with his fist [fig. 4.9], a warrior armed with an umbrella and a flamethrower [fig. 4.10], a panicked astronaut who scuttles around an empty spacecraft, a topless man in a mask created out of a plastic bottle who is lit up by the glow of a fire and a woman who twirls a mirror against a swarm of flies. Our comprehension of perspective is also altered in *#Track4*. In one clip, a

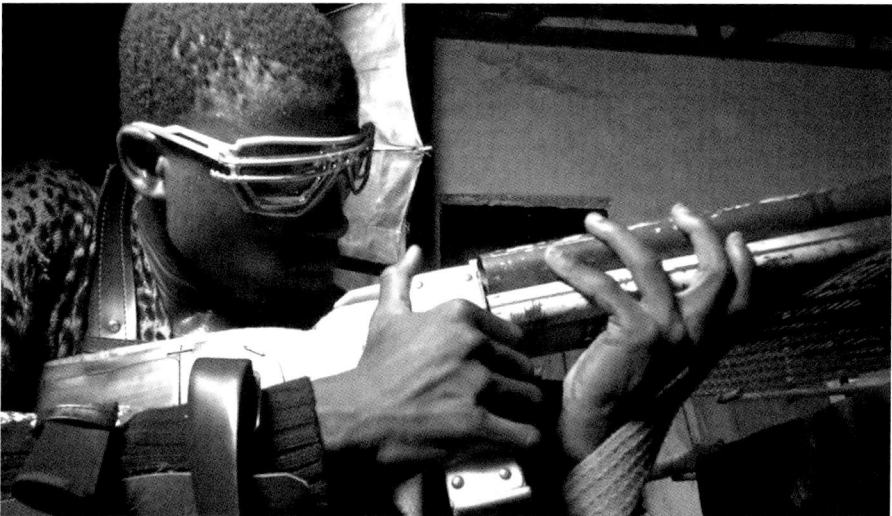

Figure 4.10: Kongo Astronauts, film still from *Postcolonial Dilemna #Track4 (Remix mix)*, 2019. © Kongo Astronauts. Courtesy of Axis Gallery, New York. (Plate 27, p. 221)

Figure 4.11: Kongo Astronauts, film still from *Postcolonial Dilemna #Track4 (Remix mix)*, 2019. © Kongo Astronauts. Courtesy of Axis Gallery, New York. (Plate 27, p. 221)

man sits on the edge of a brick wall from which the outline of a building ascends, while a flock of black birds fly across the screen [fig. 4.11]. If the viewer tries to ground themselves in the film, there is a constant destabilisation or loss of ground. In the same vein, the characters themselves appear familiar, as if emerging from the world of science fiction, cinema and comics, and yet they are without any specific source. There is a complete loss of reference points, echoing the violence done to the Congo in successive predatory regimes, colonial and postcolonial.

Making a past

Through their body of work, Kongo Astronauts prompt a consideration of the astronaut in Kinshasa. Historiography on the Congo often overlooks the Space Age as it was experienced in the country in the 1960s and 1970s, the years of which are most often chronicled through the postcolonial state's downfall after independence from Belgium. There is a certain tone to the titles that comprise this body of literature. A small sampling offers the following: *Lumumba: Africa's Lost Leader*; *Death in Congo*; *The Congo from Leopold to Kabila*; *In the Footsteps of Mr Kurtz: Living on the Brink of Disaster in the Congo*; *The Tragic State of the Congo: From Decolonisation to Dictatorship*; *Dancing in the Glory of Monsters: The Collapse of the Congo and the Great War of Africa*.[41] But there are traces in the material culture of the time that simultaneously speak to something else and complicate the standard evocations of the Congo from these years.

In 1965, the government launched a series of stamps to celebrate the centenary of the International Telecommunication Union (1865–1965), the aims of which were to promote, maintain and extend international co-operation in the field of telecommunications. The stamps showed Telstar in orbit, the world's first active communications satellite, after being launched on 10 July 1962 [fig. 4.12]. The Space Age coincided with the end of colonialism and decolonisation across Africa, and many independent states expressed their participation in the world through these kinds of stamps. The commemorative astronomical stamp was the subject of *In the Year of the Quiet Sun* (2013) – The Otolith Group's 34-minute filmic essay on the aspirations of pan-Africanism. Central to *In the Year of the Quiet Sun* is a solar phenomenon – occurring in an eleven-year cycle – when the sun's surface cools sufficiently to allow scientists to study it. Between November 1964 and November 1965, many emergent African states launched commemorative stamps to observe the event. Reproduced in the filmic essay, these spheres of saturated yellow and red seem to shine a light on the orbiting earth alongside a symbolisation of stars, spheres, roundels and flags. The scale of these stamps is expanded by the Otolith Group to the size of the screen. The stamps themselves emerge from an American context where they were generated and distributed as suggested in their schematic design, the simplified graphics of 1960s commercial art and advertising

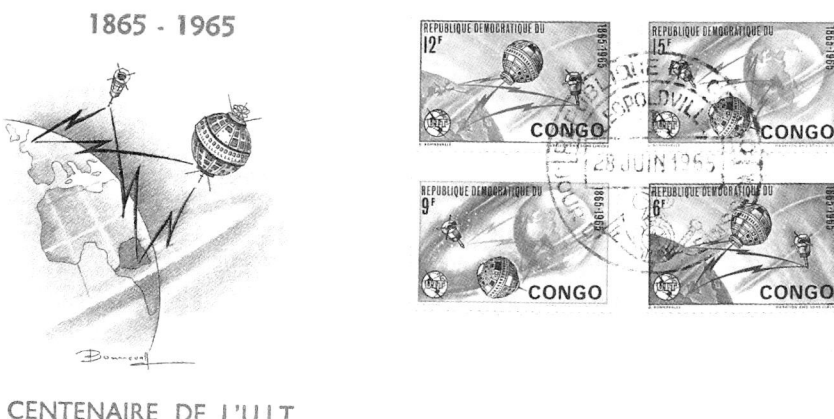

Figure 4.12: Four stamps of the Telstar satellite franked on the first day the issue was authorised for use in the Congo, 28 June 1965. Source: https://rammb.cira.colostate.edu/dev/hillger/telstar.htm.

and their standardised lettering. As Garb has written: "Why, asks the voiceover, are the symbols of pan-African liberation and decolonisation designed on Wall Street? Who is the 'New York Philatelic Society'? What is the pan-African pop that the stamps seem to symbolise and suggest?".[4243] These observations, Garb contends, express the complex entanglements experienced by emerging African states in the early years of the Cold War as they were situated between their old colonial occupiers, the superpowers of East and West and pan-Africanism.[44]

First regulated and standardised in Berne in the 1870s by the Universal Postal Union, stamps came to symbolise a world of capitalist entanglements. They were designed to observe a local context as well as to secure a value so that goods and greetings could efficiently travel. They depended on contemporary technologies, streams of currency and subjects across an expanded globe. Modernity in its culture and context was conveyed through these commemorative tokens, whose colour-coded shape (oddly global in design) offer the physical traces of the cataclysmic events relayed. The stamps themselves are overdetermined signifiers whose graphics are situated firmly in the languages of the time. Universalism was suggested through these objects – a tone already set by the Bandung Conference in April 1955. By participating in these global events, African states were levelling themselves against other contemporaneous superpowers – they were sharing in the same world. In 2014, French-Algerian artist Kader Attia completed a series of paintings entitled *Independence disillusion* [fig. 4.13] in which he reproduced and

Figure 4.13: Kader Attia, *Independence disillusion*, 2014. Oil on canvas, 40 × 31.97 cm. Courtesy of GALLERIA CONTINUA. Photo: Miguel Ángel Emérico. (Plate 28, p. 222)

enlarged African stamps from the 1960s onwards that conveyed aspects of space travel. Though obviously bound up with earthly conflicts, we could conceive of space travel as an attempt to escape the confines of the terrestrial, a bid whose shortcomings were already inscribed in the origins of the stamps and the competition of the Space Race. In an era of the Cold War where the West and the East attempted to expand their control and a group of Asian and African states set themselves apart through the Non-Alignment Movement, the Space Age coincided with decolonisation across Africa, operating as a construct through which other worlds were envisioned. If space travel was tenable, then so was the liberated state's actualisation and its success.

Returning to the Congolese context in the 1960s and 1970s, after the success of Apollo 11, Mobutu asked the crew of the American spaceship to visit the Congo. The country was the only African state to welcome the space travellers.[45] Mobutu even provided the German engineer Lutz Thilo Kayster with a testing site to develop space rockets in the hope of eventually launching a Congolese communications satellite.[46] Writing on Congolese comics, Hunt has described a comparable enthusiasm for space travel. She observed: "When Neil Armstrong took his first steps on the moon in 1970, *Zaïre*'s editors [a semi-glossy news magazine published in Kinshasa] printed an image of Tintin walking on the moon from Hergé's 1954 album, and the lead story was titled 'Armstrong: 15 years after Tintin'".[47] Hunt's observation is part of a larger consideration of *Tintin au Congo*'s reception in the Belgian Congo and by postcolonial Congolese.[48] Following the end of colonial rule in 1960, the comic's Belgian publisher, Casterman, was active in trying to prove the acceptability of *Tintin au Congo*. In 1969, Hergé gifted the 1947 version of the comic to *Zaïre*. Prior to the consolidation of *authenticité*, the *Mobutiste* magazine viewed it as a publishing coup and a holiday gift to thousands of readers and their children.[49] The editors did note that the "colonial authorities" had stopped the circulation of *Tintin au Congo* in the late 1950s to avoid offending the Congolese.[50] However, *Zaïre* had taken a survey to see what Congolese "from seven to seventy-seven years" thought, and many considered Tintin as "an integral part of their patrimony", even a "national hero".[51] Moreover, the Congolese found material in the comic by which "to ridicule the white 'who saw them like that!'".[52] Taking cues from Tintin whose journey to outer space had been published by *Zaïre*, a comic character called "Apolosa" was developed on the streets of Kinshasa around the same time.[53] This enthusiasm for the Space Age also occurred in Kinshasa's clubs, as observed by Pierre Cary Kazadi, the success of Apollo 11 led the country's youth to start staging the Apollo.[54] Imitating Neil Armstrong's spacewalk, the Apollo was seen in the city's clubs for as long as the Space Race was of contemporary significance. Music was specifically created to accompany the Apollo and was played in concerts by well-known Congolese orchestras, such as OK Jazz, Vévé and Rock-'n'-Band, throughout this time.

The collapse of the country from the 1960s onwards is complicated by the vertical energy suggested in the legs and arms lifted for the Apollo throughout the city's clubs and the spaceships launched elsewhere that echoed across the Congo. The later adoption of the astronaut by Kongo Astronauts complicates the way in which global events are confined to certain spaces. The Congo is often appended to accounts of the Cold War, as there is perhaps more of a willingness to associate the country with the suggested violence entailed in these struggles. However, as we have seen, a global enthusiasm for space travel occurred alongside these transnational conflicts. The latter-day landings staged by the collective in Kinshasa assert the occurrence of the Space Age in the city, emphasising that it had transpired in the Congo as it did elsewhere. The body of work created by Kongo Astronauts creates a speculative counter-archive. The collective prompts one to consider the way in which these events were experienced beyond the conventional "centre".

In emphasising the occurrence of the space age in Kinshasa, Kongo Astronauts connect the space of the city with the wider world. Other artists are similarly invested in these same global connections across the 1960s and 1970s. As previously mentioned, in *One. Two. Three* [fig. 4.14], Meessen developed a version of a protest song written by a Congolese Situationist in May 1968 that was subsequently videoed in the Kinshasa club Un Deux Trois. The fragmented cinematographic display of the

Figure 4.14: Vincent Meessen, *One. Two. Three*, 2015. Exhibition view at WIELS, 2016. Photo: Sven Laurent. Courtesy of the artist.

work offers a spatial translation of this collective arrangement of subjectivities. The work produced by Kongo Astronauts is available through a comparable fragmented cinematography: their short films and collaborations can be viewed on Vimeo and YouTube across countless tabs from anywhere in the world. This configuration allows one to consider the way in which the figure of the astronaut was shared around the world. The employment of several screens and an accessible website challenges the conception of a single source from which everything emerges.

We could conceive of Meessen's *One. Two. Three* as a kind of *lieu de mémoire* or "a site of memory", as coined by Pierre Nora.[55] Monumental in size, the three-screens employed by Meessen create a space in which viewers congregate to witness the events from 1968 as they occurred outside of a Euro-American context, and we could say the same of Kongo Astronauts. Furthermore, the employment of lens-based culture engages the visual economy contemporaneous to the events themselves, from May 1968 to the various Apollo voyages. A film or photograph can often compensate for absence in the historical record. Marc Ferro has argued that cinema is an "agent and source of history".[56] Popular visions held as historical epitomes often emerge from the constructions of cinema, for example, the stills from Eisenstein's scene of the 1917 storming of the Winter Palace in *October* (1928) surfaced in school textbooks without any acknowledgement of the original source.

Historians often feel the compulsion to discuss *October* if only to address its errors. The work produced by Kongo Astronauts, as well as Meessen's *One. Two. Three*, come to compete with and stand alongside contemporaneous photography and newsreel footage through the visual economy of the camera and, significantly, the online search engine. This alignment is even more so the case with Kongo Astronauts as our visions of outer space are so contingent on the photographs captured by satellites and other vessels.

"One world"

In the 1920s, the Belgian mining company Union Minière circulated several photographs that showed Katanga in a state of transformation. Photographs in a 1926 annual report sent back to Brussels convey the opening of the earth for its exploitation [fig. 4.15]. Heaps of ground are shifted by African workers equipped with shovels, as they are caught in various stages of action, slowly dispersing the soil. The earth is displaced as the workers descend in elevation through their exertions. Another photograph from "*Rapports direction générale - 1931*" shows a more advanced stage of earthwork in the shape of a valley created by the company [fig. 4.16]. The caption states "*Panda - terrassements usine reduction*". The French word "*terrassements*" suggests the work of reshaping the earth by shifting large amounts of soil, stones, by-products and so on, as well as the changes enacted on its topography. These photographs circulated by Union Minière serve to shift attention away from the surface of the earth, the environments that were overturned and the existences displaced, to the untapped mineral wealth that lay beneath the ground. This type of photography exceeds Union Minière, for example, it is also seen in the archives of the De Beers Corporation in South Africa, shaping an actuality in which land was viewed as an entity for exploitation.[57]

Gabrielle Hecht has written on the tremendous reordering of technopolitics during the Cold War, a time in which technological development emerged as the central concern to many countries. Laws, treaties and other textual orders were created to reenvision Africa as a site of extraction.[58] There were spaces where world events occurred and from which they were controlled and ones that were simultaneously siphoned off for extraction. The Space Age and Africa's status as a site of extraction are often treated as two autonomous phenomena. However, the body of work created by Kongo Astronauts seeks to connect these circuits, closing their supposed gap. Minerals from Katanga enabled the very space travel cited by the collective as well as the construction of space stations. Cobalt was singled out in

Figure 4.15: Photographs labelled "*Mine de Busanga – vue des chantiers d'exploitation*". Union Minière report, *Direction générale: rapport annual 1926*. Belgian National Archives 2–Joseph Cuvelier repository. Photo: Gabriella Nugent.

Figure 4.16: Photograph labelled "*Panda – terrassements usine reduction*". Union Minière report, *Rapports direction générale – 1931*. Belgian National Archives 2–Joseph Cuvelier repository. Photo: Gabriella Nugent.

an excited memorandum sent back to the United States in 1960 as essential for success in the Space Race waged against the Soviets at the time.[59] As early as 1950, a company owned by the Rockefeller family had taken a one-fifth share in Union Minière.[60] Minerals from the Congo today endure as the bedrock of contemporary digital technology.

These extensive circuits of extraction are suggested in Kongo Astronauts' *Postcolonial Dilemna #Track2*. There is a clip of a barge carrying ore played several times in the film [fig. 4.5]. The container is captured from above as it crosses over water, appearing as if it were endless in length. As we have seen, these scenes cut to the graphics of a video game whose gun shots echo across the screen and a clip that shows the lights of a city as if it were taken from an airplane window at night. Over the lights, a one-sided telephone conversation ensues through the calling sounds of Skype. An automated voice speaks in French, "*appelle un autre fois*". While another automated female voice with an English accent states: "The number you have dialled does not exist. Please check it and redial". There is the sound of a call ending over Skype and an attempted connection to someone else. The automated voice of an American woman answers: "Sorry, the number that you have dialled does

Figure 4.17: *The Blue Marble* from Apollo 17, 7 December 1972. Image courtesy of NASA Johnson Space Center, Gateway to Astronaut Photography of Earth.

not exist. Check the number and dial again". Various geographies are connected through these voices and accents. The collective grounds the virtual space of video games and Skype in the physical space and the extractions that enable its very existence. These connections continue through the collective's collaborations. In Baloji's "Capture", the lyrics speak to the shortcomings of technology and the precarity experienced by *creuseurs*: "The Holy Grail is mineral" and "While brothers sacrifice their lives / For phones that contain their blood".

There were certain aspirations that emerged in the West around the Space Age that were widely seen as an attempt to redress these expropriations. The classic views back onto earth from space were enshrined in the iconic photographs from the 1968 and 1972 Apollo spaceflights entitled *Earthrise* and *The Blue Marble* [fig. 4.17]. As Kelly Oliver has observed, in the depths of the Cold War, and over a decade after the Soviets had launched the first satellite to orbit earth, Sputnik, these photographs were framed by rhetoric about the "unity of mankind" travelling together on a "lonely" sphere in space.[61] Seeing earth from space also spawned ecological concerns. Heralded as man's greatest triumph, the spaceflights led to speculations on the technological control of the cosmos. While visions of earth from space caused some to wax poetic about earth, it led others to envision life off-world elsewhere. Over the course of twenty or so years, as Oliver contends, the world had travelled from world war, genocide and the threat of atomic weapons to Sputnik and the Lunar Orbiter, the Apollo spaceflights and photographs of earth from space: "the *world* gave way to the *planetary* and the *global*".⁶² The photographs of earth created a transition from thinking about a world at war to thinking its oneness. However, the only oneness seen in the work created by Kongo Astronauts is in the commercial circuits of exchange created by the extraction of minerals from the Congo and their eventual return as discarded electronic devices to the country from which they originated. In one of the photographs taken by the collective [fig. 4.2], the astronaut is captured outside a second-hand electronics store, making these connections visible.

The sentiments prompted by *Earthrise* and *Blue Marble* were only thinkable from the Global North, specifically United States whose space programme launched these photographers to outer space. The techno-optimism that surrounded space travel endures and recurs in the aspirations connected to cyberspace, again contingent on mineral extractions from the Congo crucial to electronic devices. In February 1996, cyberlibertarian John Perry Barlow wrote and circulated online "A Declaration of the Independence of Cyberspace" from Davos, Switzerland:

> Governments of the Industrial World, you weary giants of flesh and steel, I come from Cyberspace, the new home of Mind. On behalf of the future, I ask you of the past to leave us alone. You are not welcome among us. You have no sovereignty where we gather.⁶³

This opening statement conveys an attempt to conceive of cyberspace as providing a break with the past. Novelty was similarly espoused by the creator of the World Wide Web, Tim Berners-Lee, who described cyberspace as a tool through which to exceed the constraints of time and geographic space.⁶⁴ And yet the language employed by Barlow evidences a trend in which communications technologies and their evocation of the virtual are couched in the language of colonial and westward expansion, complicating the view that there is any escape from the past. These technologies are subject to the earthly conditions that enable their existence. Imaginaries created by virtual space are largely grounded in global corporations that pillage the Congo.

This theme of optimism and distrust in technology is explored in Baloji's 14-minute short film, *Zombies* (2019), which considers the contemporary obsession with being ever-connected and always-on through our mobile phones. Kongo Astronauts make an appearance in a street procession in *Zombies*, alongside a creature dressed in a costume of brightly coloured bottle caps and another constructed from condoms [fig. 4.18]. The rubber of the latter is evocative of the atrocities committed in King Leopold II's Congo Free State where forced labour met the spike in demand for rubber prompted by the invention of the inflatable bicycle tire and spurred on by

Figure 4.18: Baloji, film stills from *Zombies*, 2019. Courtesy of Baloji and NOWNESS.

the rise of the automobile. From the history of rubber to the circuit boards that comprise the astronaut's suit, Baloji's film spotlights the raw materials from the Congo that have enabled technological developments in the Global North. These connections are similarly played out in Kongo Astronaut's photographic series *Capital SCrashed.exe* where the astronaut is captured leaning against a heap of car debris surrounded by tyres [fig. 4.19]. In Baloji's film, the other zombie-like figure comprised of bottle caps evokes a discourse of recycling, most notably repurposed in contemporary art through El Anatsui's sculptural installations. Baloji's *Zombies* debuted against the backdrop of Extinction Rebellion and the promise of a Green New Deal, both of which emerged out of the United States and Europe. However, the so-called green revolution is simultaneously implicated in extractivism, and these global environmental movements fall short of drawing connections between their own political and economic systems and colonial histories.[65] Cobalt is the essential component for lithium-ion batteries that power electronic vehicles. The three figures in *Zombies* accordingly represent three different epochs in Western technological development dependent on the Congo: the industrial economy, the digital revolution and green energy. *Zombies* ends with the limp body of Papa Bolo, a big chief politician whose white suit has been bloodied, being laid to rest on a trash heap [fig. 4.20]. Closing credits play over this scene in the style of texts sent via Apple's iMessage. Like the astronaut's suit, the end of *Zombies* connects waste in Kinshasa, discarded bodies and global technological developments.

Figure 4.19: Kongo Astronauts, *Untitled [-4]* from *Capital SCrashed.exe* series, 2021. © Kongo Astronauts. Courtesy of Axis Gallery, New York. (Plate 29, p. 223)

As previously mentioned, one of the central concerns of Kongo Astronauts is "*le cyborg contemporain*" or "the contemporary cyborg", as in, following Haraway, "a hybrid creature, composed of organism and machine", which is again evoked through the creatures or zombies in Baloji's short film.[66] Imaginations of the cyborg have existed in literature, cinema and popular culture since the early 1960s, contemporaneous to when whole organism cloning, IVF and gene sequencing were first developed. The word "cyborg" is widely attributed to the NASA scientists Manfred E. Clynes and Nathan S. Kline who employed the term in 1960 to describe a series of experiments that explored ways to technologically enhance the human body in order to allow for space travel.[67] However, in the 1980s, the concept of the cyborg was adopted in more theoretical applications as a way to express the interface between technology and the body. The astronaut can be seen as a hybrid creature reminiscent of Haraway's cyborg. However, whether it is a creature "enhanced" by technology is complicated by Kongo Astronauts. Only 13 per cent of the Congolese population has access to electricity and the country's authorities reserve the right to implement internet blackouts.[68] The title of the collective's photographic series, *Capital SCrashed.exe*, evokes both a crash landing and a virus. The shortcut ".exe" is a common filename extension denoting an executable file for Microsoft Windows, but .exe files are often used to distribute viruses and other types of malicious software that

Figure 4.20: Baloji, film still from *Zombies*, 2019. Courtesy of Baloji and NOWNESS.

infect devices and steal information. The title of the series accordingly denotes a virus, which we could interpret as the pillage of the Congo's mineral resources for the benefit of electronic technologies elsewhere, which are then dumped as e-waste in Kinshasa. To this end, the collective's costumes are made of thick, heavy materials – they are excruciatingly hot. Wearing this costume in Kinshasa's tropical climate is gruelling.[69] Ironically, the spacesuit, which is designed to allow astronauts to breath in outer space, is adapted by Kongo Astronauts to create a feeling of asphyxiation or suffocation.[70] The heavily adorned costume limits the movements of the astronaut, while the space traveller's vision is simultaneously obscured by the bucket-cum-helmet. Bearing the weight of the loaded ensemble, the astronaut walks slowly around the city. Through this cumbersome figure, Kongo Astronauts challenge who can take advantage of technology and cyberspace and the freedoms espoused by both. In *System K*, the camera captures the collective staging an appearance in the middle of traffic – a UN van speeds by the astronaut. Ekeba's voice can be heard: "Hello? Hello? Mayday! Respond! Kongo Astronauts calling Kinshasa. I need oxygen suitable for breathing". He receives a reply "natural element spotted", but the connection is aborted: "Hello? Hello? Wi-Fi connection – disconnection".[71]

Past futures

By calling our attention to the Space Age, Kongo Astronauts evoke a time of shared optimism across Africa. Futures that never arrived, but were once imagined, glimmer in the body of work created by the collective. They are invoked through the figure of the astronaut, who seems to be transported in time from the heroic moment of space exploration to the streets of contemporary Kinshasa. As we have seen, the Space Age coincided with the era of decolonisation and a sense of excitement and optimism that it enshrined as well as its concomitant violence. Freedom, it could be imagined then, extended to the exploration of space. The collective's astronaut appears to stage a spacewalk throughout the city; its arms are outstretched in the photographs as if contending with zero gravity. This action conveys an egalitarian gesture as zero gravity offers an opportunity for weightlessness that exceeds external signifiers. This evocation of an egalitarian world is echoed in the contents of the Voyager Golden Records, which were two phonograph records sent aboard both Voyager spacecrafts launched in 1977. Music and sounds were selected to convey the diversity of life and culture on earth. They were intended for any extra-terrestrials as a sort of time capsule. The American astronomer Carl Sagan asserted: "The spacecraft will be encountered and the record played only if there are advanced space-faring civilisations in interstellar space, but the launching of this 'bottle' into the cosmic 'ocean' says something very hopeful about life on this planet".[72] The audio section contained spoken greetings in 55 languages. The sounds of the earth selection was similarly varied, from the "Alima Song" of the Mbuti ethnic group in the Democratic Republic of Congo, "Cengunmé" from Benin, "Barnumbirr" and "Moikoi Song" performed by the Milingimbi Mission in the Northern Territory of Australia to orchestral compositions from Germany, Belgium and Austria as well as the Americans Chuck Barry and Louis Armstrong. This was a vision of the world with which the liberated African state could engage and to which it could contribute as an equal to outer space developments.

The Angolan artist Kiluanji Kia Henda turned to space travel for the subject of his installation, *Icarus 13: The First Journey to the Sun* (2007) [fig. 4.21], which is comprised of eight photographs, a tiny scale model of a spacecraft and an accompanying commentary explaining a fictitious mission to the sun. In the photographs, the mausoleum of the first Angolan president Agostinho Neto is reminiscent of a space rocket, while the green rays of a light show over a football stadium during the celebrations of Angola's team qualifying for the 2006 World Cup evoke the illumination of a spaceship taking off. Through the dream of an Angolan space programme, the work recalls an earlier experience of optimism proposed by African socialism prior to the country's corrupt elite siphoning off its vast oil supply. However, apropos the suggestion of Icarus, these aspirations, and indeed Angola's aspirations to assume a different position in the global political economy, are shown to be essentially doomed. It is in these complex entanglements of "counterfutures" that the work of Kongo Astronauts is similarly situated. As we have seen, Mbembe's

Figure 4.21: Kiluanji Kia Henda, *Icarus 13: The First Journey to the Sun*, 2007. Installation view from the exhibition *There is Always a Cup of Sea to Sail*, 29th São Paulo Biennial, 2010. Courtesy of the artist and Goodman Gallery.

construction of the postcolony comprises multiple temporalities.[73] Both Kongo Astronauts and Kia Henda engage past visions of the future that endure in the present, a gesture that complicates the view of time as self-contained and events as firmly fixed in chronology. Questions still linger as to what accomplishments could have occurred had another course been taken by the Congo, or even if the country had escaped Western intervention in the context of the Cold War and the assassination of Lumumba.

History as told by both Kia Henda and Kongo Astronauts emerges through the sentiment of "what might have been" as opposed to concrete events and actors. Their turn to a subjunctive state seems to work against a historical determinism often employed in the case of the Congo, which we could argue acts as a type of neocolonial control. As observed by Eshun: "African social reality is overdetermined by intimidating global scenarios, doomsday economic projections, weather predictions, medical reports on AIDS and life-expectancy forecasts, all of which predict decades of immiseration".[74] On 17 February 2018, the cover of the UK financial weekly *The Economist* declared that the Congo was "in peril" and that it was "heading back to hell". These assertions were accompanied by a black and white photograph of soldiers, one of whom turns back over a gun-laden shoulder to gaze towards the camera. The photograph is evocative of liberation struggles across Africa in the 1960s. The journal's logo and contents appear in red above the black and white photograph, as if to evoke what is in store for the soldiers and country, the bloodshed and abyss that threatens to descend like a storm in the sky. The editorial on the Congo entitled "Waiting to erupt" chronicles the cyclical character of civil war which engulfed the country from 1996 until 1997 and again from 1998 until 2003. The Congo is compared to a volcano always on the verge of eruption. Misery is concluded as that which awaits the country, and, through the photograph, what was already waiting for the country in the 1960s. This sense of certainty is disturbed by the cited artistic engagements with the Space Age in Africa. Furthermore, the suggestion of an alternative as conveyed by the shared optimism of the time emphasises that which actually did occur. The artworks under discussion complicate the outright acceptance of certain world orders. On the contrary, there were a variety of potential alternative outcomes possible from these same years. Through the speculative "what-if", we are taken back to the apprehensions and contingencies of the world as experienced by contemporaries and the events studied. These engagements offer a sense of awareness of the occupations and concerns of an era. Kongo Astronauts' turn to the Space Age allows for a sense of indeterminacy that challenges the assuredness through which the Congo's downfall is charted.

Opacity

In his well-known essay "For Opacity", Glissant defined transparency as the ground for "'understanding' people and ideas from the perspective of Western thought".[75] Reduction and standardisation occur through transparency, as Glissant stated: "in order to understand and thus accept you, I have to measure your solidity with the ideal scale providing me with grounds to make comparisons and, perhaps, judgements. I have to reduce".[76] Complex subjects are transformed into categorisable objects of Western knowledge. However, through the project of "creolisation", Glissant eschews the worldwide spread of transparency and the projection of Western thought as an "objective" and "rational" system of evaluation. For Glissant, "the opaque is not the obscure", but rather that which "cannot be reduced" or rendered intelligible according to Western epistemologies and systems. Drawing from Glissant, the events orchestrated by the collective operate through opacity, challenging the demand for transparency. The perambulating astronaut prompts conjecture, guesswork and supposition from its audience. Their appearances occur without any given agenda and even the photographs and short films produced by the collective lack a clear storyline. Helmets conceal the performer's identity from confused onlookers. The work produced by Kongo Astronauts opposes the extractive structures that characterise the country as open and accessible for Western demands, as well as the "easy-to-read" photographs that circulate in the media.

The sense of opacity deployed by the collective operates against a drive for knowledge that was associated with exploration and space travel. The search of outer space and colonialism both shared the so-called spirit of adventure and a desire to explore "virgin" lands and spheres. By the logic of capitalist accumulation, colonialism chased saleable assets for extraction, and this search for territory yet to be explored and exploited continued to outer space. The photographs of outer space produced by satellites and other vessels comprised what Elizabeth DeLoughrey, citing Martin Jay, called one of many "scopic regimes of modernity".[77] Dennis Cosgrove contended: "To imagine the earth as a globe is essentially a visual act".[78] The photographs of earth taken from outerspace created an Apollonian eye as in one that was "synoptic and omniscient, intellectually detached".[79] This global view, as argued by Cosgrove, emerged from the aerial perspective of aircrafts that was associated with the disembodied avatar central to the Cold War. In contrast to the limited vision of the astronaut, "satellite eyes are omnipresent and omniscient", producing what Peter Sloterdijk described as "an inverted astronomy [that] has thus come into being, looking down from space onto the earth rather than from the ground up into the skies".[80] This perspective was associated with aerial photography as employed for warfare in which the earth is rendered as a surface exposed for observation and surveillance. There was an efficiency associated with these photographs. However, in the work created by Kongo Astronauts, Sloterdijk's "inverted astronomy" is overturned and the efficiency demanded to compute a terrain is denied. The photographs and short films created by the collective are consciously earthbound and even look towards the sky as if to acknowledge the status of the astronaut on solid ground. Horizons are obscured from view as walls and gates act as obstacles to the eye. Their work challenges the topographic maps of aerial photography that are organised to see the whole earth or even all of Kinshasa. For the artwork produced by the collective conjures opacity. We could even say the same of the cast of characters adopted by the collective whose appearances emerge from the world of science fiction, cinema and comics. They are generic and vague as opposed to specific in their allusions. Through these strategies of opacity, Kongo Astronauts create a body of work that resists an easy comprehension and intelligibility. The logic of their artwork operates against the omniscient eye of colonialism that extended to the exploration of outer space, as well as an extractivism that opens up the earth. Kongo Astronauts avoid the same kind of accrual, and, in doing so, they create what we could term an anti-extraction aesthetic.

The Congo in, of and as the world

Kongo Astronauts engage the absurd: their events centre around an astronaut who is earthbound. However, the alien-like silver cosmonaut compels viewers to see Kinshasa and the surrounding environment with fresh eyes, as if they were looking at outer space. In doing so, as I have argued, the collective challenges stereotypical and preconceived conceptions of the city, as well as cliched assumptions that circumscribe various geographies and events. The artwork produced by the collective joins together colonialism, global extractive economies, the avant-garde, the Space Age, independence movements across Africa, contemporary digital technologies and the Internet. In the work produced by the collective and their several collaborations, the astronaut travels to earth to evoke a consideration of the world, specifically the way in which the Congo connects to and even enables the events associated with the 1960s and 1970s as well as contemporary digital existences that operate through computers and android devices. The collective captures a sentiment of optimism associated with the end of colonialism, the Space Age and the Internet, all of which purported a more equal and shared world, and yet Kongo Astronauts simultaneously suggest its downfall through e-waste and the global corporations that pillage the country's mineral resources. Ultimately, what the performances, photographs, short films and collaborations produced by Kongo Astronauts evidence is the interconnectedness of our world, from the local experiences of shared global events exemplified in the Space Age to the minerals and materials that circulate across it. Nothing is without cause and effect: the collective ground any consideration of contemporary technologies in the violence through which they are created and their afterlives elsewhere. The abstract entity of the Internet and global appetites for digital consumption are given physical shape through an astronaut dressed in a costume constructed from e-waste that walks the streets of Kinshasa.

CODA

Between History and individual histories

In the introduction to this book, I mentioned Michèle Magema's installation, *Mémoires Hévéa, entre Histoire et histoires individuelles* (2015) [fig. 5.1], the title of which translates to "*Hevea* Memories, between History and individual histories". The installation is comprised of three large photographic portraits surrounded by 34 drawings. At the centre of installation is a portrait of Magema's maternal grandmother, Anne Kilonga, who was born in 1921. The artist discovered her grandmother's 1974 studio portrait amongst family heirlooms, and she used it as the basis from which to stage photographs of herself and her own mother, Marie-José Mbongo Ngudi Mpassi, who was born in 1952. This archival photograph performs a temporal movement that the other works studied in this book also engage: the past punctuates

Figure 5.1: Michèle Magema, *Mémoires Hévéa, entre Histoire et histoires individuelles*, 2015. 2016.44.1, collection RMCA Tervuren. Photo J. Van de Vyver, RMCA Tervuren ©. © ADAGP, Paris and DACS, London, 2021.

the present. The oscillating time of images infuses the present with a past. The sepia-toned photographs of Magema and her mother appear on either side of Kilonga's portrait, creating a triptych of three generations of women. They are each dressed in the same Congolese style of outfit: a wrapped skirt, a blouse, an apron of varying textiles, a headwrap and flip-flops on their feet. The women are seated, tilting slightly forward, with their hands on their thighs, and they look straight toward the camera.

The photographs of the women are surrounded by drawings, 12 of which are text-based. Several of the drawings depict historical male figures [fig. 5.2], some of which are based on photographs, including King Leopold II, Lumumba, Kasa-Vubu, Mobutu and Kabila senior and junior, and others, such as, King Baudouin, the King of Belgium from 1951–1993, and Simon Kimbangu, a Congolese religious leader who founded the Christian religious movement Kimbanguism. Other drawings suggest the country's colonial history, from a rubber tree being tapped to a *chicotte* whip, which was used to coerce Congolese who refused to supply labour to rubber extraction. The reference to the rubber tree in the work's title, "*hévéa*" ("*hevea*") as in its scientific genus, calls up this history, as well as the elastic nature of memory. There are also views rendered by Magema of Kinshasa and Lubumbashi and depictions of the country's flags since independence. On either side of the photographs are text-based drawings, which acknowledge events in Magema's family, including the wedding of her parents and grandparents, the language of Kikongo (Magema's maternal tongue) and the dates surrounding her family's immigration to France. There are also a handful of text-based drawings that refer to political events and parties in the Congo such as "INDEPENDENCE" and "ABAKO" and others associated with Mobutu's *authenticité* programme, such as "ZAÏRE" and "SHABA", the name Mobutu gave to Katanga.

Through the installation's textual and visual components, Magema weaves together her personal and familial memories with official Congolese histories, as suggested in the subtitle of the installation: "between History and individual histories". The drawings evoke a typical timeline of the country, one charted through male political figures and defining events, while the photographs and some of the text-based drawings convey the life of a family, of individuals, lived against this background. These two threads convey the way in which the Congo is constructed for those who grow up in the diaspora, as somewhere between "History" and memory. Moreover, these official histories are embodied by Magema. Her hand translates them into drawings, conveying how the history of the country entered her family's own timeline. For example, Magema's grandmother was a devout Kimbanguist, while her father was a member of the ABAKO opposition party and consequently fled the country due to Mobutu's oppression. Like the other artists included in this study, Magema captures the lived dimensions of history, the complexities of which

Figure 5.2: Michèle Magema, detail of *Mémoires Hévéa, entre Histoire et histoires individuelles*, 2015. Courtesy of the artist. © ADAGP, Paris and DACS, London, 2021.

are obscured by the "Heart of Darkness" trope that circumscribes the Congo, and resuscitates them through visual art. Moreover, in *Mémoires Hévéa,* these national events come to exist as intergenerational memories, passed down through the family, as suggested by the connectedness of the three women whose appearances echo one another, as well as the drawings themselves which appear stylistically like grains in wood, evoking the concentric layers of a tree, a family tree of sorts.

At the start of this book, I adopted Rancière's contention that visual art changes what is seeable, sayable and knowable. The globalisation of the art world and the expansion of its centres of production and exhibition has led to the proliferation of critical perspectives around Belgium's colonial past from those who lived through its aftermath in the Congo. The democratic access of digital technologies has similarly opened up these debates, challenging whose voices are heard, and these perspectives consequently come to circulate in a global art world where they encounter new audiences. Following *Mémoires Hévéa*, the artworks foregrounded in this study call our attention to individual histories, to people and events occluded from dominant narratives, from the lives of miners, past and present, to women in *animation* performances, fans of Lumumba, the global phenomenon of the Space Age and the lifecycle of electronic devices. Through these different frames, the selected artists offer a re-reading of the colonial and immediate post-independence past, and they consequently shed light on the banal and everyday ways in which the history of colonialism permeates the present, from experiences of time to the waste that litters the streets of Kinshasa. This is the significance of art. It can reconstitute the past and the present in order to see them anew, connecting previously overlooked circuits.

This book has dealt primarily with the relationship between the past and the present: the artists studied here look back to earlier moments and images that remain in the present, echoing the afterlives and mutations of colonialism. But there is simultaneously a future orientation to the selected artworks. As noted in the introduction, these artworks create new images from older ones, or even sometimes from their absence, and, in doing so, they generate a new visual record for the future, one that attests to the ramifications of the colonial past across time. The works studied here ask one to bear witness to the people and events pictured and therefore to the unfinished work of decolonisation. They productively question or challenge our present. As we have seen, it was photographs that led to a global outcry around the atrocities committed in King Leopold II's personal property of Congo Free State in the early twentieth century and its takeover by the Belgian state in 1908. In the same vein, the selected works bring to consciousness a history of inequality, domination and oppression that clings to the present, and, from there, they invite viewers to act in the knowledge of the colonial structures that have profoundly shaped our world.

Notes

Introduction

1. Andreas Huyssen, *Present Pasts: Urban Palimpsests and the Politics of Memory* (Stanford: Stanford University Press, 2003), 156; Bogumil Jewsiewicki, "Denial and Challenge of Modernity: Suffering, Recognition, and Dignity in Photographs by Sammy Baloji", *Suffering, Art and Aesthetics*, eds. M. Nijhawan and R. Hadj-Moussa (New York: Palgrave Macmillan, 2014), 51-74 (55).
2. Huyssen (2003), 156.
3. T.J. Demos and Hilde Van Gelder (eds.), *In and Out of Brussels: Figuring Postcolonial Africa and Europe in the Films of Herman Asselberghs, Sven Augustijnen, Renzo Martens and Els Opsomer* (Leuven: Leuven University Press, 2012); T.J. Demos, *Return to the Postcolony: Spectres of Colonialism in Contemporary Art* (Sternberg Press: Berlin, 2013).
4. Sharon Sliwinski, "The Childhood of Human Rights: The Kodak on the Congo", *Journal of Visual Culture*, Vol. 5, No. 3 (2006): 333-363.
5. Sliwinski (2006), 335.
6. Amandine Lauro, "Maintenir l'Ordre dans la 'Colonie-modèle': Note sur les Désordres Urbains et la Police des Frontières Raciales au Congo Belge", *Crime, Histoire & Sociétés* 15:2 (2011): 97-121.
7. See N'Goné Fall (ed.), *Photo Kinshasa* (Paris: Revue Noire, 2001), 60; Sandrine Colard, "The Afterlife of a Colonial Photographic Archive: The Subjective Legacy of InforCongo", *Critical Interventions*, Vol. 12, No. 2 (2018): 117-139 (119).
8. Colard (2018), 135.
9. See Julien Truddaïu, "Representing Lumumba (1956-1961): The Twists and Turns of Belgian Colonial Propaganda", *Lumumba in the Arts*, ed. Matthias De Groof (Leuven: Leuven University Press, 2002), 388-407 (389-390).
10. See Ludo De Witte, *The Assassination of Lumumba*, trans. Ann Wright and Renée Fenby (Verso: London, 2001), 58.
11. Tamar Garb, "Archiving the In-Between", *Àsìkò: On the Future of Artistic and Curatorial Pedagogies in Africa*, ed. Stephanie Baptist (Lagos: Centre for Contemporary Art, 2017), 115-128 (121); Jonathan Harris, *The Global Contemporary Art World* (Hoboken: Wiley Blackwell, 2017), 10.
12. Erin Haney, *Photography and Africa* (London: Reaktion, 2010), 24-25.
13. Roland Barthes, *Camera Lucida: Reflections on Photography*, trans. Richard Howard (New York: Hill & Wang, 1980; repr. London: Vintage Books, 2000), 93; Susan Sontag, *On Photography* (New York: Delta, 1977), 15.
14. Karen E. Milbourne, "Senses of Time: Video and Film-Based Arts of Africa", *African Arts*, Vol. 48, No. 4 (2015): 72-84.
15. Achille Mbembe, *On the Postcolony* (Berkeley, Los Angeles and London: University of California Press, 2001), 14, original emphasis.
16. Jacques Derrida, *Archive Fever: A Freudian Impression*, trans. Eric Prenowitz (Chicago: Chicago University Press, 1996). Ann Laura Stoler notes that the critical interest in the archive preceded

Derrida's publication. See Stoler, *Along the Archival Grain: Epistemic Anxieties and Colonial Common Sense* (Princeton: Princeton University Press, 2009), 44.

17. Michel Foucault, *The Archaeology of Knowledge*, trans. A.M. Sheridan Smith (London: Routledge 1972), 146.
18. Stoler (2009), 44.
19. Hal Foster, "An Archival Impulse", *October*, Vol. 110 (2004): 3-22.
20. See Ingrid Schaffner and Matthias Winzen, *Deep Storage: Collecting, Storing and Archiving Contemporary Art* (New York: Prestel, 1998); Sylvie Mokthari et al. (eds.), *Les artistes contemporains et l'archive: interrogation sur le sens du temps et de la mémoire à l'ère de la numérisation* (Rennes: Presses Universitaires de Rennes, 2004); Charles Mereweather (ed.), *The Archive* (London: Whitechapel; Cambridge: MIT Press, 2006); Okwui Enwezor, "Archive Fever: Photography between History and Monument", *Archive Fever: Uses of the Document in Contemporary Art* (New York: International Centre of Photography; Göttingen: Steidl Publishers, 2008), 11-51.
21. There are exceptions, see Tamar Garb (ed.), *Distance and Desire: Encounters with the African Archive. African Photography from The Walter Collection* (New York: The Walther Collection; Göttingen: Steidl, 2013); Maëline Le Lay, Dominique Malaquais and Nadine Siegert (eds.), *Archive (re)mix: Vues d'Afrique*, eds. (Rennes: Presses Universitaires de Rennes, 2015). With regards to the South African context, see Lauri Firstenberg and John Peffer, *Translation/Seduction/Displacement: Post-Conceptual and Photographic Work by Artists from South Africa* (Portland: Institute of Contemporary Art at Maine College of Art, 2000); Carolyn Hamilton et al. (eds.), *Refiguring the Archive* (Dordecht, Boston and London: Kluwer Publishers, 2002); Brendan Maart (ed.), *Imaginary Fact. Contemporary South African Art and the Archive* (Grahamstown: National Arts Festival, 2013).
22. See also Darren Newbury et al., *Women and Photography in Africa: Creative Practices and Feminist Challenges* (London: Routledge, 2021), 10.
23. Lorena Rizzo, *Photography and History in Colonial Southern Africa: Shades of Empire* (London: Routledge, 2020); Jennifer Bajorek, *Unfixed: Photography and Decolonial Imagination in West Africa* (London and Durham, Duke University Press, 2020).
24. Eduardo Cadava, *Words of Light: Theses on the Photography of History* (Princeton: Princeton University Press, 1997); Annie Coombes, *History After Apartheid: Visual Culture and Public Memory in a Democratic South Africa* (Durham and London: Duke University Press, 2003); Ferdinand de Jong and Michael Rowlands, *Alternative Imaginaries of Memory in West Africa* (London: Routledge 2007); Patricia Hayes, "The Colour of History: Photography and the Public Sphere in Southern Africa", *The Public Sphere from Outside the West*, eds. Sanil V. and Divya Dwivedi (London: Bloomsbury, 2015), 147-163.
25. Cadava (1997), 61, emphasis added.
26. Geoffrey Batchen, "Seeing and Saying: A Response to Incongruous Images", *History and Theory*, Vol. 48, No. 4: 26-33 (26).
27. Matthew Stanard, *The Leopard, the Lion and the Cock: Colonial Memories and Monuments in Belgium* (Leuven: Leuven University Press, 2019), 265.
28. Debora Silverman has chronicled the museum's engagement with the politics and culture of colonial memory in Belgium and my account draws from and expands her own. See Silverman, "Diasporas of Art: History, the Tervuren Royal Museum for Central Africa and the Politics of Memory in Belgium, 1885-2014", *The Journal of Modern History*, Vol. 87, No. 3 (2015): 615-667.
29. Silverman (2015), 627.

30. Adam Hochschild, *King Leopold's Ghost: A Story of Greed, Terror and Heroism in Colonial Africa* (Boston and New York: Houghton Mifflin Company, 1999).
31. Daniel Vangroenweghe, *Du sang sur les lianes: Léopold II et son Congo* (Brussels: Didier Hatier, 1996); Jules Marchal, *L'etat libre du Congo: paradis perdu: l'histoire du Congo 1876-1900*, vol. 1 and 2 (Borgloon: Éditions Paula Bellings, 1996); Marchal, *E.D. Morel contre Léopold II: L'histoire du Congo 1900-1910*, vol 1 and 2 (Paris: Éditions L'Harmattan, 1996).
32. Stephen Bates, "The hidden holocaust", *The Guardian* (13 May 1999), https://www.theguardian.com/theguardian/1999/may/13/features11.g22.
33. For a summary of these issues, see Georgius Verbeeck, "Un génocide s'est-il déroulé dans l'État indépendant du Congo?", *Le Congo Colonial. Une Histoire en Questions*, eds. Idesbald Godderis, Amandine Lauro and Guy Vanthemsche (Paris: La Renaissance du Livre, 2020), 45-61.
34. Bates (1999).
35. See Robert Storr, Philippe Pirotte and Jan Hoet, *Luc Tuymans: Mwana Kitoko (Beautiful White Man)* (Ghent: S.M.A.K. Stedelijk Museum voor Actuele Kunst, 2001).
36. See Johan Lagae and Sabine Cornelis (eds.), *Sammy Baloji & Patrick Mudekereza en residence au Musée royal de l'Afrique centrale: Congo Far West: Arts, sciences et collections* (Milan: Silvana, 2011).
37. On the successes and failures of this project, see Maëline Le Lay, "Performer l'archive pour réécrire l'histoire: l'exposition Congo Far West au Musée royal de l'Afrique central de Tervuren", *Archive (re)mix: Vues d'Afrique*, eds. Maëline La Lay, Dominique Malaquais and Nadine Siegert (Rennes: Presses Universitairs de Rennes, 2015), 107-123.
38. See Patrick Mudekereza, "Biennial culture or grassroots globalisation?: the challenge of the Picha art centre, as a tool for building local relevance for the Rencontres Picha, Biennale de Lubumbashi", Research Report for Master of Arts in History of Art (University of the Witwatersrand, 2017), http://wiredspace.wits.ac.za/handle/10539/24575; Mudekereza, "Picha: The Second Biennial of Photography and Video Art Lubumbashi, Democratic Republic of the Congo, October 2010", trans. Allen F. Roberts, *African Arts*, Vol. 44, No. 3 (2011): 68-75.
39. The exhibition resulted in an artist's book, see Lotte Arndt and Asger Taiaksev (eds.), *Hunting and Collecting: Sammy Baloji* (Ostend: Mu.ZEE; Paris: Galerie Imane Farès, 2016).
40. Jacques Rancière, *The Politics of Aesthetics*, trans. Gabriel Rockhill (London: Bloomsbury, 2004), 7-14.
41. Jacques Rancière, *Disagreement: Politics and Philosophy*, trans. Julie Rose (Minneapolis and London: University of Minnesota Press, 1999), 29.
42. Rancière (1999), 29.
43. Rancière (1999), 29-30; Rancière (2004), 14.
44. Rancière (1999), 29-30.
45. Rancière (2004), 59.
46. Édouard Glissant, *Poetics of Relation*, trans. Betsy Wing (Ann Arbor: Michigan University Press, 1997): 183.
47. Jacques Rancière, *Dissensus: On Politics and Aesthetics*, ed. and trans. Steven Corcoran (London: Continuum, 2010), 2.
48. Rancière (2010), 140.
49. Rancière (2010), 141.
50. Kevin C. Dunn, *Imagining the Congo: The International Relations of Identity* (New York: Palgrave Macmillan, 2003).
51. Dunn (2003), 4.
52. Hunt, *A Nervous State: Violence, Remedies and Reverie in Colonial Congo* (Durham: Duke University Press, 2016), 3.

53. Filip De Boeck and Sammy Baloji, *Suturing the City: Living Together in Congo's Urban Worlds* (London: Autograph ABP, 2016), 33-34.
54. David Van Reybrouck, *Congo: The Epic History of a People*, trans. Sam Garrett (London: Fourth Estate, 2014).
55. De Boeck and Baloji (2006), 34.
56. Hunt (2016), 3.
57. Okwui Enwezor, "Introduction: Travel Notes: Living, Working and Travelling in a Restless World", *Trade Routes: History and Geography: 2nd Johannesburg Biennale 1997*, ed. Okwui Enwezor (Johannesburg: Greater Johannesburg Metropolitan Council; Den Haag, Netherlands: Prince Claus Fund for Culture and Development, 1997), 7-12 (11-12).
58. Debora Silverman, "Art Nouveau, Art of Darkness: African Lineages of Belgian Modernism, Part I", *West 86th: A Journal of Decorative Arts, Design History and Material Culture*, Vol. 18, No. 2 (2011): 139-181; Debora Silverman, "Art Nouveau, Art of Darkness: African Lineages of Belgian Modernism, Part II, *West 86th: A Journal of Decorative Arts, Design History and Material Culture*, Vol. 19, No. 2 (2012): 175-195; Debora Silverman "Art Nouveau, Art of Darkness: African Lineages of Belgian Modernism, Part III", *West 86th: A Journal of Decorative Arts, Design History and Material Culture*, Vol. 20, No. 2 (2013): 22-61.
59. Silverman (2021).
60. This dependence on theories of photography centred on its European and North American histories is also discussed by Bajorek (2020), 18-20.

Chapter 1. Mining Lubumbashi: Sammy Baloji's *Mémoire*

1. Bruce Fetter, *The Creation of Elisabethville 1910-1940* (Stanford, CA: Hoover Institution Press, 1976), 12-27.
2. Jean-Luc Vellut, "Hégémonies en construction: Articulations entre etat et entreprises dans le bloc colonial belge (1908-1960)", *Revue canadienne des études africaines/Canadian Journal of African Studies*, Vol. 16, No. 2 (1982): 313-330.
3. See Donald Reid, "Industrial Paternalism: Discourse and Practice in Nineteenth-Century French Mining and Metallurgy", *Comparative Studies in Society and History*, Vol. 27, No. 4 (1985): 579-607; Nancy Rose Hunt, "Le bébé en brousse': European Women, African Birth Spacing, and Colonial Intervention in Breast Feeding in the Belgian Congo", *International Journal of African Historical* Studies, Vol. 21, No. 3 (1988): 401-432.
4. Van Reybrouck (2014), 189-191.
5. Gabrielle Hecht, *Being Nuclear: Africans and the Global Uranium Trade* (Cambridge and London: MIT Press, 2012), 23.
6. Miles Larmer, "Permanent Precaity: Capital and Labour in the Central African Copperbelt", *Labor History*, Vol. 58, No. 2 (2017): 170-184.
7. In 2003 Gécamines, at the insistence of the IMF and the World Bank, had fired eleven thousand superfluous workers. See Colette Braeckman, *Vers la deuxième indépendance du Congo* (Brussels: Le Cri Edition, 2009), 158-159.
8. See Sabine Sorgel, "The Global Politics of Faustin Linyekula's Dance Theatre: From Congo to Berlin and Back Again via Brussels and Avignon", *Moving (Across) Borders: Performing Translation, Intervention, Participation*, eds. Gabriele Brandstetter and Holgar Hartung (Bielefeld: Transcript, 2017), 79-91.
9. Alphonse Tiérou, in cooperation with the French government sponsored arts initiative "*Pour une danse Africaine Contemporaine*", conducted a series of lectures and workshops across the continent. These workshops laid the groundwork for the development of choreographic competitions

NOTES

designed to stimulate a uniquely African choreography culture. See Tierou, *Si sa danse bouge, l'Afrique bougera* (Paris: Maisonneuve and Larose, 2001), 57.

10. Gilbert Douglas et al., "Under Fire: Defining a contemporary African dance aesthetic – can it be done?", *Critical Arts*, Vol. 20, No. 2 (2006): 102-115 (103).
11. Bogumil Jewsiewicki, *The Beautiful Time: Photography by Sammy Baloji* (New York: Museum for African Art, 2010), 13-14.
12. These photographs are not unique (there are copies in Belgium), but they were unknown in Katanga. Jewsiewicki (2010), 12-13.
13. Mbembe (2001), 4.
14. Mbembe (2001), 4.
15. Achille Mbembe, "Necropolitics", *The Unhomely: Phantom Scenes in Global Society*, trans. Libby Meintjes, ed. Okwui Enwezor (Seville: BIACS, 2006), 32-51 (39-40).
16. Jewsiewicki (2010), 13-14.
17. Jewsiewicki (2010), 8, 34.
18. Tate Modern, "Contested Terrains: Sammy Baloji", http://www.tate.org.uk/whats-on/tate-modern/display/level-2-gallery-contested-terrains/contested-terrains-sammy-baloji.
19. Jewsiewicki (2010), 10.
20. Ann Laura Stoler, "'The Rot Remains': From Ruins to Ruination", *Imperial Debris: On Ruins and Ruination*, ed. Ann Laura Stoler (Durham: Duke University Press, 2013), 1-35.
21. Jennifer Robinson, "Living in Dystopia: Past, Present, and Future in Contemporary African Cities", *Noir Urbanisms: Dystopic Images of the Modern City*, ed. Gyan Prakash (Princeton: Princeton University Press, 2010), 218-240 (222, 226).
22. Jean-Luc Vellut, "Mining in the Belgian Congo", *History of Central Africa*, eds. David Birmingham and Phyllis M. Martin (London and New York: Longman, 1983), 126-162 (153-154).
23. Jules Marchal, *Forced Labour in the Gold and Copper Mines: A History of Congo Under Belgian Rule, 1910-1945*, trans. Ayi Kwei Armah (Popenguine: Per Ankh, 2003), 78.
24. Fetter (1976), 110-112; Vellut (1983), 156-157; Hunt (1988), 416-421.
25. Fetter (1976), 112, 125-126; Vellut (1983), 156-157.
26. Jewsiewicki (2010).
27. See Charles Perrings, *Black Mineworkers in Central Africa: Industrial Strategies and the Evolution of an African Proletariat in the Copperbelt, 1911-41* (New York: Africana Publishing, 1979); John Higginson, *A Working Class in the Making: Belgian Colonial Labour Policy, Private Enterprise and the African Mineworker, 1907-1951* (Madison: University of Wisconsin Press, 1989).
28. Higginson (1989), 3, 6, 11, 13.
29. Perrings (1979); Higginson (1989).
30. Vellut (1983), 154.
31. Elizabeth Edwards (ed.), *Anthropology and Photography, 1860-1920* (New Haven and London: Yale University Press, 1992).
32. See David Green, "Veins of Resemblance: Photography and Eugenics", *Oxford Art Journal*, Vol. 7, No. 2 (1984): 3-16.
33. Deborah Poole, "An Excess of Description: Ethnography, Race, and Visual Technologies", *Annual Review of Anthropology*, Vol. 34 (2005): 159-179 (164).
34. Poole (2005), 164.
35. Catherine Lutz and Jane Collins, "The Photograph as an Intersection of Gazes: The Example of National Geographic", *Visual Anthropology Review*, Vol. 7, No. 1 (1991): 134-149 (139).
36. ""*Type bon, sauf quelques indigènes du Ruanda d'un type mince, faible et élancé*" (original text, all translations are my own).

37. Ian Baucom, *Spectres of the Atlantic: Finance Capital, Slavery, and the Philosophy of History* (Durham and London: Duke University Press, 2005), 9.
38. Baucom (2005), 61.
39. Baucom (2005), 40.
40. Baucom (2005), 105.
41. Vellut (1983), 154.
42. Jewsiewicki (2014), 53.
43. Jewsiewicki (2014), 68. This is not always the case though; there is a long-standing tradition of women from many different African states resorting to naked protest.
44. Johannes Fabian, *Time and the Other: How Anthropology Makes its Object* (New York: Columbia University Press, 1983), 60-63; Ch. Didier Gondola, *Tropical Cowboys: Westerns, Violence, and Masculinity in Kinshasa* (Indianapolis: Indiana University Press, 2016), 41.
45. Gondola, *Tropical Cowboys* (2016), 41.
46. Paul Gilroy, *Small Acts: Thoughts of the Politics of Black Cultures* (London: Serpent's Tail, 1993), 179.
47. Ernest Cole, *House of Bondage* (New York: Random House, 1967), 28-29.
48. Danny Lyons, *Conversations with the Dead* (New York: Holt, Rinehart and Winston, 1971), 169.
49. Cedric Robinson, *Black Marxism: The Making of the Black Radical Tradition* (London: Zed Press, 1983; repr. Chapel Hill: University of North Carolina Press, 2000), 2.
50. Robinson (2000), 2.
51. Robinson (2000), 2.
52. Jodi Melamed, "Racial Capitalism", *Critical Ethnic Studies*, Vol. 1, No. 1 (2015): 76-85 (77).
53. Melamed (2015), 77.
54. Van Reybrouck (2014), 7.
55. Van Reybrouck (2014), 7.
56. Van Reybrouck (2014), 7.
57. V.Y. Mudimbe, *The Invention of Africa: Gnosis, Philosophy, and the Order of Knowledge* (Bloomington and Indianapolis: Indiana University Press, 1988), 2.
58. Hunt (2016), 102.
59. Vanessa Ogle, *The Global Transformation of Time: 1870-1950* (Cambridge: Harvard University Press, 2015), 93.
60. E.P. Thompson, *The Making of the English Working Class* (Harmondsworth: Penguin, 1968); Jean Comaroff and John L. Comaroff, *Of Revelation and Revolution: Christianity, Colonialism and Consciousness in South Africa* (Chicago and London: The University of Chicago Press, 1991); Frederick Cooper, "Colonising Time: Work Rhythms and Labour Conflict in Colonial Mombasa", *Colonialism and Culture*, ed. Nicholas B. Dirks (Ann Arbor: University of Michigan, 1994), 209-245; Giordano Nanni, *Colonisation of Time: Ritual, Routine and Resistance in the British Empire* (Manchester: Manchester University Press, 2012).
61. Thompson (1968); Comaroff and Comaroff (1991).
62. Omari H. Kokole, "Time, Language and the Oral Tradition: An African Perspective", *Time in the Black Experience*, ed. Joseph K. Adjaye (Westport and London: Greenwood Press, 1994), 35-54 (46).
63. Alamin Mazrui and Lupenga Mphande, "Time and Labour in Colonial Africa: The Case of Kenya and Malawi", *Time in the Black Experience*, ed. Joseph K. Adjaye (Westport and London: Greenwood Press, 1994), 97-119 (98).
64. Fetter (1976), 35.
65. Hunt (1988), 401.
66. "*Il est deux heures*", "*cinq heures*", "*six heures*", and "*six heures et demie*" (original).

67. "*Il est dix heures. Plus aucun bruit ne s'entend*" (original).
68. "*Le noir est matinal, il peut parfaitement se lever a six heures du matin*" (original).
69. "*Levez-vous, levez-vous, l'heure est arrivée, attention les retardataires!*" (original).
70. Frantz Fanon, *The Wretched of the Earth*, trans. Constance Farrington (New York: Grove Press, 1963; repr. New York: Grove Weidenfeld, 1965), 235.
71. Sammy Baloji, "Sammy Baloji: The Past in Front of Us", Louisiana Channel (2015), https://vimeo.com/132212385.
72. Mazrui and Mphande (1994), 99.
73. Mazrui and Mphande (1994), 99. See also John Mbiti, "Eschatology", *Biblical Revelation and African Beliefs*, eds. Kwesi Dickson and Paul Ellingworth (London: Lutterworth, 1969), 159-184 (159); Mbiti, *New Testament Eschatology in an African Background* (London: Oxford University Press, 1971), 24-32; Mbiti, *African Religions and Philosophy* (Oxford: Heinemann, 1969; repr. 1990), 15-28.
74. Mazrui and Mphande (1994), 98.
75. Dominique Zahan, *Religion, spiritualité et pensée Africaines* (Paris: Payot, 1970), 76.
76. Mazrui and Mphande (1994), 99.
77. Mbiti (1969), 159; Zahan (1970), 141; Mbiti (1971), 241.
78. Newell S. Booth, Jr., "Time and Change in African Traditional Thought", *Journal of Religion in Africa*, Vol. 7, No. 2 (1975): 81-91 (84-85).
79. Balandier (1968) attests to the retention of the Kongo week in the face of Christianity as the former regulated traditional cults, which occurred alongside "the religion of Sunday" and governed the economic week. Hunt (1988) similarly suggests that alternate temporal practices endured. She observes that Congolese women continued to nurse their infants at night, rejecting a tight and regular time schedule. My emphasis on the specificity of time is a case against literature that comprehends temporality in the postcolony solely through Derridean ghosts, see Demos (2013).
80. Fanon (1965), 53.
81. Fanon (1965), 53.
82. Darieck Scott, *Extravagant Abjection: Blackness, Power and Sexuality in the African American Literary Imagination* (New York: New York University Press, 2010), 58-65.
83. Scott (2010), 58.
84. Scott (2010), 63.
85. Scott (2010), 65.
86. See Johannes Fabian, *Jamaa* (Evanston: Northwestern University Press, 1971); Higginson (1989), 12.
87. Derek Gregory, *The Colonial Present* (Oxford: Blackwell, 2004), 7.
88. Gregory (2004), 7.
89. Alberto Acosta, "Post-Extractivism: From Discourse to Practice – Reflections for Action", *Alternative Pathways to Sustainable Development: Lessons from Latin America*, International Development Policy Series, No. 9 (Geneva: Graduate Institute Publications; Boston: Brill-Nijhoff, 2017), 77-101.
90. Hochschild (1999), 180.
91. Delinda Collier, "Obsolescing Analogue Africa: A Re-reading of the 'Digital' in Digital Art", *Critical Interventions*, Vol. 8, No. 3 (2014): 279-289.
92. On time as a theoretical model in video art, see Karen Milbourne, "Senses of Time: Video and Film-Based Arts of Africa", *African Arts*, Vol. 48, No. 4 (2015): 72-84.
93. Ariel Osterweis Scott, "Performing Acupuncture on a Necropolitical Body: Choreographer Faustin Linyekula's Studios Kabako in Kisangani, Democratic Republic of Congo", *Dance Research Journal*, Vol. 42, No. 2 (2010): 13-27 (18).

94. Scott (2010), 18.
95. Pierre Petit and Georges Mulumbwa Mutambwa, "'La crise': Lexicon and Ethos of the Second Economy in Lubumbashi", *Africa*, Vol. 75, No. 4 (2005): 467–87 (268).
96. Petit and Mutambwa (2005), 474.
97. Donatien Dibwe dia Mwembu, *Bana Shaba abandonnés par leur père. Structures de l'autorité et histoire sociale de la famille ouvrière au Katanga (1910-1997)* (Paris: L'Harmattan, 2001).
98. Mbembe (2006), 39-40.
99. Petit and Mutambwa (2005), 474.
100. Petit and Mutambwa (2005), 474.
101. Petit and Mutambwa (2005), 474-75.
102. Petit and Mutambwa (2005), 474-75.
103. Collier (2020), 165.
104. Collier (2020), 165.
105. Gabriella Nugent, "Mining Time in Sammy Baloji's *Mémoire*", *African Arts*, Vol. 52, No. 3 (2019): 62-71.

Chapter 2. The Maintenance of Mobutu's Zaire: Michèle Magema's *Oyé Oyé*

1. Julie Crenn, "Michèle Magema: Without Echo, There Is No Meaning", *n.paradoxa: international feminist art journal*, Vol. 13 (2013): 15-22 (15).
2. Studies of state power and nationalism more generally have called for more attention to the gendered dimensions and meanings of nationalist discourse, see Geoff Eley and Ronald Grigot Suny (eds.), *Becoming National* (Oxford: Oxford University Press, 1996).
3. Ester Boserup, *Woman's Role in Economic Development* (London: George Allen and Unwin Ltd, 1970), 17. See also Francille Rusan Wilson, "Reinventing the Past and Circumscribing the Future: *Authenticité* and the Negative Image of Women's Work in Zaire", *Women and Work in Africa*, ed. Edna G. Bay (Boulder: Westview Press, 1982), 153-170; Gertrude Mianda, "Women and Garden Produce of Kinshasa: The Difficult Quest for Autonomy", *Women, Work and Gender Relations in Developing Countries: A Global Perspective*, eds. Parvin Ghorayshi and Claire Bélanger (Westport and London: Greenwood Press, 1996) 91-101 (94); Rosalie Malu Muswamba, *Le travail des femmes en République démocratique du Congo: exploitation ou promesse d'autonomie?* (Paris: UNESCO, 2006), 24. The division of labour in the Kingdom of Kongo was traditionally gender specific and women were in control of agriculture, see John K. Thornton, *The Kingdom of Kongo: Civil War and Transition, 1641-1718* (Madison: University of Wisconsin Press, 1983), 29-30; Thornton, *A Cultural History of the Atlantic World, 1250-1820* (Cambridge: Cambridge University Press, 2012), 65-66.
4. Jane Freedman, *Gender, Violence and Politics in the Democratic Republic of Congo* (London and New York: Routledge, 2016), 22.
5. Malu Mushwamba (2006), 25.
6. Freedman (2016), 22.
7. Wilson (1982), 153.
8. Amina Mama, "Sheroes and Villains: Conceptualising Colonial and Contemporary Violence Against Women in Africa", *Feminist Genealogies, Colonial Legacies and Democratic Futures*, eds. M. Jacqui Alexander and Chandra Talpade Mohanty (New York and London: Routledge, 1997), 46-62 (54).
9. Karen Bouwer, *Gender and Decolonisation in the Congo: The Legacy of Patrice Lumumba* (New York: Palgrave Macmillan, 2010), 16.

10. Barbara A. Yates, "Colonialism, Education and Work: Sex Differentiation in Colonial Zaire", *Women and Work in Africa*, ed. Edna G. Bay (Boulder: Westview Press, 1982), 127-152 (131).
11. Yates (1982), 131.
12. Yates (1982), 131.
13. Gertrude Mianda, "Colonialism, Education and Gender Relations in the Belgian Congo: The Évolué Case", *Women in African Colonial Histories*, eds. Jean Allman, Susan Geiger and Nakanyike Muisi (Bloomington: Indiana University Press, 2002), 144-163 (146-148).
14. Yates (1982), 131.
15. Gertrude Mianda, "Dans l'ombre de la 'démocratie' au Zaire: la remise en question de l'emancipation Mobutiste de la femme", *Canadian Journal of African Studies*, Vol. 29, No. 1 (1995): 51-78 (54); Bouwer (2010), 43.
16. Wilson (1982), 155.
17. Mbembe (2001), 107-108.
18. Crawford Young and Thomas Turner, *The Rise and Decline of the Zairian State* (Madison: University of Wisconsin Press, 1985), 211.
19. Young and Turner (1985), 212.
20. On the transformations carried out by Mobutu's government, see Ghislain C. Kabwit, "Zaïre: The Roots of the Continuing Crisis", *Journal of Modern African Studies*, Vol. 17, No. 3 (1979): 381-407.
21. Georges Nzongola-Ntalaja, *The Congo: From Leopold to Kabila: A People's History* (London and New York: Zed Books, 2002), 166.
22. Achille Mbembe, "Provisional Notes on the Postcolony", *Africa*, Vol. 62, No. 1 (1992): 3-37 (25). This characteristic of familial organisation distinguished the MPR from classical political parties, see Michael G. Shatzberg, *The Dialectics of Oppression in Zaire* (Bloomington: Indiana University Press, 1988), 71, 89-90.
23. Crawford Young, "Zaire: The Shattered Illusion of the Integral State", *The Journal of Modern African Studies*, Vol. 32, No. 2 (1994): 247-263 (248).
24. Young (1994), 248.
25. Young (1994), 247, 262.
26. Gérard Prunier, *Africa's World War: Congo, the Rwandan Genocide, and the Making of a Continental Catastrophe* (Oxford: Oxford University Press, 2009), 135-142.
27. William Renoe, "From State Collapse to 'Absolutism', to State Failure", *Third World Quarterly*, Vol. 27, No. 1 (2006): 43-56.
28. Jan Vansina, *Paths in the Rainforest: Toward a History of Political Tradition in Equatorial Africa* (Madison: University Wisconsin Press, 1990).
29. Leopard skin was part of the precolonial regalia of Kongo kings, see Suzanne Preston Blier, *The Royal Arts of Africa: The Majesty of Form* (New York: H. N. Abrams, 1998), 229.
30. Mbembe (2001), 128.
31. Bob W. White, *Rumba Rules: The Politics of Dance Music in Mobutu's Zaire* (Durham: Duke University Press, 2008), 219.
32. Wilson (1982), 161.
33. Wilson (1982), 162.
34. Terri F. Gould, "Value Conflict and Development: The Struggle of the Professional Zairian Woman", *Journal of Modern African Studies*, Vol. 16, No. 1 (1978): 133-140 (136).
35. On *femmes libres*, see Susanne Comhaire-Sylvain, *Femmes de Kinshasa hier et aujourd-hui* (Paris: Mouton, 1968), 44-51; Ch. Didier Gondola, "Popular Music, Urban Society and Changing Gender Relations in Kinshasa, Zaire", *Gendered Encounters*, eds. Maria Luise Grosz-Ngaté and Omari H. Kokole (New York: Routledge, 1997), 65-86 (75-76).

36. See Pierre-Joseph Proudhon Proudhon, *Systems of Economical Contradictions: or, The Philosophy of Misery*, trans. Benjamin R. Tucker (Boston, MA: B.R. Tucker, 1888; orig. 1846). On the figuration of this dichotomy in art historical discourse, see Tamar Garb, 'Renoir and the Natural Woman', *Oxford Art Journal*, Vol. 8, No. 2 (1985): 3-15.
37. See Thomas Callaghy, *The State-Society Struggle: Zaire in Comparative Perspective* (New York: Columbia University Press, 1984).
38. Young and Turner (1985), 213-215. See Placide Tempels, *La philosophie bantoue* (Paris: Présence Africaine, 1945); Jan Vansina "Recording the Oral History of the Bakuba-I. Methods", *The Journal of African History*, Vol. 1, No. 1 (1960): 43-53; Vansina, "Recording the Oral History of the Bakuba-II. Results", *The Journal of African History*, Vol. 1, No. 1 (1960): 257-270; Vansina, *De la tradition orale: essai de méthode historique* (Tervuren: Musée Royal de l'Afrique Centrale, 1961).
39. White (2008), 70.
40. White (2008), 70.
41. Gazungil Sang'Amin Kapalanga, *Les spectacles d'animation politique en République du Zaire* (Louvain-la-Neuve: Cahiers theatre Louvain, 1989), 20.
42. White (2008), 73.
43. See H. Thassinda Uba Thassinda, *Zaire, les princes de l'invisible: L'Afrique noire bâillonnée par le parti unique* (Caen, France: Editions C'est-à-dire, 1992); Kapalanga (1989); Joan Huckstep, "Embodied Nationalism 'Animation Politique' (Political Dance) in Zaire: A Case Study of the Dimensionality and Agency of Dance as the Spirit of Individual, Community, and National Identity", PhD dissertation (Temple University, 2005); White (2008).
44. Lisa Gilman, *The Dance of Politics: Gender, Performance and Democratisation in Malawi* (Philadelphia: Temple University Press, 2009).
45. Yolanda Covington-Ward, *Gesture and Power: Religion, Nationalism and Everyday Performance in Congo* (Durham and London: Duke University Press, 2017); Lesley Nicole Braun, "Dancing ambiguities in the Democratic Republic of Congo", *Critical African Studies*, Vol. 11, No. 1 (2019): 1-18.
46. Covington-Ward (2016), 169.
47. Covington-Ward (2016), 170.
48. Covington-Ward (2016), 170.
49. Nzongola-Ntalaja (2002), 167; White (2008), 78; Covington-Ward (2016), 172-173; Braun (2019), 8.
50. Covington-Ward (2016), 180.
51. Covington-Ward (2016), 167-168.
52. Nzongola-Ntalaja (2002); Leo Zeilig, *Lumumba: Africa's Lost Leader* (London: Haus, 2008).
53. Anne McClintock, *Imperial Leather: Race, Gender and Sexuality in the Colonial Contest* (New York and London: Routledge, 1995), 359.
54. Lesley Nicole Braun similarly turns to Cixous to discuss Magema's work. Braun describes the artist's oeuvre as "the fragmented images of women". However, I would argue that Braun's account looks for a tidy coherence around Magema's body of work at the expense of the work's complexity. Little thought is given to Magema's reworking of archival footage in *Oyé Oyé*, as well as the interaction between the two screens. Her analysis of *Mémoire Hévéas* is also determined by this try at coherence. Referencing its current display at the Royal Museum for Central Africa, Braun strangely contends that the frontal appearance of the women's hands and feet in the photographs offers a counter to the mutilated limbs of Leopold's Congo Free State. She excludes the drawings from her description of the work and only reproduces the installation's photographic component.

See Lesley Nicole Braun, "The Moving Parts in Michèle Magema's Body of Work", *African Arts*, Vol. 53, No. 3 (2019): 22-29.

55. Simon Baker, "The Thinking Man and the femme sans tête: Collective Perception and Self-Representation", *RES: Anthropology and Aesthetics*, No. 38 (2000): 186-210 (192).
56. Hélène Cixous, "Castration or Decapitation?", trans. Annette Kuhn, *Signs*, Vol. 7, No. 1 (1981): 41-55 (42).
57. Cixous (1981), 42-43.
58. Comhaire-Sylvain (1968), 253-288.
59. Covington-Ward (2016), 171-172.
60. Elleke Boehmer, *Stories of Women: Gender and Narrative in the Postcolonial Nation* (Manchester: Manchester University Press, 2005), 29.
61. Boehmer (2005), 29.
62. Cixous (1981), 43, original emphasis.
63. Eric Hobsbawm, "Introduction: Inventing Traditions", *The Invention of Tradition*, eds. Eric Hobsbawm and Terence Ranger (Cambridge: Cambridge University Press, 1983), 1-14 (4).
64. Isidore Ndaywel è Nziem, *Histoire générale du Congo: De l'héritage ancien à la République Démocratique du Congo* (Paris: Duculot, 1998), 665-804.
65. Johan Lagae and Kim De Raedt, "Building for 'l'Authenticité': Eugène Palumbo and the Architecture of Mobutu's Congo", *Journal of Architectural Education*, Vol. 68, No. 2 (2014): 178-189 (179).
66. Lisa Gilman, "The Traditionalisation of Women's Dancing, Hegemony and Politics in Malawi", *Journal of Folklore Research*, Vol. 41, No. 1 (2004): 33-60; Gilman (2008), 33-39.
67. McClintock (1995), 359; Gilman (2004), 45.
68. Benedict Anderson, *Imagined Communities: Reflections on the Origin and Spread of Nationalism* (London: Verso, 1983).
69. McClintock (1995), 374.
70. Braun (2019), 8.
71. McClintock (1995), 374.
72. Covington-Ward (2016), 175.
73. Covington-Ward (2016), 175.
74. Covington-Ward (2016), 175.
75. Comhaire-Sylvain (1968), 14-15; Wilson (1982), 155-156.
76. Florence Stratton, "How Could Things Fall Apart For Whom They Were Not Together?", *Contemporary African Literature and the Politics of Gender* (London and New York: Routledge, 1994), 22-38 (38).
77. Mama (1997), 56.
78. Elleke Boehmer, "Stories of Women and Mothers: Gender and Nationalism in the Early Fiction of Flora Nwapa", *Motherlands: Black Women's Writing from Africa, the Caribbean and South Asia*, ed. Susheila Nasta (London: The Women's Press Limited, 1991), 3-23 (7).
79. Jewsiewicki (2010), 10, 13-14.
80. Jewsiewicki (2014), 52.
81. Donatien Didwe dia Mwembu, *Bana Shaba abdonnés par leur père: structures d'autorité et histoire sociale de la famille ouvière au Katanga 1910-1997* (Paris: L'Harmatten, 2001), 65.
82. Didwe dia Mwembu (2001), 61-62.
83. Didwe dia Mwembu (2001), 68.
84. Bouwer (2010), 48.
85. Bouwer (2010), 48.
86. Wilson (1982), 154.

87. Barthes (2000), 77.
88. Barthes (2000), 80.
89. Barthes (2000), 96, original emphasis.
90. Barthes (2000), 96, original emphasis.
91. Rachel Donadio, "Exploring a Century of Art from Congo", *The New York Times* (24 July 2015), https://www.nytimes.com/2015/07/25/arts/design/exploring-a-century-of-art-from-congo.html?_r=0.
92. Séverine Kodjo-Grandvaux, "*Beauté Congo*, un certain regard sur l'histoire culturelle de la RDC", *Jeune Afrique* (20 July 2015), http://www.jeuneafrique.com/mag/247901/culture/arts-beaute-congo-un-certain-regard-sur-lhistoire-culturelle-de-la-rdc.
93. Mierle Laderman Ukeles, "Manifesto for Maintenance Art, 1969", Arnolfini, https://www.arnolfini.org.uk/blog/manifesto-for-maintenance-art-1969.
94. Lisa Baraitser, "Touching Time: Maintenance, Endurance, Care", *Psychosocial Imaginaries: Perspectives on Temporality, Subjectivities and Activism*, ed. Stephen Frosh (London and New York: Palgrave Macmillan, 2015), 21–47 (21).
95. Bruce Fetter, "Relocating Central Africa's Biological Reproduction, 1923–1963", *International Journal of African Historical Studies*, Vol. 19, No. 3 (1986): 463–475 (466); Hunt (1988).
96. In the 1970s, Bobi Ladawa became the mistress of President Mobutu and had children with him before the death of his first wife, Marie Antoinette, in 1977.
97. Bob W. White, "The Political Undead: Is It Possible to Mourn for Mobutu's Zaire?", Mourning and the Imagination of Political Time in Contemporary Central Africa [special issue], eds. Bogumil Jewsiewicki and Bob W. White, *African Studies Review*, Vol. 48, No. 2: 65–85.
98. Sarah Van Beurden, *Authentically African: Arts and the Transnational Politics of Congolese Culture* (Athens: Ohio University Press, 2015), 153–158, 199–205.
99. Tamar Garb, "Painting/Politics/Photograph: Marlene Dumas, Mme Lumumba and the Image of the African Woman", *Art History*, Vol. 43, No. 3 (2020): 588–611.
100. Mudimbe (1988), 48.
101. Van Reybrouck (2014), 216.
102. Van Reybrouck (2014), 216.
103. Van Reybrouck (2014), 216.
104. Nancy Rose Hunt, "Domesticity and Colonialism in Belgian Africa: Usumbura's Foyer Social, 1946–1960", *Signs*, Vol. 15, No. 3 (1990): 447–474.
105. *Time*, "How to Appear Évolué", Vol. 84, No. 13 (25 September 1964), 35.
106. *Time* (25 September 1964), 35.
107. See, for example, Jean-Louis Comolli, "Mechanical Bodies, Ever More Heavenly", trans. Annette Michelson, *October*, No. 83 (1998): 19–24; Harun Farocki, "Workers Leaving the Factory", trans. Laurent Faasch-Ibrahim, *Harun Farocki: Working on the Sight-Lines*, ed. Thomas Elsaesser (Amsterdam: Amsterdam University Press, 2004), 237–244; Elena Gorfinkel, "Waiting: Enduration and Art Cinema's Tired Bodies", *Discourse*, Vol. 34, No. 2/3 (2012): 311–347.
108. Farocki (2004), 238.
109. Commolli (1998), 20–21.
110. Michel Foucault, *Discipline and Punish: The Birth of the Prison*, trans. Alan Sheridan (New York: Pantheon Books 1977; repr. New York: Vintage Books, 1995), 139.
111. Foucault (1995), 140.
112. My discussion of detail is indebted to Briony Fer's paper "A history of detail – or thinking small" presented at The Courtauld Institute of Art on 15 January 2018.
113. Mbembe (2001), 105.
114. Mbembe (2001), 106.

115. Mbembe (2001), 106.
116. Mbembe (2001), 106.
117. Mbembe (2001), 106.
118. Bennetta Jules-Rosette, "Afro-Pessimism's Many Guises", *Public Culture*, Vol. 14, No. 2 (2002): 603–605 (604).
119. Jules-Rosette (2002), 604.
120. Ukeles (1969).
121. Jean Omasombo Tshonda and Benoît Verhaegen, *Patrice Lumumba: Jeunesse et Apprentissage Politique 1925-1956* (Tervuren: Institut Africain-CEDAF; Paris: Haramttan, 1998), 139. "*Mon mari et ma souer ont eu tout à m'apprendre. Lumumba m'avait prié d'aller me cacher, chaque fois que je le voyais arriver, dans la chamber à coucher où il venait me retourver pour juger me tenue*" (original, all translations are my own).
122. Bouwer (2010), 202.
123. Achille Mbembe, "On the Power of the False", *Public Culture*, Vol. 14, No. 2 (2002): 629–641 (631).
124. Mbembe (2002), 631.
125. I suggest small in subject because, while the cartoons and caricatures with which Mbembe engages are physically small, the way in which they take on the state is sizable as is their circulation. See Mbembe (2001), 102–141.
126. The depiction of Félicité echoes that of other female characters in Senegalese cinema, like Collé in Sembène's film *Moolade* (2004) and Karmen in Gaï Ramaka's *Karmen Geï* (2001).
127. Wendy Ide, "Félicité review – musical, magnetic portrait of Kinshasa life", *The Observer*, https://www.theguardian.com/film/2017/nov/12/felicite-review-musical-magnetic-kinshasa-life-alain-gomis, original emphasis.

Chapter 3. The Image of Lumumba: Georges Senga's *Une vie après la mort*

1. In 2013, *Une vie après la mort* was exhibited at ASBL Dialogues in Lubumbashi in collaboration with l'Institut Français de Lubumbashi, l'Ecole Française de Lubumbashi and Rencontres Picha. For this exhibition, Senga produced a pamphlet which included an artist statement as well as a testimony from Kayembe Kilobo. See Georges Senga, *Une vie après la mort*, ed. Marie-Aude Delafoy (Lubumbashi: ASBL Dialogues, 2013). "*J'étais un fan de la première heure de l'homme politique... Cela fut le début d'une grande aventure pour moi*" (original, all translations are my own).
2. Kayembe in Senga (2013). "*L'indépendance est accordée a celui qui la veut*" (original).
3. Senga, email correspondence (9 July 2018).
4. Georges Nzongola-Ntalaja, "Patrice Lumumba: The Most Important Assassination of the 20th Century", *The Guardian* (17 January 2011), https://www.theguardian.com/global-development/poverty-matters/2011/jan/17/patrice-lumumba-50th-anniversary-assassination.
5. Kayembe in Senga (2013). "*L'idée du départ, était de faire une fiction sur la vie de Lumumba après 1961, tout en se pausant une question. Que serait devenu Patrice Lumumba s'il avait survécu à son destin? Serait-il devenu un homme riche et corrompu regardant le Congo se transformer avec cet esprit d'injustice; ou aurait-il été un homme riche de ce qu'il a tenté de faire pour le Congo en se battant pour son l'indépendance? Un homme modeste qui aurait continué de défendre le droit contre l'absence de droit?*" (original).
6. Emmanuel Gerard and Bruce Kuklick, *Death in the Congo: Murdering Patrice Lumumba* (Cambridge and London: Harvard University Press, 2015), 122.
7. On Augustijnen's *Spectres* (2011), see Demos (2013), 19–47.
8. Senga (2018).

9. Senga (2013). "Au delà du fantasme, que reste t-il?" (original).
10. On the circulation of Lumumba's image, see Bogumil Jewsiewicki, "Popular Painting in Contemporary Katanga: Painters, Audiences, Buyers and Sociopolitical Contexts", *A Congo Chronicle: Patrice Lumumba in Urban Art*, ed. Bogumil Jewsiewicki (New York: Museum for African Art, 1999), 13-27 (16).
11. Senga (2013).
12. Alphonse Mbuyamba Kankolongo, "Quelques témoignages sur Lumumba", *Lumumba entre dieu et diable: Un héros africain dans ses images*, eds. Pierre Halen and János Riesz (Paris: L'Harmattan, 1997), 129-135 (135).
13. Pedro Monaville, "Decolonising the University: Postal Politics, The Student Movement and Global 1968 in the Congo", PhD dissertation (University of Michigan, 2013), 108.
14. Monaville (2013), 108.
15. Thomas Kanza, *The Rise and Fall of Patrice Lumumba: Conflict in the Congo* (London: Rex Collings, 1978), 12.
16. A photograph of Lumumba was published in the March 1954 issue of *La voix du congolais*. See Jean-Marie Mutamba Makombo, "La destinée politique de Patrice Lumumba (1925-1961)", *À la redécouverte de Patrice Emery Lumumba*, eds. Mabiala Mantuba Ngoma (Kinshasa: Institut de Formation et d'Études Politiques, 1996), 11-52 (49).
17. Monaville (2013), 108.
18. Kabwit (1979), 390.
19. Van Reybrouck (2014), 352.
20. Senga (2013). "*Mon style, ma coiffure, et mon pseudo pouvaient aussi me faire tuer*" (original).
21. Van Reybrouck (2014), 237.
22. Gondola, *Tropical Cowboys* (2016), 160-161.
23. De Boeck and Plissart (2004), 39.
24. Van Reybrouck (2014), 354.
25. On the development of "*la Sape*", see Ch. Didier Gondola, "Dream and Drama: The Search for Elegance Among Congolese Youth", *African Studies Review*, Vol. 42, No. 1 (1999): 23-48.
26. Santu Mofokeng, "The Black Photo Album / Look at Me: 1890-1950", *Events of the Self: Portraiture and Social Identity. Contemporary African Photography from the Walther Collection*, ed. Okwui Enwezor (Göttingen: Steidl, 2010), 171-172.
27. Jennifer Bajorek, "Then and Now: Santu Mofokeng's *Black Photo Album*", *Distance and Desire: Encounters with the African Archive. African Photography from The Walter Collection*, ed. Tamar Garb (New York: The Walther Collection; Göttingen: Steidl, 2013), 221-227 (226).
28. Fabian (1983), 25-35.
29. My thanks to Hélène Neveu Kringelbach for this observation.
30. Fall (2001), 10.
31. Z.S. Strother, "A Photograph Steals the Soul", *Portraiture and Photography in Africa*, eds. John Peffer and Elisabeth L. Cameron (Bloomington: Indiana University Press, 2013), 177-212 (195).
32. Jewsiewicki, "Popular Painting in Contemporary Katanga" (1999), 16.
33. Jewsiewicki, "Popular Painting in Contemporary Katanga" (1999), 16.
34. Mary Nooter Roberts and Allen Roberts, *Memory: Luba Art and the Making of History* (New York and Munich: Museum of African Art, 1996), 117-149.
35. Jewsiewicki, "Popular Painting in Contemporary Katanga" (1999), 16.
36. Jewsiewicki, "Popular Painting in Contemporary Katanga" (1999), 16.
37. Manthia Diawara, "Talk of the Town", *Artforum*, Vol. 36, No. 6 (February 1998): 64-71 (70).
38. Hunt (1990), 469. See also Homi Bhabha, "Of Mimicry and Man: The Ambivalence of Colonial Discourse", *October*, No. 28 (1984): 125-133.

39. Hunt (1990), 469.
40. Bhabha (1984), 127.
41. Bogumil Jewsiewicki, "Painting in Zaire: From the Invention of the West to the Representation of Social Self", *Readings in African Popular*, ed. Karin Barber (Bloomington: Indiana University Press, 1997), 99-110 (105, 107).
42. Esther Marijnen, "Public Authority and Conservation in Areas of Armed Conflict: Virunga National Park as a 'State within a State' in Eastern Congo", *Development and Change*, Vol. 49, No. 3 (2018): 790-814 (798-800).
43. On the image of Lumumba in the mass media, see Isabelle De Rezende, "History as Spectacle", *Lumumba in the Arts* (Leuven: Leuven University Press, 2020), 26-43.
44. Huyssen (2003), 156.
45. *Time*, "Belgian Congo: Democracy with Spears", Vol. 75, No. 22 (30 May 1960), 25.
46. Dunn (2003), 83.
47. Dunn (2003), 83.
48. Christine Masuy, "Du portrait au personage: La diabolisation symbolique de Patrice Lumumba dans La Libre Belgique", *Lumumba entre dieu et diable: Un héros africain dans ses images*, eds. Pierre Halen and János Riesz (Paris: L'Harmattan, 1997), 199-213.
49. Masuy (1997), 205.
50. Patrice Lumumba, *Lumumba Speaks: The Speeches and Writings of Patrice Lumumba, 1958-1961*, ed. Jean Van Lierde, trans. Helen R. Lane (Boston and Toronto: Little, Brown and Company, 1972), 220-225 (221-222).
51. Dunn (2003), 84.
52. Dunn (2003), 84.
53. See Madeleine G. Kalb, *The Congo Cables: The Cold War in Africa - From Eisenhower to Kennedy* (New York: Macmillan, 1982), 49; Serge Michel, *Uhru Lumumba* (Paris: René Julliard, 1962), 110-111.
54. De Witte, (2001); Zeilig (2008); Van Reybrouck (2014); Gerard and Kucklick (2015).
55. Van Reybrouck (2014), 309.
56. Van Reybrouck (2014), 309.
57. Pedro Monaville, "A History of Glory and Dignity: Patrice Lumumba in Historical Imagination and Postcolonial Genealogies", *Lumumba in the Arts*, ed. Matthias De Groof (Leuven: Leuven University Press, 2020), 62-77 (69-70).
58. Monaville (2020), 70.
59. Monaville (2020), 70. See Jean-Claude, Willame, *Patrice Lumumba: La crise congolaise revisitée* (Paris: Karthala, 1990), 469-482.
60. In the 1950s, as a young *évolué* with *immatriculé* status, Lumumba wrote a letter to the editors of *La croix du Congo* disapproving of the "new fashion" for wearing shirts with their edges outside of the trousers ("*la chemise pendante*"). Lumumba, "La mode masculine à Stanleyville", *La croix du Congo* (20 May 1951).
61. White (2008), 250-251.
62. De Witte (2001), 58.
63. De Witte (2001), 140-141.
64. De Witte (2001), 58.
65. BBC, "1961: Ex-Congo PM declared dead" (13 February 1961), http://news.bbc.co.uk/onthisday/hi/dates/stories/february/13/newsid_2541000/2541053.stm.
66. On the mobilisation of Lumumba's image in the direct aftermath of the assassination, see Quinn Slobodian, *Foreign Front: Third World Politics in Sixties West Germany* (Durham and London: Duke University Press, 2012), 61-67.

67. Erin Haney makes a similar observation in a chapter from her book on African photography which deals with the intersections between painting, printing, and photography. See Haney (2010), 131. A small body of scholarship has addressed the connections between photography and sculpture, see Stephen F. Sprague, "Yoruba Photography: How the Yoruba See Themselves", *African Arts*, Vol. 12, No. 1 (1978): 52-59, 107; Olu Oguibe, "Photography and the Substance of the Image", *In/sight: African Photographers 1940 to the Present*, eds. Clare Bell et al. (New York: Guggenheim Museum, 1996), 231-250; Tobias Wendl, "Entangled Traditions: Photography and the History of Media in Southern Ghana", *RES: Anthropology and Aesthetics*, No. 39 (2001): 78-101.
68. Jewsiewicki (1997), 99; Johannes Fabian, *Moments of Freedom: Anthropology and Popular Culture* (Charlottesville and London: University Press of Virginia, 1998), 52. In the case of Lumumba, see Bogumil Jewsiewicki, "Congolese Memories of Lumumba: Between Cultural Hero and Humanity's Redeemer", *A Congo Chronicle: Patrice Lumumba in Urban Art*, ed. Jewsiewicki (New York: Museum of African Art, 1999), 73-91.
69. Jewsiewicki (1997), 105, 107.
70. Johannes Fabian, *Remembering the Present: Painting and Popular History in Zaire* (Berkeley, Los Angeles and London: University of California Press, 1996), ix-x.
71. The relationship between Congolese painters and European patrons has been discussed by Jean-Luc Vellut. See Vellut, "La peinture du Congo-Zaïre et la recherche de l'Afrique innocente: présentation du livre de J. A. Cornet, R. De Cnodder, I. Dierickx, et W. Toebosch: 60 ans de peinture au Zaïre", *Bulletin des séances* 36, No. 4 (1990): 633-59.
72. Fabian (1996), 119.
73. Gabriella Nugent, "From Camera to Canvas: The Case of Patrice Lumumba and Congolese Popular Painting", *Nka: Journal of Contemporary African Art*, No. 47 (2020): 82-93.
74. Jewsiewicki, "Popular Painting in Contemporary Katanga" (1999), 16.
75. Jewsiewicki (1997), 107.
76. Jewsiewicki (1997), 107.
77. Nancy Rose Hunt, "Tintin and the Interruptions of Congolese Comics", *Images and Empires: Visuality in Colonial and Postcolonial Africa* (Berkeley and Los Angeles: University of California Press), 90-123 (103).
78. Tshibumba worked as Burozi's apprentice from 1970-71. Jewsiewicki, "Popular Painting in Contemporary Katanga" (1999), 23.
79. Fabian (1996), 263-265; Jewsiewicki (1997), 100, 107; Jewsiewicki, "Popular Painting in Contemporary Katanga" (1999) 16; Jewsiewicki, "Congolese Memories of Lumumba" (1999), 84-85. There are photographs included in the exhibition catalogue for *Congo Art Works: Popular Painting*; however, there is little said about the relationship between photography and popular painting. See Bambi Ceuppens and Sammy Baloji (eds.), *Congo Art Works: Popular Painting* (Brussels: Éditions Racine, 2017).
80. Liese Van der Watt, "Echoes of Zaire: Popular Painting from Lubumbashi, DRC", *Africa is a Country* (2 July 2015), https://africasacountry.com/2015/07/echoes-of-zaire-popular-painting-from-lubumbashi-drc-by-liese-van-der-watt/.
81. Haney (2010), 149.
82. Jewsiewicki offers an alternative reading. He sees the image and the writing as expressing two divergent truths: "the legend reproduces the official state version, but the image signifies what is known through other channels, including rumour". He associates written text and explicit references to writing as an allusion to state control. Jewsiewicki (1997), 107.
83. The same image has been reproduced by Tshibumba under other titles such as *Le 17 janv 1961 / Bob Denard a tué Lumumb-Mpolo-Okito*. This alternate title refers to rumours that a French

soldier called Bob Denard had murdered Lumumba in cooperation with Katangese authorities. See Fabian (1996), 121-122.
84. Haney (2010), 149.
85. The court of the Merina kingdom in Madagascar is one of the few places on the continent known thus far where there was an established tradition of painted portraiture in place before the first European photographers arrived. Haney (2010), 127.
86. Van der Watt (2 July 2015).
87. Walter Benjamin, "The Work of Art in the Age of Mechanical Reproduction", *Illuminations*, ed. Hannah Arendt, trans. Harry Zorn (New York: Schocken Books, 1969; repr. London: Pimlico, 1999), 211-244 (217).
88. Jewsiewicki, "Popular Painting in Contemporary Katanga" (1999), 21-22.
89. Fabian (1996), 122.
90. Jewsiewicki, "Congolese Memories of Lumumba" (1999), 88.
91. Marie-Jose Hoyet, "Quelques images de Patrice Lumumba dans la literature du monde noir d'expression francaise," *Patrice Lumumba entre dieu et diable: Un heros africain dans ses images*, eds. Pierre Halen and Janos Riesz (Paris: L'Harmattan, 1997), 49-80 (53).
92. This concept of the contact zone was developed by Mary Louise Pratt. See Pratt, "Arts of the Contact Zone", *Profession* (1991): 33-40.
93. Jewsiewicki, "Popular Painting in Contemporary Katanga" (1999), 26.
94. *Lumumba, la mort du prophète*, dir. Raoul Peck (Velvet Films, 1991).
95. Georgia Popplewell, "Raoul Peck: A Vision of His Own", *Caribbean Beat*, 60 (March/April 2003), https://www.caribbean-beat.com/issue-60/vision-his-own#axzz5MH66Etnl.
96. Popplewell (2003).
97. Bouwer (2010), 163.
98. Katrien Pype, "Geographies of the Occult and the Divine – Pentecostal Semiotics of Urban Space in Kinshasa", *Witchcraft, Demons and Deliverance*, eds. Claudia Währisch-Oblau and Henning Wrogemann (Zurich: Lit Verlag, 2015), 69-92 (87).
99. Filip De Boeck and Marie-Françoise Plissart, *Kinshasa: Tales of the Invisible City* (Ghent: Ludion, 2004; repr. Leuven: Leuven University Press, 2014), 109.
100. Bouwer (2010), 190.
101. Zeitgeist Films, *Lumumba* press kit (2001), https://zeitgeistfilms.com/media/films/5/presskit.pdf.
102. The staging of paintings in film is an often-employed technique, see Alexander Korda's *Remembrandt* (1936), Vincente Minnelli's biopic on Vincent van Gogh, *Lust for Life* (1970), and Derek Jarman's *Caravaggio* (1986).
103. Fabian (1996), 158.
104. Jewsiewicki (1997), 105, 107; Fabian (1998), 64.
105. Elvira Dyangani Ose, telephone conversation (4 July 2019).
106. Dyangani Ose (4 July 2019).
107. Johannes Fabian, "Popular Culture in Africa: Findings and Conjectures", *Africa*, Vol. 48, No. 4 (1978): 315-334; Karen Barber, "Popular Arts in Africa", *African Studies Review*, Vol. 30, No. 3 (1987): 1-78.
108. Bajorek (2020), 241.
109. Bajorek (2020), 241.
110. Nancy Rose Hunt, *A Colonial Lexicon: Of Birth Ritual, Medicalisation and Mobility in the Congo* (Durham and London: Duke University Press, 1999), 176.
111. Senga (2013). "*Je me suis orienté vers l'agriculture artisanale pour payer les études de mes enfants et me suis acheté un petit vélo comme moyen de déplacement. C'était une honte pour moi*" (original).
112. *Lumumba, la mort du prophète* (1991).

113. Matthias De Groof, "Introduction: The Iconography of Patrice Emery Lumumba", *Lumumba in the Arts*, ed. Matthias De Groof (Leuven: Leuven University Press, 2020), 6-23.
114. Paolo Magagnoli, *Documents of Utopia: The Politics of Experimental Documentary* (London and New York: Wallflower Press, 2015).
115. Magagnoli (2015), 9.
116. Malcolm Chase and Christopher Shaw (eds.), "The Dimensions of Nostalgia", *The Imagined Past: History and Nostalgia* (Manchester: Manchester University Press, 1989), 1-17.

Chapter 4. From Kinshasa to the Moon: Kongo Astronauts

1. My reconstruction of these events is indebted to Dominique Malaquais's account of Kongo Astronauts. See Malaquais, "Postcolonial Dilemma: Parts I-III", *Ellipses Journal of Creative Research*, http://www.ellipses.org.za/project/postcolonial-dilemma-parts-i-iii/.
2. Kongo Astronauts, "Kongo Astronauts", https://kongoastronauts.wordpress.com/about-kongo-astronauts-kinshasa-rdcongo-2013-2019/. "*[Le] cyborg contemporain*", "*une tentative de résistance aux ghettos psychiques qui recouvrent multiples réalités postcoloniales*", "*la globalisation digitale où le passé, le future et le present s'entrechoquent*" and "*[le] rhytme d'un HIP HOP déjanté*" (original, all translations are my own).
3. Alyssa Klein, "Baloji's Love Letter To The Congo Is The Most Stunning Music Video Of The Year", *OkayAfrica* (3 September 2015) <https://www.okayafrica.com/baloji-capture-64-bits-and-malachite-music-video/; Jake Hulyer, "How Baloji traced his Congolese roots to hear another side of Africa", *FACT Magazine* (27 November 2015), https://www.factmag.com/2015/11/27/baloji-interview/.
4. Mark Dery, "Black to the Future: Interviews with Samuel R. Delany, Greg Tate, and Tricia Rose", *Flame Wars: The Discourse of Cyberculture*, ed. Mary Dery (Durham and London: Duke University Press, 1994), 179-222 (180).
5. Dery (1994), 180.
6. Alondra Nelson, "Introduction: Future Texts", *Social Text*, Vol. 20, No. 2 (2002): 1-15.
7. Kodwo Eshun, "Further Considerations on Afrofuturism", *CR: The New Centennial Review*, Vol. 3, No. 2 (2003): 287-302.
8. Zoé Whitley, "The Place is Space: Afrofuturism's Transnational Geographies", *The Shadows Took Shape*, eds. Naima J. Keith and Zoé Whitley (New York: The Studio Museum in Harlem, 2013), 19-25 (20).
9. Whitley (2013), 20.
10. Whitley (2013), 21.
11. On batik, see Nancy Hynes and John Picton, "Yinka Shonibare: Re-Dressing History/Undressing Ethnicity", *African Arts*, Vol. 34, No. 3 (2001): 60-95.
12. See Ian Bourland, "Afronauts: Race in Space", *Third Text*, Vol. 24, No. 2: 209-229.
13. Mohale Mashigo, "Afrofuturism: Ayashis' Amateki", *The Johannesburg Review of Books* (1 October 2018), https://johannesburgreviewofbooks.com/2018/10/01/afrofuturism-is-not-for-africans-living-in-africa-an-essay-by-mohale-mashigo-excerpted-from-her-new-collection-of-short-stories-intruders/.
14. Mashigo (2018).
15. Mashigo (2018).
16. Mashigo (2018).
17. Mashigo (2018).
18. Mashigo (2018).

19. Eléonore Hellio, "The Anti-Art of Kongo Futurism", Pan African Space Station (April 2013), https://panafricanspacestation.org.za/tag/bebson-elemba/.
20. See Alisa LaGamma (ed.), *Kongo: Power and Majesty* (New York: Metropolitan Museum of Art; New Haven and London: Yale University Press, 2015).
21. These quotes are taken from the collective's website. "*...élargit les champs d'action de KA au moyen d'improbables branchements. Communications inter-espaces et espèces, phénomènes paranormaux, cybernétique dilettante, dissidence cognitive forgent sa pratique de la video*" (original).
22. "*...incarne KA via une action qui procède d'états modifiés de conscience, de dérives urbaines, de télescopages*" (original).
23. "*Il fabrique des combinaisons spatiales avec de vieux circuits électroniques chargés de cobalt, de cuivre et de coltan, les met en action, traversant la ville, ses rues, ses rond-points*" (original).
24. "*...compositeur, inventeur d'instruments, performeur, incitateur*" (original).
25. In a letter dated 24 July 1960 and addressed to André Frankin, Guy Debord expressed his concern for the Congo: "Are we going towards colonial recapture, that is, a new Korean War?". Debord, who predicted Lumumba's assassination, also wrote in the letter: "What has been happening in the Congo in the past 12 days will have to be studied for a long time and in all aspects, and seems to me to be an essential experimentation of the revolutionary conditions of the third world". See Debord, *Correspondance, tome 1: juin 1957-août 1960* (Paris: Fayaed, 1999), 356–357. In an unsigned article entitled "Géopolitique de l'hibernation", the author, probably Debord, described the Congolese people's reaction in 1960 as a total refusal of the colonial rationality and a "most dignified continuation of Dadaism". He called Lumumba a poet who hijacked the language of the master to transform the world. See "Géopolitique de l'hibernation", *Internationale Situationiste*, No. 7 (April 1962): 3–10.
26. On the interactions between Congolese exchange students in Paris and members of the SI, see Monaville (2013), 222–227.
27. Monaville (2013), 220–21. Andrew Hussey, one of Debord's biographers, notes the Situationists' interest in the Congo, but only parenthetically as a near incongruity, and describes the Congo as one of the "most far-fling and unlikely parts of the world". See Hussey, *The Game of War: The Life and Death of Guy Debord* (London: Jonathan Cape, 2001), 180.
28. Ken Knabb (ed. and trans.) *Situationist-International Anthology* (Berkeley: Bureau of Public Secrets, 1981), 1–8.
29. Paul Henry Chombart de Lauwe, "Paris et l'agglomération parisienne" (1952), *Paris: essais de sociologie, 1952-1964* (Paris: Éditions ouvrières, 1965), 19–101.
30. Tom McDonough (ed. and trans.), *The Situationists and the City* (London: Verso, 2009), 78.
31. McDonough (2009), 88.
32. McDonough (2009), 88.
33. McDonough (2009), 78.
34. De Boeck and Plissart (2004), 133.
35. Donna Haraway, *When Species Meet* (Minneapolis and London: University of Minnesota Press, 2008), 238.
36. Karol Sienkiewicz, "Pawel Althamer", *Culture.pl*, https://culture.pl/en/artist/pawel-althamer.
37. De Boeck and Baloji (2016), 95. See also Gauthier de Villers (ed.), *Phénomènes informels et dynamiques culturelles en Afrique* (Tervuren/Paris: Institut-Africain-CEDAF/L'Harmattan: 1996).
38. *System K*, dir. Renaud Barret (Les Films en Vrac and La Belle Kinoise, 2019).
39. Sergei Eisenstein, "Montage of Attractions: For 'Enough Stupidity in Every Wiseman'", trans. Daniel Gerould, *The Drama Review*, Vol. 18, No. 1 (1974): 77–85.
40. Sergei Eisenstein, *Film Form: Essays in Film Theory*, ed. and trans. Jay Leyda (New York: Harcourt, Brace & World, 1949), 170–171.

41. Zeilig (2008); Nzongola-Ntalaja (2002); Michela Wrong, *In the Footsteps of Mr Kurtz: Living on the Brink of Disaster in Mobutu's Congo* (London: Fourth Estate, 2001); Jeanne Haskin, *The Tragic State of the Congo: From Decolonisation to Dictatorship* (New York: Algora Publishing, 2005); Jason Stearns, *Dancing in the Glory of Monsters: The Collapse of the Congo and the Great War of Africa* (New York: PublicAffairs, 2012).
42. Tamar Garb, "Of States and Stamps: The Otolith Group at the Delfina Foundation", *Contemporary And* (10 December 2014), https://www.contemporaryand.com/magazines/of-states-and-stamps-the-otolith-group-at-the-delfina-foundation/.
43. Garb (2014).
44. Garb (2014).
45. See William Close, *Beyond the Storm: Treating the Powerless and Powerful in Mobutu's Congo/Zaire*, (Marbleton: Meadowlark Springs Productions, 2007), 251; Van Reybrouck (2014), 344–345.
46. Sammy Baloji et al., "On the exhibition *Congo Stars*. Introduction by the curators", *Congo Stars*, eds. Barbara Steiner and Nicole Fritz (Cologne: Buchandlung Walther König, 2018), 11-12 (12).
47. Hunt (2002), 94.
48. *Tintin au Congo*'s global reception alternates between the colonial banning and commercial quarantining of the comic in the late 1950s (as seen in the United Kingdom) and the argument that the comic sold better in the Congo than anywhere else. Harry Thomspon reported in 1991: "The bigger market of all was in the Belgian Congo, and it continues to sell in great numbers in independent Zaire today. Zairian children, it seems, consider it an honour that Tintin included their country in his list of those meriting a visit". See Thompson, *Tintin: Hergé and His Creation* (London: Hodder & Stoughton, 1991), 42.
49. Hunt (2002), 94.
50. Hunt (2002), 94.
51. Hunt (2002), 94.
52. Hunt (2002), 94.
53. Hunt (2002), 94.
54. Pierre Cary Kazadi, "Trends of Nineteenth and Twentieth Century Music in the Congo Zaire", *Musikkulturen Asiens, Afrikas und Ozeaniens im 19. Jahrhundert*, ed. Robert Günther (Regensberg: Gustav Bosse Verlag, 1973), 267-283 (276).
55. Pierre Nora, *Les lieux de mèmoire* (Paris: Gallimard, 1997).
56. Marc Ferro, *Cinema and History*, trans. Naomi Greene (Detroit: Wayne State University Press, 1988), 14-20.
57. Karen E. Milbourne, *Earth Matters: Land as Material and Metaphor in the Arts of Africa* (New York: Monacelli Press; Washington, D.C.: National Museum of African Art, 2013), 130.
58. Hecht (2012), 22, 25-29.
59. David Renton, David Seddon and Leo Zeilig, *The Congo: Plunder and Resistance* (London and New York: Zed Books, 2007), 96.
60. M.D. Markovitz, *Cross and Sword: The Political Role of Christian Missions in the Belgian Congo 1908-1960* (Stanford: Hoover Institution Press, 1973), 22, 26, 115.
61. Kelly Oliver, *Earth & World: Philosophy After the Apollo Missions* (New York: Columbia University Press, 2015), 1-3.
62. Oliver (2015), 3, original emphasis.
63. John Perry Barlow, "A Declaration of the Independence of Cyberspace", Electronic Frontier Foundation, https://www.eff.org/cyberspace-independence.
64. Paul Virilio, *The Lost Dimension*, trans. Daniel Mosherberg (New York: Semiotext(e), 1991), 15.

65. Thandi Loewenson, "Daring to Dream with Eyes Wide Open: review of Baloji's Zombies", *ROAPE* (7 June 2019), https://roape.net/2019/06/07/daring-to-dream-with-eyes-wide-open-review-of-balojis-zombies/.
66. Donna J. Haraway, *Simians, Cyborgs and Women: The Reinvention of Nature* (New York: Routledge, 1991), 1.
67. Manfred E. Clynes and Nathan S. Kline, "Cyborgs and space", *Astronautics* (September 1960): 26–27, 74–76.
68. Lighting Africa, "Democratic Republic of Congo: A fledging off-grid market in a difficult context" (January 2018), https://www.lightingafrica.org/country/democratic-republic-of-congo/
69. As also noted by Dominique Malaquais, "Kongo Astronauts: Collectif embarqué", *Multitudes*, Vol. 4, No. 77 (2019): 20–26 (22).
70. Malaquais (2019), 23.
71. *System K* (2019).
72. Carl Sagan, "Voyager will carry 'earth sounds' record", *NASA* (August 1977), https://www.jpl.nasa.gov/releases/70s/release_1977_0800.html.
73. Mbembe (2001), 16.
74. Eshun (2003), 291.
75. Glissant (1997): 189–190.
76. Glissant (1997), 190.
77. Elizabeth DeLoughrey, "Satellite Planetarity and the Ends of the Earth", *Public Culture*, Vol. 26, No. 2 (2014): 257–280 (260).
78. Denis Cosgrove, *Apollo's Eye: A Cartographic Genealogy of the Earth in the Western Imagination* (Baltimore: Johns Hopkins University Press, 2001), 15.
79. Cosgrove (2001), 15.
80. Wolfgang Sachs, *Planet Dialectics: Explorations in Environment and Development* (London: Zed Books, 1999), 115, 110.

Bibliography

Acosta, Alberto, "Post-Extractivism: From Discourse to Practice—Reflections for Action", *Alternative Pathways to Sustainable Development: Lessons from Latin America*, International Development Policy Series, No. 9 (Geneva: Graduate Institute Publications; Boston: Brill-Nijhoff, 2017), 77-101.

Anderson, Benedict, *Imagined Communities: Reflections on the Origin and Spread of Nationalism* (London: Verso, 1983).

Arndt, Lotte and Asger Taiaksev (eds.), *Hunting and Collecting: Sammy Baloji* (Ostend: Mu.ZEE; Paris: Galerie Imane Farès, 2016).

Bajorek, Jennifer, "Then and Now: Santu Mofokeng's *Black Photo Album*", *Distance and Desire: Encounters with the African Archive. African Photography from The Walter Collection*, ed. Tamar Garb (New York: The Walther Collection; Göttingen: Steidl, 2013), 221-227.

—— *Unfixed: Photography and Decolonial Imagination in West Africa* (London and Durham, Duke University Press, 2020).

Baker, Simon, "The Thinking Man and the femme sans tête: Collective Perception and Self-Representation", *RES: Anthropology and Aesthetics*, No. 38 (2000): 186-210.

Baloji, Sammy, "Sammy Baloji: The Past in Front of Us", Louisiana Channel (2015), https://vimeo.com/132212385.

Baloji, Sammy et al., "On the exhibition *Congo Stars*. Introduction by the curators", *Congo Stars*, eds. Barbara Steiner and Nicole Fritz (Cologne: Buchandlung Walther König, 2018), 11-12.

Baraitser, Lisa, "Touching Time: Maintenance, Endurance, Care", *Psychosocial Imaginaries: Perspectives on Temporality, Subjectivities and Activism*, ed. Stephen Frosh (London and New York: Palgrave Macmillan, 2015), 21-47.

Barber, Karen, "Popular Arts in Africa", *African Studies Review*, Vol. 30, No. 3 (1987): 1-78.

Barlow, John Perry, "A Declaration of the Independence of Cyberspace", Electronic Frontier Foundation, https://www.eff.org/cyberspace-independence.

Barthes, Roland, *Camera Lucida: Reflections on Photography*, trans. Richard Howard (New York: Hill & Wang, 1980; repr. London: Vintage Books, 2000).

Batchen, Geoffrey, "Seeing and Saying: A Response to Incongruous Images", *History and Theory*, Vol. 48, No. 4: 26-33.

Bates, Stephen, "The hidden holocaust", *The Guardian* (13 May 1999), https://www.theguardian.com/theguardian/1999/may/13/features11.g22.

Baucom, Ian, *Spectres of the Atlantic: Finance Capital, Slavery, and the Philosophy of History* (Durham and London: Duke University Press, 2005).

BBC, "1961: Ex-Congo PM declared dead" (13 February 1961), http://news.bbc.co.uk/onthisday/hi/dates/stories/february/13/newsid_2541000/2541053.stm.

Benjamin, Walter, "The Work of Art in the Age of Mechanical Reproduction", *Illuminations*, ed. Hannah Arendt, trans. Harry Zohn (New York: Schocken Books, 1969; repr. London: Pimlico, 1999), 211-244.

Bhabha, Homi, "Of Mimicry and Man: The Ambivalence of Colonial Discourse", *October*, No. 28 (1984): 125-233.

Blier, Suzanne Preston, *The Royal Arts of Africa: The Majesty of Form* (New York: H. N. Abrams, 1998).

Boehmer, Elleke, "Stories of Women and Mothers: Gender and Nationalism in the Early Fiction of Flora Nwapa", *Motherlands: Black Women's Writing from Africa, the Caribbean and South Asia*, ed. Susheila Nasta (London: The Women's Press Limited, 1991), 3-23.

—— *Stories of Women: Gender and Narrative in the Postcolonial Nation* (Manchester: Manchester University Press, 2005).

Booth, Jr., Newell S., "Time and Change in African Traditional Thought", *Journal of Religion in Africa*, Vol. 7, No. 2 (1975): 81-91.

Boserup, Ester, *Woman's Role in Economic Development* (London: George Allen and Unwin Ltd, 1970).

Bourland, Ian, "Afronauts: Race in Space", *Third Text*, Vol. 24, No. 2: 209-229.

Bouwer, Karen, *Gender and Decolonisation in the Congo: The Legacy of Patrice Lumumba* (New York: Palgrave Macmillan, 2010).

Braeckman, Colette, *Vers la deuxième indépendance du Congo* (Brussels: Le Cri Edition, 2009).

Braun, Lesley Nicole, "Dancing ambiguities in the Democratic Republic of Congo", *Critical African Studies*, Vol. 11, No. 1 (2019): 1-18.

—— "The Moving Parts in Michèle Magema's Body of Work", *African Arts*, Vol. 53, No. 3 (2019): 22-29.

Callaghy, Thomas, *The State-Society Struggle: Zaire in Comparative Perspective* (New York: Columbia University Press, 1984).

Ceuppens, Bambi and Sammy Baloji (eds.), *Congo Art Works: Popular Painting* (Brussels: Éditions Racine, 2017).

Chase, Malcolm and Christopher Shaw (eds.), "The Dimensions of Nostalgia", *The Imagined Past: History and Nostalgia* (Manchester: Manchester University Press, 1989), 1-17.

Chombart de Lauwe, Paul Henry, "Paris et l'agglomération parisienne" (1952), *Paris: essais de sociologie, 1952-1964* (Paris: Éditions ouvrières, 1965), 19-101.

Cixous, Hélène, "Castration or Decapitation?", trans. Annette Kuhn, *Signs*, Vol. 7, No. 1 (1981): 41-55.

Close, William, *Beyond the Storm: Treating the Powerless and Powerful in Mobutu's Congo/Zaire*, (Marbleton: Meadowlark Springs Productions, 2007).

Clynes, Manfred E. and Nathan S. Kline, "Cyborgs and space", *Astronautics* (September 1960): 26-27, 74-76.

Colard, Sandrine, "The Afterlife of a Colonial Photographic Archive: The Subjective Legacy of InforCongo", *Critical Interventions*, Vol. 12, No. 2 (2018): 117-139.

Cole, Ernest, *House of Bondage* (New York: Random House, 1967).

Collier, Delinda, "Obsolescing Analogue Africa: A Re-reading of the 'Digital' in Digital Art", *Critical Interventions*, Vol. 8, No. 3 (2014): 279-289.

—— *Media Primitivism: Technological Art in Africa* (Durham and London: Duke University Press, 2020).

Comaroff, John L. and Jean Comaroff, *Of Revelation and Revolution: Christianity, Colonialism and Consciousness in South Africa* (Chicago and London: The University of Chicago Press, 1991).

Comhaire-Sylvain, Susanne, *Femmes de Kinshasa hier et aujourd'hui* (Paris: Mouton, 1968).

Comolli, Jean-Louis, "Mechanical Bodies, Ever More Heavenly", trans. Annette Michelson, *October*, No. 83 (1998): 19-24.

Coombes, Annie, *History After Apartheid: Visual Culture and Public Memory in a Democratic South Africa* (Durham and London: Duke University Press, 2003).

Cooper, Frederick, "Colonising Time: Work Rhythms and Labour Conflict in Colonial Mombasa", *Colonialism and Culture*, ed. Nicholas B. Dirks (Ann Arbor: University of Michigan, 1994), 209-245.

Cosgrove, Denis, *Apollo's Eye: A Cartographic Genealogy of the Earth in the Western Imagination* (Baltimore: Johns Hopkins University Press, 2001).

Covington-Ward, Yolanda, *Gesture and Power: Religion, Nationalism and Everyday Performance in Congo* (Durham and London: Duke University Press, 2017).

Crenn, Julie, "Michèle Magema: Without Echo, There Is No Meaning", *n.paradoxa: international feminist art journal*, Vol. 13 (2013): 15-22.

De Boeck, Filip and Marie-Françoise Plissart, *Kinshasa: Tales of the Invisible City* (Ghent: Ludion, 2004; repr. Leuven: Leuven University Press, 2014).

De Boeck, Filip and Sammy Baloji, *Suturing the City: Living Together in Congo's Urban Worlds* (London: Autograph ABP, 2016).

De Groof, Matthias (ed.), *Lumumba in the Arts* (Leuven: Leuven University Press, 2020).

De Jong, Ferdinand and Michael Rowlands, *Alternative Imaginaries of Memory in West Africa* (London: Routledge 2007).

De Rezende, Isabelle, "History as Spectacle", *Lumumba in the Arts* (Leuven: Leuven University Press, 2020), 26-43.

De Villers, Gauthier (ed.), *Phénomènes informels et dynamiques culturelles en Afrique* (Tervuren/Paris: Institut-Africain-CEDAF/L'Harmattan: 1996).

De Witte, Ludo, *The Assassination of Lumumba*, trans. Ann Wright and Renée Fenby (Verso: London, 2001).

Debord, Guy, *Correspondance, tome 1: juin 1957-août 1960* (Paris: Fayaed, 1999).

DeLoughrey, Elizabeth, "Satellite Planetarity and the Ends of the Earth", *Public Culture*, Vol. 26, No. 2 (2014): 257-280.

Demos, T.J., *Return to the Postcolony: Spectres of Colonialism in Contemporary Art* (Berlin: Sternberg Press, 2013).

Demos, T.J. and Hilde Van Gelder (eds.), *In and Out of Brussels: Figuring Postcolonial Africa and Europe in the Films of Herman Asselberghs, Sven Augustijnen, Renzo Martens and Els Opsomer* (Leuven: Leuven University Press, 2012).

Derrida, Jacques, *Archive Fever: A Freudian Impression*, trans. Eric Prenowitz (Chicago: Chicago University Press, 1996).

Dery, Mark, "Black to the Future: Interviews with Samuel R. Delany, Greg Tate, and Tricia Rose", *Flame Wars: The Discourse of Cyberculture*, ed. Mark Dery (Durham and London: Duke University Press, 1994), 179-222.

Diawara, Manthia, "Talk of the Town", *Artforum*, Vol. 36, No. 6 (February 1998): 64-71.

Didwe dia Mwembu, Donatien, *Bana Shaba abdonnés par leur père: structures d"autorité et histoire sociale de la famille ouvière au Katanga 1910-1997* (Paris: L'Harmatten, 2001).

Donadio, Rachel, "Exploring a Century of Art from Congo", *The New York Times* (24 July 2015), https://www.nytimes.com/2015/07/25/arts/design/exploring-a-century-of-art-from-congo.html?_r=0.

Douglas, Gilbert et al., "Under Fire: Defining a contemporary African dance aesthetic – can it be done?", *Critical Arts*, Vol. 20, No. 2 (2006): 102-115.

Dunn, Kevin C., *Imagining the Congo: The International Relations of Identity* (New York: Palgrave Macmillan, 2003).

Dyangani Ose, Elvira, telephone conversation (4 July 2019).

Edwards, Elizabeth (ed.), *Anthropology and Photography, 1860-1920* (New Haven and London: Yale University Press, 1992).

Eisenstein, Sergei, *Film Form: Essays in Film Theory*, ed. and trans. Jay Leyda (New York: Harcourt, Brace & World, 1949).

—— "Montage of Attractions: For 'Enough Stupidity in Every Wiseman'", trans. Daniel Gerould, *The Drama Review*, Vol. 18, No. 1 (1974): 77-85.

Eley, Geoff and Ronald Grigot Suny (eds.), *Becoming National* (Oxford: Oxford University Press, 1996).

Enwezor, Okwui, "Introduction: Travel Notes: Living, Working and Travelling in a Restless World", *Trade Routes: History and Geography: 2nd Johannesburg Biennale 1997*, ed. Okwui Enwezor

(Johannesburg: Greater Johannesburg Metropolitan Council; Den Haag, Netherlands: Prince Claus Fund for Culture and Development, 1997), 7-12.

——— "Archive Fever: Photography between History and Monument", *Archive Fever: Uses of the Document in Contemporary Art* (New York: International Centre of Photography; Göttingen: Steidl Publishers, 2008), 11-51.

Eshun, Kodwo, "Further Considerations on Afrofuturism", *CR: The New Centennial Review*, Vol. 3, No. 2 (2003): 287-302.

Fabian, Johannes, *Jamaa* (Evanston: Northwestern University Press, 1971).

——— "Popular Culture in Africa: Findings and Conjectures", *Africa*, Vol. 48, No. 4 (1978): 315-334.

——— *Time and the Other: How Anthropology Makes its Object* (New York: Columbia University Press, 1983).

——— *Remembering the Present: Painting and Popular History in Zaire* (Berkeley, Los Angeles and London: University of California Press, 1996).

——— *Moments of Freedom: Anthropology and Popular Culture* (Charlottesville and London: University Press of Virginia, 1998).

Fall, N'Goné (ed.), *Photo Kinshasa* (Paris: Revue Noire, 2001).

Fanon, Frantz, *The Wretched of the Earth*, trans. Constance Farrington (New York: Grove Press, 1963; repr. New York: Grove Weidenfeld, 1965).

Farocki, Harun, "Workers Leaving the Factory", trans. Laurent Faasch-Ibrahim, *Harun Farocki: Working on the Sight-Lines*, ed. Thomas Elsaesser (Amsterdam: Amsterdam University Press, 2004), 237-244.

Fer, Briony, "A history of detail - or thinking small", The Courtauld Institute of Art (15 January 2018).

Ferro, Marc, *Cinema and History*, trans. Naomi Greene (Detroit: Wayne State University Press, 1988).

Fetter, Bruce, *The Creation of Elisabethville 1910-1940* (Stanford, CA: Hoover Institution Press, 1976).

——— "Relocating Central Africa's Biological Reproduction, 1923-1963", *International Journal of African Historical Studies*, Vol. 19, No. 3 (1986): 463-475.

Firstenberg, Lauri and John Peffer, *Translation/Seduction/Displacement: Post-Conceptual and Photographic Work by Artists from South Africa* (Portland: Institute of Contemporary Art at Maine College of Art, 2000).

Foster, Hal, "An Archival Impulse", *October*, Vol. 110 (2004): 3-22.

Foucault, Michel, *The Archaeology of Knowledge*, trans. A.M. Sheridan Smith (London: Routledge 1972).

——— *Discipline and Punish: The Birth of the Prison*, trans. Alan Sheridan (New York: Pantheon Books, 1977; repr. New York: Vintage Books, 1995).

Freedman, Jane, *Gender, Violence and Politics in the Democratic Republic of Congo* (London and New York: Routledge, 2016).

Garb, Tamar, "Renoir and the Natural Woman", *Oxford Art Journal*, Vol. 8, No. 2 (1985): 3-15.

——— "Of States and Stamps: The Otolith Group at the Delfina Foundation", *Contemporary And* (10 December 2014), https://www.contemporaryand.com/magazines/of-states-and-stamps-the-otolith-group-at-the-delfina-foundation/.

——— "Archiving the In-Between", *Àsìkò: On the Future of Artistic and Curatorial Pedagogies in Africa*, ed. Stephanie Baptist (Lagos: Centre for Contemporary Art, 2017), 115-128.

——— "Painting/Politics/Photograph: Marlene Dumas, Mme Lumumba and the Image of the African Woman", *Art History*, Vol. 43, No. 3 (2020): 588-611.

Garb, Tamar (ed.), *Distance and Desire: Encounters with the African Archive. African Photography from The Walter Collection* (New York: The Walther Collection; Göttingen: Steidl, 2013).

"Géopolitique de l'hibernation", *Internationale Situationiste*, No. 7 (April 1962): 3-10.

Gerard, Emmanuel and Bruce Kuklick, *Death in the Congo: Murdering Patrice Lumumba* (Cambridge and London: Harvard University Press, 2015).

Gilman, Lisa, "The Traditionalisation of Women's Dancing, Hegemony and Politics in Malawi", *Journal of Folklore Research*, Vol. 41, No. 1 (2004).
—— *The Dance of Politics: Gender, Performance and Democratisation in Malawi* (Philadelphia: Temple University Press, 2009).
Gilroy, Paul, *Small Acts: Thoughts of the Politics of Black Cultures* (London: Serpent's Tail, 1993).
Glissant, Édouard, *Poetics of Relation*, trans. Betsy Wing (Ann Arbor: Michigan University Press, 1997).
Gondola, Ch. Didier, "Popular Music, Urban Society and Changing Gender Relations in Kinshasa, Zaire", *Gendered Encounters*, eds. Maria Luise Grosz-Ngaté and Omari H. Kokole (New York: Routledge, 1997), 65-86.
—— "Dream and Drama: The Search for Elegance Among Congolese Youth", *African Studies Review*, Vol. 42, No. 1 (1999): 23-48.
—— *Tropical Cowboys: Westerns, Violence, and Masculinity in Kinshasa* (Indianapolis: Indiana University Press, 2016).
Gorfinkel, Elena, "Waiting: Endurance and Art Cinema's Tired Bodies", *Discourse*, Vol. 34, No. 2/3 (2012): 311-47.
Gould, Terri F., "Value Conflict and Development: The Struggle of the Professional Zairian Woman", *Journal of Modern African Studies*, Vol. 16, No. 1 (1978): 133-140.
Green, David, "Veins of Resemblance: Photography and Eugenics", *Oxford Art Journal*, Vol. 7, No. 2 (1984): 3-16.
Gregory, Derek, *The Colonial Present* (Oxford: Blackwell, 2004).
Hamilton, Carolyn et al. (eds.), *Refiguring the Archive* (Dordecht, Boston and London: Kluwer Publishers, 2002).
Haney, Erin, *Photography and Africa* (London: Reaktion Books, 2010).
Haraway, Donna J., *Simians, Cyborgs and Women: The Reinvention of Nature* (New York: Routledge, 1991).
—— *When Species Meet* (Minneapolis and London: University of Minnesota Press, 2008).
Harris, Jonathan, *The Global Contemporary Art World* (Hoboken: Wiley Blackwell, 2017).
Haskin, Jeanne, *The Tragic State of the Congo: From Decolonisation to Dictatorship* (New York: Algora Publishing, 2005).
Hayes, Patricia, "The Colour of History: Photography and the Public Sphere in Southern Africa", *The Public Sphere from Outside the West*, eds. Sanil V. and Divya Dwivedi (London: Bloomsbury, 2015), 147-163.
Hecht, Gabrielle, *Being Nuclear: Africans and the Global Uranium Trade* (Cambridge and London: MIT Press, 2012).
Hellio, Eléonore, "The Anti-Art of Kongo Futurism", Pan African Space Station (April 2013), https://panafricanspacestation.org.za/tag/bebson-elemba/.
Higginson, John, *A Working Class in the Making: Belgian Colonial Labour Policy, Private Enterprise and the African Mineworker, 1907-1951* (Madison: University of Wisconsin Press, 1989).
Hobsbawm, Eric, "Introduction: Inventing Traditions", *The Invention of Tradition*, eds. Eric Hobsbawm and Terence Ranger (Cambridge: Cambridge University Press, 1983), 1-14.
Hochschild, Adam, *King Leopold's Ghost: A Story of Greed, Terror and Heroism in Colonial Africa* (Boston and New York: Houghton Mifflin Company, 1999).
Hoyet, Marie-Jose, "Quelques images de Patrice Lumumba dans la literature du monde noir d'expression francaise", *Patrice Lumumba entre dieu et diable: Un héros africain dans ses images*, eds. Pierre Halen and János Riesz (Paris: L'Harmattan, 1997), 49-80.
Huckstep, Joan, "Embodied Nationalism 'Animation Politique' (Political Dance) in Zaire: A Case Study of the Dimensionality and Agency of Dance as the Spirit of Individual, Community, and National Identity", PhD dissertation (Temple University, 2005).

Hulyer, Jake, "How Baloji traced his Congolese roots to hear another side of Africa", *FACT Magazine* (27 November 2015), https://www.factmag.com/2015/11/27/baloji-interview/.

Hunt, Nancy Rose, "'Le bébé en brousse': European Women, African Birth Spacing, and Colonial Intervention in Breast Feeding in the Belgian Congo", *International Journal of African Historical Studies*, Vol. 21, No. 3 (1988): 401-432.

—— "Domesticity and Colonialism in Belgian Africa: Usumbura's Foyer Social, 1946-1960", *Signs*, Vol. 15, No. 3 (1990): 447-474.

—— *A Colonial Lexicon: Of Birth Ritual, Medicalisation and Mobility in the Congo* (Durham and London: Duke University Press, 1999).

—— "Tintin and the Interruptions of Congolese Comics", *Images and Empires: Visuality in Colonial and Postcolonial Africa*, eds. Paul S. Landau and Deborah D. Kaspin (Berkeley, Los Angeles and London: University of California Press, 2002): 90-123.

—— *A Nervous State: Violence, Remedies and Reverie in Colonial Congo* (Durham: Duke University Press, 2016).

Hussey, Andrew, *The Game of War: The Life and Death of Guy Debord* (London: Jonathan Cape, 2001).

Huyssen, Andreas, *Present Pasts: Urban Palimpsests and the Politics of Memory* (Stanford: Stanford University Press, 2003).

Hynes, Nancy and John Picton, "Yinka Shonibare: Re-Dressing History/Undressing Ethnicity", *African Arts*, Vol. 34, No. 3 (2001): 60-95.

Ide, Wendy, "Félicité review – musical, magnetic portrait of Kinshasa life", *The Observer*, https://www.theguardian.com/film/2017/nov/12/felicite-review-musical-magnetic-kinshasa-life-alain-gomis.

Jewsiewicki, Bogumil, "Painting in Zaire: From the Invention of the West to the Representation of Social Self", *Readings in African Popular*, ed. Karin Barber (Bloomington: Indiana University Press, 1997).

—— "Congolese Memories of Lumumba: Between Cultural Hero and Humanity's Redeemer", *A Congo Chronicle: Patrice Lumumba in Urban Art*, ed. Bogumil Jewsiewicki (New York: Museum of African Art, 1999), 73-91.

—— "Popular Painting in Contemporary Katanga: Painters, Audiences, Buyers and Sociopolitical Contexts", *A Congo Chronicle: Patrice Lumumba in Urban Art*, ed. Bogumil Jewsiewicki (New York: Museum for African Art, 1999), 13-27.

—— *The Beautiful Time: Photography by Sammy Baloji* (New York: Museum for African Art, 2010).

—— "Denial and Challenge of Modernity: Suffering, Recognition, and Dignity in Photographs by Sammy Baloji", *Suffering, Art and Aesthetics*, eds. M. Nijhawan and R. Hadj-Moussa (New York: Palgrave Macmillan, 2014), 51-74.

Jules-Rosette, Bennetta, "Afro-Pessimism's Many Guises", *Public Culture*, Vol. 14, No. 2 (2002): 603-605.

Kabwit, Ghislain C., "Zaïre: The Roots of the Continuing Crisis", *Journal of Modern African Studies*, Vol. 17, No. 3 (1979): 381-407.

Kalb, Madeleine G., *The Congo Cables: The Cold War in Africa-From Eisenhower to Kennedy* (New York: Macmillan, 1982).

Kanza, Thomas, *The Rise and Fall of Patrice Lumumba* (London: Rex Collings, 1978).

Kapalanga, Gazungil Sang'Amin, *Les spectacles d'animation politique en République du Zaire* (Louvain-la-Neuve: Cahiers theatre Louvain, 1989).

Kazadi, Pierre Cary, "Trends of Nineteenth and Twentieth Century Music in the Congo Zaire", *Musikkulturen Asiens, Afrikas und Ozeaniens im 19. Jahrhundert*, ed. Robert Günther (Regensberg: Gustav Bosse Verlag, 1973), 267-283.

Klein, Alyssa, "Baloji's Love Letter To The Congo Is The Most Stunning Music Video Of The Year", *OkayAfrica* (3 September 2015), https://www.okayafrica.com/baloji-capture-64-bits-and-malachite-music-video/.

Knabb, Ken (ed. and trans.), *Situationist-International Anthology* (Berkeley: Bureau of Public Secrets, 1981).

Kodjo-Grandvaux, Séverine, "*Beauté Congo*, un certain regard sur l'histoire culturelle de la RDC", *Jeune Afrique* (20 July 2015), http://www.jeuneafrique.com/mag/247901/culture/arts-beaute-congo-un-certain-regard-sur-lhistoire-culturelle-de-la-rdc.

Kokole, Omari H., "Time, Language and the Oral Tradition: An African Perspective", *Time in the Black Experience*, ed. Joseph K. Adjaye (Westport and London: Greenwood Press, 1994), 35–54.

Kongo Astronauts, "Kongo Astronauts", https://kongoastronauts.wordpress.com/about-kongo-astronauts-kinshasa-rdcongo-2013-2019/.

Kopytoff, Igor, *Ancestors as Elders in Africa* (New York: Bobbs-Merill, 1971).

Lagae, Johan and Sabine Cornelis (eds.), *Sammy Baloji & Patrick Mudekereza en residence au Musée royal de l'Afrique centrale: Congo Far West: Arts, sciences et collections* (Milan: Silvana, 2011).

Lagae, Johan and Kim De Raedt, "Building for 'l'Authenticité': Eugène Palumbo and the Architecture of Mobutu's Congo", *Journal of Architectural Education*, Vol. 68, No. 2 (2014): 178–189.

LaGamma, Alisa (ed.), *Kongo: Power and Majesty* (New York: Metropolitan Museum of Art; New Haven and London: Yale University Press, 2015).

Larmer, Miles, "Permanent Precaity: Capital and Labour in the Central African Copperbelt", *Labor History*, Vol. 58, No. 2 (2017): 170–184.

Le Lay, Maëline, Dominique Malaquais and Nadine Siegert (eds.), *Archive (re)mix: Vues d'Afrique*, eds. (Rennes: Presses Universitaires de Rennes, 2015).

Le Lay, Maëline, "Performer l'archive pour réécrire l'histoire: l'exposition Congo Far West au Musée royal de l'Afrique central de Tervuren", *Archive (re)mix: Vues d'Afrique*, eds. Maéline La Lay, Dominique Malaquais and Nadine Siegert (Rennes: Presses Universitairs de Rennes, 2015), 107–123.

Lighting Africa, "Democratic Republic of Congo: A fledging off-grid market in a difficult context" (January 2018), https://www.lightingafrica.org/country/democratic-republic-of-congo/.

Loewenson, Thandi, "Daring to Dream with Eyes Wide Open: review of Baloji's Zombies", *ROAPE* (7 June 2019), https://roape.net/2019/06/07/daring-to-dream-with-eyes-wide-open-review-of-balojis-zombies/.

Lumumba, Patrice, "La mode masculine à Stanleyville", *La croix du Congo* (20 May 1951).

—— *Lumumba Speaks: The Speeches and Writings of Patrice Lumumba, 1958–1961*, ed. Jean Van Lierde, trans. Helen R. Lane (Boston and Toronto: Little, Brown and Company, 1972).

Lumumba, la mort du prophète, dir. Raoul Peck (Velvet Films, 1991).

Lutz, Catherine and Jane Collins, "The Photograph as an Intersection of Gazes: The Example of *National Geographic*", *Visual Anthropology Review*, Vol. 7, No. 1 (1991): 134–149.

Lyons, Danny, *Conversations with the Dead* (New York: Holt, Rinehart and Winston, 1971).

Maart, Brendan (ed.), *Imaginary Fact. Contemporary South African Art and the Archive* (Grahamstown: National Arts Festival, 2013).

Magagnoli, Paolo, *Documents of Utopia: The Politics of Experimental Documentary* (London and New York: Wallflower Press, 2015).

Malaquais, Dominique, "Postcolonial Dilemma: Parts I–III", *Ellipses Journal of Creative Research*, http://www.ellipses.org.za/project/postcolonial-dilemma-parts-i-iii/.

—— "Kongo Astronauts: Collectif embarqué", *Multitudes*, Vol. 4, No. 77 (2019): 20–26.

Mama, Amina, "Sheroes and Villains: Conceptualising Colonial and Contemporary Violence Against Women in Africa", *Feminist Genealogies, Colonial Legacies and Democratic Futures*, eds. M. Jacqui Alexander and Chandra Talpade Mohanty (New York and London: Routledge, 1997).

Marchal, Jules, *L'etat libre du Congo: paradis perdu: l'histoire du Congo 1876-1900*, vol. 1 and 2 (Borgloon: Éditions Paula Bellings, 1996).

—— *E.D. Morel contre Léopold II: L'histoire du Congo 1900-1910*, vol 1 and 2 (Paris: Éditions L'Harmattan, 1996).
—— *Forced Labour in the Gold and Copper Mines: A History of Congo Under Belgian Rule, 1910-1945*, trans. Ayi Kwei Armah (Popenguine: Per Ankh, 2003).
Marijnen, Esther, "Public Authority and Conservation in Areas of Armed Conflict: Virunga National Park as a 'State within a State' in Eastern Congo", *Development and Change*, Vol. 49, No. 3 (2018): 790-814.
Markovitz, M.D., *Cross and Sword: The Political Role of Christian Missions in the Belgian Congo 1908-1960* (Stanford: Hoover Institution Press, 1973).
Mashigo, Mohale, "Afrofuturism: Ayashis' Amateki", *The Johannesburg Review of Books* (1 October 2018), https://johannesburgreviewofbooks.com/2018/10/01/afrofuturism-is-not-for-africans-living-in-africa-an-essay-by-mohale-mashigo-excerpted-from-her-new-collection-of-short-stories-intruders/.
Masuy, Christine, "Du portrait au personage: La diabolisation symbolique de Patrice Lumumba dans La Libre Belgique", *Lumumba entre dieu et diable: Un héros africain dans ses images*, ed. by Pierre Halen and János Riesz (Paris: L'Harmattan, 1997), 199-213.
Mazrui, Alamin and Lupenga Mphande, "Time and Labour in Colonial Africa: The Case of Kenya and Malawi", *Time in the Black Experience*, ed. Joseph K. Adjaye (Westport and London: Greenwood Press, 1994), 97-119.
Mbembe, Achille, "Provisional Notes on the Postcolony", *Africa*, Vol. 62, No. 1 (1992): 3-37.
—— *On the Postcolony* (Berkeley, Los Angeles and London: University of California Press, 2001).
—— "On the Power of the False", *Public Culture*, Vol. 14, No. 2 (2002): 629-641.
—— "Necropolitics", *The Unhomely: Phantom Scenes in Global Society*, trans. Libby Meintjes, ed. Okwui Enwezor (Seville: BIACS, 2006), 32-51.
Mbiti, John, "Eschatology", *Biblical Revelation and African Beliefs*, eds. Kwesi Dickson and Paul Ellingworth (London: Lutterworth, 1969), 159-184.
—— *New Testament Eschatology in an African Background* (London: Oxford University Press, 1971).
—— *African Religions and Philosophy* (Oxford: Heinemann, 1969; repr. 1990).
Mbuyamba Kankolongo, Alphonse, "Quelques témoignages sur Lumumba", *Lumumba entre dieu et diable: Un héros africain dans ses images*, eds. Pierre Halen and János Riesz (Paris: L'Harmattan, 1997), 129-135.
McClintock, Anne, *Imperial Leather: Race, Gender and Sexuality in the Colonial Contest* (New York and London: Routledge, 1995).
McDonough, Tom (ed. and trans.), *The Situationists and the City* (London: Verso, 2009).
Melamed, Jodi, "Racial Capitalism", *Critical Ethnic Studies*, Vol. 1, No. 1 (2015): 76-85.
Mereweather, Charles (ed.), *The Archive* (London: Whitechapel; Cambridge: MIT Press, 2006).
Mianda, Gertrude, "Dans l'ombre de la 'démocratie' au Zaire: la remise en question de l'emancipation Mobutiste de la femme", *Canadian Journal of African Studies*, Vol. 29, No. 1 (1995): 51-78.
—— "Women and Garden Produce of Kinshasa: The Difficult Quest for Autonomy", *Women, Work and Gender Relations in Developing Countries: A Global Perspective*, eds. Parvin Ghorayshi and Claire Bélanger (Westport and London: Greenwood Press, 1996), 91-101.
—— "Colonialism, Education and Gender Relations in the Belgian Congo: The Évolué Case", *Women in African Colonial Histories*, eds. Jean Allman, Susan Geiger and Nakanyike Muisi (Bloomington: Indiana University Press, 2002), 144-163.
Milbourne, Karen E., *Earth Matters: Land as Material and Metaphor in the Arts of Africa* (New York: Monacelli Press; Washington D.C.: National Museum of African Art, 2013).
—— "Senses of Time: Video and Film-Based Arts of Africa", *African Arts*, Vol. 48, No. 4 (2015): 72-84.

Mofokeng, Santu, "The Black Photo Album/Look at Me: 1890-1950", *Events of the Self: Portraiture and Social Identity. Contemporary African Photography from the Walther Collection*, ed. Okwui Enwezor (Göttingen, Germany: Steidl, 2010), 171-172.

Mokthari, Sylvie et al. (eds), *Les artistes contemporains et l'archive: interrogation sur le sens du temps et de la mémoire à l'ère de la numérisation* (Rennes: Presses Universitaires de Rennes, 2004).

Monaville, Pedro, "Decolonising the University: Postal Politics, The Student Movement and Global 1968 in the Congo", PhD dissertation (University of Michigan, 2013).

—— "A History of Glory and Dignity: Patrice Lumumba in Historical Imagination and Postcolonial Genealogies", *Lumumba in the Arts*, ed. Matthias De Groof (Leuven: Leuven University Press, 2020), 62-77.

Mudekereza, Patrick, "Picha: The Second Biennale of Photography and Video Art Lubumbashi, Democratic Republic of the Congo, October 2010", trans. Allen F. Roberts, *African Arts*, Vol. 44, No. 3 (2011): 68-75.

—— "Biennial culture or grassroots globalisation?: the challenge of the Picha art centre, as a tool for building local relevance for the Rencontres Picha, Biennale de Lubumbashi", research report for Master of Arts in History of Art (University of the Witwatersrand, 2017), http://wiredspace.wits.ac.za/handle/10539/24575.

Mudimbe, V.Y., *The Invention of Africa: Gnosis, Philosophy, and the Order of Knowledge* (Bloomington and Indianapolis: Indiana University Press, 1988).

Muswamba, Rosalie Malu, *Le travail des femmes en République démocratique du Congo: exploitation ou promesse d'autonomie?* (Paris: UNESCO, 2006).

Mutamba Makombo, Jean-Marie, "La destinée politique de Patrice Lumumba (1925-1961)", *À la redécouverte de Patrice Emery Lumumba*, eds. Mabiala Mantuba Ngoma (Kinshasa: Institut de Formation et d'Études Politiques, 1996), 11-52.

Nanni, Giordano, *Colonisation of Time: Ritual, Routine and Resistance in the British Empire* (Manchester: Manchester University Press, 2012).

Ndaywel è Nziem, Isidore, *Histoire générale du Congo: De l'héritage ancien à la République Démocratique du Congo* (Paris: Duculot, 1998).

Nelson, Alondra, "Introduction: Future Texts", *Social Text*, Vol. 20, No. 2 (2002): 1-15.

Newbury, Darren, et al., *Women and Photography in Africa: Creative Practices and Feminist Challenges* (London: Routledge, 2021).

Nora, Pierre, *Les lieux de mèmoire* (Paris: Gallimard, 1997).

Nugent, Gabriella, "Mining Time in Sammy Baloji's *Mémoire*", *African Arts*, Vol. 52, No. 3 (2019): 62-71.

—— "From Camera to Canvas: The Case of Patrice Lumumba and Congolese Popular Painting", *Nka: Journal of Contemporary African Art*, No. 47 (2020): 82-93.

Nzongola-Ntalaja, Georges, *The Congo: From Leopold to Kabila: A People's History* (London and New York: Zed Books, 2002).

—— "Patrice Lumumba: The Most Important Assassination of the 20th Century", *The Guardian* (17 January 2011), https://www.theguardian.com/global-development/poverty-matters/2011/jan/17/patrice-lumumba-50th-anniversary-assassination.

Ogle, Vanessa, *The Global Transformation of Time: 1870-1950* (Cambridge: Harvard University Press, 2015).

Oguibe, Olu, "Photography and the Substance of the Image", *In/sight: African Photographers 1940 to the Present*, eds. Clare Bell et al. (New York: Guggenheim Museum, 1996), 231-250.

Oliver, Kelly, *Earth & World: Philosophy After the Apollo Missions* (New York: Columbia University Press, 2015).

Omasombo Tshonda, Jean and Verhaegen, Benoît, *Patrice Lumumba: Jeunesse et Apprentissage Politique 1925-1956* (Tervuren: Institut Africain-CEDAF; Paris: Haramttan, 1998).

Perrings, Charles, *Black Mineworkers in Central Africa: Industrial Strategies and the Evolution of an African Proletariat in the Copperbelt, 1911-41* (New York: Africana Publishing, 1979).

Petit, Pierre, and Georges Mulumbwa Mutambwa, "'La crise': Lexicon and Ethos of the Second Economy in Lubumbashi," *Africa*, Vol. 75, No. 4 (2005): 467-87.

Poole, Deborah, "An Excess of Description: Ethnography, Race, and Visual Technologies", *Annual Review of Anthropology*, Vol. 34 (2005): 159-179.

Popplewell, Georgia, "Raoul Peck: A Vision of His Own", *Caribbean Beat*, 60 (March/April 2003), https://www.caribbean-beat.com/issue-60/vision-his-own#axzz5MH66Etnl.

Pratt, Mary Louise, "Arts of the Contact Zone", *Profession* (1991): 33-40.

Proudhon, Pierre-Joseph, *Systems of Economical Contradictions: or, The Philosophy of Misery*, trans. Benjamin R. Tucker (Boston, MA: B.R. Tucker, 1888).

Prunier, Gérard, *Africa's World War: Congo, the Rwandan Genocide, and the Making of a Continental Catastrophe* (Oxford: Oxford University Press, 2009).

Pype, Katrien, "Geographies of the Occult and the Divine – Pentecostal Semiotics of Urban Space in Kinshasa", *Witchcraft, Demons and Deliverance*, eds. Claudia Währisch-Oblau and Henning Wrogemann (Zurich: Lit Verlag, 2015), 69-92.

Rancière, Jacques, *Disagreement: Politics and Philosophy*, trans. Julie Rose (Minneapolis and London: University of Minnesota Press, 1999).

—— *The Politics of Aesthetics*, trans. Gabriel Rockhill (London: Bloomsbury, 2004).

—— *Dissensus: On Politics and Aesthetics*, ed. and trans. Steven Corcoran (London: Continuum, 2010).

Reid, Donald, "Industrial Paternalism: Discourse and Practice in Nineteenth-Century French Mining and Metallurgy", *Comparative Studies in Society and History*, Vol. 27, No. 4 (1985): 579-607.

Renoe, William, "From State Collapse to 'Absolutism', to State Failure", *Third World Quarterly*, Vol. 27, No. 1 (2006): 43-56.

Renton, David, David Seddon and Leo Zeilig, *The Congo: Plunder and Resistance* (London and New York: Zed Books, 2007).

Rizzo, Lorena, *Photography and History in Colonial Southern Africa: Shades of Empire* (London: Routledge, 2020).

Roberts, Mary Nooter and Allen Roberts, *Memory: Luba Art and the Making of History* (New York and Munich: Museum of African Art, 1996).

Robinson, Cedric, *Black Marxism: The Making of the Black Radical Tradition* (London: Zed Press, 1983; repr. Chapel Hill: University of North Carolina Press, 2000).

Robinson, Jennifer, "Living in Dystopia: Past, Present, and Future in Contemporary African Cities", *Noir Urbanisms: Dystopic Images of the Modern City*, ed. Gyan Prakash (Princeton: Princeton University Press, 2010), 218-240.

Sachs, Wolfgang, *Planet Dialectics: Explorations in Environment and Development* (London: Zed Books, 1999).

Sagan, Carl, "Voyager will carry 'earth sounds' record", *NASA* (August 1977), https://www.jpl.nasa.gov/releases/70s/release_1977_0800.html.

Schaffner, Ingrid and Matthias Winzen, *Deep Storage: Collecting, Storing and Archiving Contemporary Art* (New York: Prestel, 1998).

Scott, Darieck, *Extravagant Abjection: Blackness, Power and Sexuality in the African American Literary Imagination* (New York: New York University Press, 2010).

Scott, Ariel Osterweis, "Performing Acupuncture on a Necropolitical Body: Choreographer Faustin Linyekula's Studios Kabako in Kisangani, Democratic Republic of Congo", *Dance Research Journal*, Vol. 42, No. 2 (2010), 13-27.

Senga, Georges, *Une vie après la mort*, ed. Marie-Aude Delafoy (Lubumbashi: ASBL Dialogues, 2013).

—— email correspondence (9 July 2018).

Shatzberg, Michael G., *The Dialectics of Oppression in Zaire* (Bloomington: Indiana University Press, 1988).
Silverman, Debora, "Art Nouveau, Art of Darkness: African Lineages of Belgian Modernism, Part I", *West 86th: A Journal of Decorative Arts, Design History and Material Culture*, Vol. 18, No. 2 (2011): 139-181.
—— "Art Nouveau, Art of Darkness: African Lineages of Belgian Modernism, Part II, *West 86th: A Journal of Decorative Arts, Design History and Material Culture*, Vol. 19, No. 2 (2012): 175-195.
—— "Art Nouveau, Art of Darkness: African Lineages of Belgian Modernism, Part III", *West 86th: A Journal of Decorative Arts, Design History and Material Culture*, Vol. 20, No. 2 (2013): 22-61.
—— "Diasporas of Art: History, the Tervuren Royal Museum for Central Africa, and the Politics of Memory in Belgium, 1885-2014", *The Journal of Modern History*, Vol. 87, No. 3 (2015): 615-667.
—— "Black Lives Matter in Belgium: Reckoning with Legacies of Colonialism, Violence and Contemporary Racism", UCLA (16 April 2021).
Sliwinski, Sharon, "The Childhood of Human Rights: The Kodak on the Congo", *Journal of Visual Culture*, Vol. 5, No. 3 (2006): 333-363.
Slobodian, Quinn, *Foreign Front: Third World Politics in Sixties West Germany* (Durham and London: Duke University Press, 2012).
Sorgel, Sabine, "The Global Politics of Faustin Linyekula's Dance Theatre: From Congo to Berlin and Back Again via Brussels and Avignon", *Moving (Across) Borders: Performing Translation, Intervention, Participation*, eds. Gabriele Brandstetter and Holgar Hartung (Bielefeld: Transcript, 2017), 79-91.
Sprague, Stephen F., "Yoruba Photography: How the Yoruba See Themselves", *African Arts*, Vol. 12, No. 1 (1978): 52-59, 107.
Stanard, Matthew, *The Leopard, the Lion and the Cock: Colonial Memories and Monuments in Belgium* (Leuven: Leuven University Press, 2019).
Stearns, Jason, *Dancing in the Glory of Monsters: The Collapse of the Congo and the Great War of Africa* (New York: PublicAffairs, 2012).
Storr, Robert, Philippe Pirotte and Jan Hoet, *Luc Tuymans: Mwana Kitoko (Beautiful White Man)* (Ghent: S.M.A.K. Stedelijk Museum voor Actuele Kunst, 2001).
Stratton, Florence, "How Could Things Fall Apart For Whom They Were Not Together?", *Contemporary African Literature and the Politics of Gender* (London and New York: Routledge, 1994), 22-38.
Strother, Z.S., "A Photograph Steals the Soul", *Portraiture and Photography in Africa*, eds. John Peffer and Elisabeth L. Cameron (Bloomington: Indiana University Press, 2013), 177-212.
Stoler, Ann Laura, *Along the Archival Grain: Epistemic Anxieties and Colonial Common Sense* (Princeton: Princeton University Press, 2009).
—— "'The Rot Remains': From Ruins to Ruination", *Imperial Debris: On Ruins and Ruination*, ed. Ann Laura Stoler (Durham: Duke University Press, 2013), 1-35.
System K, dir. Renaud Barret (Les Films en Vrac and La Belle Kinoise, 2019).
Tate Modern, "Contested Terrains: Sammy Baloji", http://www.tate.org.uk/whats-on/tate-modern/display/level-2-gallery-contested-terrains/contested-terrains-sammy-baloji.
Tempels, Placide, *La philosophie bantoue* (Paris: Présence Africaine, 1945).
Thassinda, H. Thassinda Uba, *Zaire, les princes de l'invisible: L'Afrique noire bâillonnée par le parti unique* (Caen: Editions C'est-à-dire, 1992).
Thompson, E.P., *The Making of the English Working Class* (Harmondsworth: Penguin, 1968).
Thompson, Harry, *Tintin: Hergé and His Creation* (London: Hodder & Stoughton, 1991).
Thornton, John K., *The Kingdom of Kongo: Civil War and Transition, 1641-1718* (Madison: University of Wisconsin Press, 1983).
—— *A Cultural History of the Atlantic World, 1250-1820* (Cambridge: Cambridge University Press, 2012).
Tierou, Alphonse, *Si sa danse bouge, l'Afrique bougera* (Paris: Maisonneuve and Larose, 2001).

Time, "Belgian Congo: Democracy with Spears", Vol. 75, No. 22 (30 May 1960).

—— "How to Appear Évolué", Vol. 84, No. 13 (25 September 1964).

Truddaïu, Julien, "Representing Lumumba (1956-1961): The Twists and Turns of Belgian Colonial Propaganda", *Lumumba in the Arts*, ed. Matthias De Groof (Leuven: Leuven University Press, 2002), 388-407.

Ukeles, Mierle Laderman, "Manifesto for Maintenance Art, 1969", Arnolfini, https://www.arnolfini.org.uk/blog/manifesto-for-maintenance-art-1969.

Van Beurden, Sarah, *Authentically African: Arts and the Transnational Politics of Congolese Culture* (Athens: Ohio University Press, 2015).

Van der Watt, Liese, "Echoes of Zaire: Popular Painting from Lubumbashi, DRC", *Africa is a Country* (2 July 2015), https://africasacountry.com/2015/07/echoes-of-zaire-popular-painting-from-lubumbashi-drc-by-liese-van-der-watt/.

Van Reybrouck, David, *Congo: The Epic History of a People*, trans. Sam Garrett (London: Fourth Estate, 2014).

Vangroenweghe, Daniel, *Du sang sur les lianes: Léopold II et son Congo* (Brussels: Didier Hatier, 1996).

Vansina, Jan, "Recording the Oral History of the Bakuba-I. Methods", *The Journal of African History*, Vol. 1, No. 1 (1960): 43-53.

—— "Recording the Oral History of the Bakuba-II. Results", *The Journal of African History*, Vol. 1, No. 1 (1960): 257-70.

—— *De la tradition orale: essai de méthode historique* (Tervuren: Musée Royal de l'Afrique Centrale, 1961).

—— *Paths in the Rainforest: Toward a History of Political Tradition in Equatorial Africa* (Madison: University Wisconsin Press, 1990).

Vellut, Jean-Luc, "Hégémonies en construction: Articulations entre etat et entreprises dans le bloc colonial belge (1908-1960)", *Revue canadienne des études africaines/Canadian Journal of African Studies*, Vol. 16, No. 2 (1982): 313-330.

—— "Mining in the Belgian Congo", *History of Central Africa*, eds. David Birmingham and Phyllis M. Martin (London and New York: Longman, 1983), 126-162.

—— "La peinture du Congo-Zaïre et la recherche de l'Afrique innocente: présentation du livre de J. A. Cornet, R. De Cnodder, I. Dierickx, et W. Toebosch: 60 ans de peinture au Zaïre", *Bulletin des séances* 36, No. 4 (1990): 633-59.

Verbeeck, Georgius, "Un génocide s'est-il déroulé dans l'État indépendant du Congo?", *Le Congo Colonial. Une Histoire en Questions*, eds. Idesbald Goddeeris, Amandine Lauro and Guy Vanthemsche (Paris: La Renaissance du Livre, 2020), 45-61.

Virilio, Paul, *The Lost Dimension*, trans. Daniel Mosherberg (New York: Semiotext(e), 1991).

Wendl, Tobias, "Entangled Traditions: Photography and the History of Media in Southern Ghana", *RES: Anthropology and Aesthetics*, No. 39 (2001): 78-101.

White, Bob W., "The Political Undead: Is It Possible to Mourn for Mobutu's Zaire?", Mourning and the Imagination of Political Time in Contemporary Central Africa [special issue], eds. Bogumil Jewsiewicki and Bob W. White, *African Studies Review*, Vol. 48, No. 2: 65-85.

Whitley, Zoé, "The Place is Space: Afrofuturism's Transnational Geographies", *The Shadows Took Shape*, eds. Naima J. Keith and Zoé Whitley (New York: The Studio Museum in Harlem, 2013), 19-25.

Willame, Jean-Claude, *Patrice Lumumba: La crise congolaise revisitée* (Paris: Karthala, 1990).

Wilson, Francille Rusan, "Reinventing the Past and Circumscribing the Future: Authenticité and the Negative Image of Women's Work in Zaire", *Women and Work in Africa*, ed. Edna G. Bay (Boulder: Westview Press, 1982), 153-170.

Wrong, Michela, *In the Footsteps of Mr Kurtz: Living on the Brink of Disaster in Mobutu's Congo* (London: Fourth Estate, 2001).

Yates, Barbara A., "Colonialism, Education and Work: Sex Differentiation in Colonial Zaire", *Women and Work in Africa*, ed. Edna G. Bay (Boulder: Westview Press, 1982), 127–152.

Young, Crawford, "Zaire: The Shattered Illusion of the Integral State", *The Journal of Modern African Studies*, Vol. 32, No. 2 (1994): 247–263.

Young, Crawford and Thomas Turner, *The Rise and Decline of the Zairian State* (Madison: University of Wisconsin Press, 1985).

Zahan, Dominique, *Religion, spiritualité et pensée Africaines* (Paris: Payot, 1970).

Zeilig, Leo, *Lumumba: Africa's Lost Leader* (London: Haus, 2008).

Zeitgeist Films, *Lumumba* press kit (2001), https://zeitgeistfilms.com/media/films/5/presskit.pdf.

Index

Afrofuturism 121–123
Akerman, Chantal 76–77
Anderson, Benedict 63
animation politique et culturelle 55–56
    women in 56
anthropology
    and photography 29
Apollo missions
    Apollonian eye 149
    Apollo (type of dance in Kinshasa) 136
    Apolosa (Congolese comic character) 136
    photographs of earth from space 141–142
archive(s)
    archival turn in contemporary art 13–14
    as dominant or official institution 27, 29, 31–33, 49, 57, 138
    counter-archive 136
    in Africa 14
    personal 86, 89, 91–93
Armstrong, Neil 135–136
astronaut
    in contemporary art 122, 126
Attia, Kader 134
Augustijnen, Sven 88
authenticité 52–55
    and clothing 91
    contradictions of 54–55
Bajorek, Jennifer 93, 115, 117
Baloji (musician) 119–120, 141, 142–143
Baloji, Sammy 11
    in Belgium 17–19
    Mémoire (photomontage series) 25–39, 65-68
    Mémoire (video) 25, 40–46
    The Album 9–10
Barber, Karen 114
Barret, Renaud. *See* System K
Barthes, Roland 13, 67
Baucom, Ian 33
Beauté Congo 1926-2015:
    Congo Kitoko (exhibition) 67–68

Belgian Congo. *See* InforCongo
    as *une colonie modèle* 12
    as paternalist 22
Belgium
    colonial memories in 15–19
Benjamin, Walter 33, 108–109
Bhabha, Homi K. 94–95
Biennale de Lubumbashi
    artist participation 18
    Elvira Dyangani Ose 88, 113–114
    origins 17
big men (tradition of) 53–54, 99
Bills (youth culture) 91
Boehmer, Elleke 62, 64
Boserup, Ester 50
Bouwer, Karen 111
Braun, Lesley Nicole 56
Burozi 104–105, 107, 109
capitalism
    and racism 34
    time of 38
cinema. *See* film
Cixous, Hélène 59–62
clothing
    and *authenticité* 53, 55, 91
    and the *évolués* 73, 90
    as compliance 61–62
    as resistance 91
Cold War
    and extraction 138
    and Lumumba 85, 97
    and the Congo 85, 136
Cole, Ernest 34
Collier, Delinda 42, 46
colour vs. black and white 30–31, 57–58, 88, 102
comics 106, 135–136
Congo Free State
    afterlives of 22, 41–42, 138–141
    as imperialism 22
    human rights campaign against 11–12
    photographs of 11–12, 21
    violence in 15, 21

Congolese historiography 133, 136
    Lumumba 98, 117
    male actors 58, 152
Congolese popular painting 101-109, 110, 113-114
Congo Reform Association 11-12, 21
Conrad, Joseph 21
contact zone 109
Covington-Ward, Yolanda 56
creuseurs 26-27, 40, 42, 44-46
cyberspace 142-145
cyborg 144-145
dance
    and time 44
    animation politique 55-56
    Apollo (type of) 136
    improvisation 44-45
De Boeck, Filip 18, 21, 112, 126
Debord, Guy 125-126
decolonisation 115, 116-117
    and the Space Age 133-135, 146
    persistence of Lumumba's image 116
Derrida, Jacques 13
Dery, Mark 121-122
detail 77-82
De Witte, Ludo 16, 100
Diawara, Manthia 94
Dumas, Marlene 73-75
Dunn, Kevin 21
dystopia
    trope of 28, 122, 147-148
The Economist (newspaper) 147-148
Eisenstein, Sergei 128-129, 137
Ekeba, Michel 11, 124, 127, 145. See Kongo
    Astronauts
Enwezor, Okwui 22
Eshun, Kodwo 122, 147
ethnographic type 33
évolués 73
    and French language 73
    and photography 94-96
    appearance 73, 90
    carte d'immatriculation 73, 90, 94
    European disdain for 90
    interior decoration 95-96
    masculinity 91
    wives 75
extractivism 41-42, 138-145, 139
    Cold War technopolitics 138

Congo Free State 22, 41-42
Fabian, Johannes 39, 101-102, 111, 113, 114
Fanon, Frantz 37, 39, 98
Félicité (film) 83
femmes libres 54
film
    as agent of history 137-138
    montage 127-133
    photographs staged in 112
    women's labour 76-77
Foster, Hal 13-14
Foucault, Michel 13, 77-78
Garb, Tamar 73, 134
Gerard, Emmanuel 86, 89
Gilman, Lisa 56, 63
Glissant, Édouard 20, 148
global/globalisation
    biennials 18
    photography and video 12-13, 23
Gomis, Alain. See *Félicité*
Gondola, Ch. Didier 33
Gregory, Derek 41
Haney, Erin 105-106
Haraway, Donna 126, 144
Hecht, Gabrielle 138
Hellio, Éléonore 11, 119, 124. See Kongo
    Astronauts
Higginson, John 29, 39
Hochschild, Adam. See *King Leopold's Ghost*
Hunting and Collecting (exhibition) 18
Hunt, Nancy Rose 21, 36, 75, 94, 135-136
Huyssen, Andreas 11
L'Illustration Congolaise (magazine) 12, 93
InforCongo 12, 95, 103. See Joseph Makula
intermedia 101-109, 112, 114, 133
invention of tradition 63
Jewsiewicki, Bogumil 11, 28, 66, 103, 109, 110, 111
Jules-Rosette, Bennetta 80, 82
Kabila, Laurent-Désiré 53, 111-112
Kapalanga, Gazungil Sang'Amin 55
Kayembe Kilobo 85-88, 89-93, 95, 98-99, 106, 109, 112-118
Kia Henda, Kiluanji 146-147
King Leopold's Ghost (book) 15, 21
Kinshasa 35-36, 46, 53, 80, 83, 101, 111, 119, 121, 124, 133, 136, 143, 145
Kongo Astronauts 11, 119-150

Kongo Kingdom 123
Kuba culture 72
Kuklick, Bruce 86, 89
Lettrist International 19, 124. *See* Situationist International
Linyekula, Faustin 27
   Mémoire (video) 40-46
Luba culture 94
Lubumbashi 17-18, 26, 45-46, 85, 100, 101, 112-114
Lumumba, Patrice Émery
   amnesia around 109-114
   appearance 89-90, 99
   arrest of 100
   assassination of 16, 100-101
   Congolese independence speech 40, 97, 112
   in Congolese popular painting 101-109
   memories of 112-114
   photographs and newsreel footage of 12, 96-97, 112
   Western media representations of 97
Magema, Michèle 11, 18
   at the Biennale de Lubumbashi 18, 19
   in Belgium 19, 151
   Mémoires Hévéa 151-153
   Oyé Oyé 49-84
Magnin, André 67-68
maintenance 71-75, 77
   lapse in 81
   Lisa Baraitser on 71
   Mierle Laderman Ukeles's definition of 71, 81
Makula, Joseph 95-96
Mama, Amina 51
Marchal, Jules 15, 29
masculinity 33-34, 91, 94, 99
Mashigo, Mohale 123
Masuy, Christine 97
Mazru, Alamin 37, 38
Mbembe, Achille. *See* postcolony and necropolitics
Mbiti, John 37, 38
Mbongwana Star 119, 127
McClintock, Anne 58, 63
Meessen, Vincent 19, 124, 136-138
memory
   collective memory of Lumumba 109-114
   colonial past in Belgium 16
   personal 86, 88, 91, 93, 152-153

Michel, Thierry. *See Mobutu, roi du Zaïre*
mimicry 94-95
mining. *See* extractivism
   as violence 46, 130, 141
Mobutu, roi du Zaïre (documentary film) 49, 57-58, 68-69
   men as agents of history 58
   women as background 69
Mobutu Sese Seko
   corruption 53, 72
   cult of personality 52
   Gécamines 26
   governance 52-55
   as *le père de la nation* 53-54
   Space Age 135
   suppression under 91, 110
modernity
   and getting one's photo taken 94
   and salaried work 66
   bicycles 115-116
   European terms of 68
   scopic regimes of 149
Mofokeng, Santu 93
Monaville, Pedro 89, 90, 98
Mother Africa 64
Mphande, Lupenga 36, 37, 38
Mudekereza, Patrick 17-18
Mutambwa, Georges Mulumbwa 45
nationalism
   as visual spectacle 63
   women as generic 62
   women as symbols 63, 80
necropolitics (Mbembe) 27-28, 45, 83, 126
Nelson, Alondra 121
Nora, Pierre 137
Nos Images (magazine) 103
nostalgia 115, 117
Nzongola-Ntalaja, Georges 58, 86, 89
opacity 148-149
Opango, Pauline 73-75, 81
Otolith Group 133-134
past futures 45, 145-148
Peck, Raoul 110-111, 112, 113
   Lumumba (film) 112
   Lumumba, la mort du prophète (documentary film) 110-111, 116-117
performance art 119, 127
Petit, Pierre 45

photography
    analogue vs. digital 10, 31, 35, 37, 114
    and anthropology 29-30
    and Congolese popular painting 101-109
    and film 112
    circulation online 117, 138
    as series 34
    signs of wear and tear 91-93
    tense of 67
Plissart, Marie-Françoise 17, 18, 126
portraiture 61, 103, 106, 107, 151
postcolonial
    as temporal divison 41
    gendered terms 64-65, 68, 77, 79-82
    theory 46
postcolony (Mbembe) 13, 27-28, 52, 53, 79-82, 126, 146-147
Rancière, Jacques 19-20, 153
Robinson, Cedric 34
Robinson, Jennifer 28
Royal Museum for Central Africa 9, 15, 17, 19, 151
Sambi, Chéri 106, 109
Scott, Darieck 39
Seeley Harris, Alice 11-12, 103
Sembene, Ousmane 76
Senga, Georges 11
    at the Biennale de Lubumbashi 18, 88, 113
    in Belgium 18
    Une vie après la mort 85-118
Shonibare, Yinka 122
Silverman, Debora 22
Situationist International 19, 124-126
    and the Congo 124
    dérive 124-126
stamps 133-135
Stanard, Matthew 15
Stoler, Ann Laura 13
Stratton, Florence 64
System K (documentary film) 126, 145
Tempels, Placide 55
textiles 57, 72-73
Tillim, Guy
    Avenue Patrice Lumumba 88, 113
    Congo Democratic 79-80, 107
Time (magazine) 73, 75, 97

time/temporality
    and mining 36
    at Union Minière 36-38
    colonial transformations in 35-36
    in photography and video 13
    multiplicity of 35
    of capitalism 38
    of crisis 45
Tshibumba Kanda-Matulu 101-109, 113
Tshombe, Moïse 16, 26, 114
Tuymans, Luc 16
Union Minière du Haut Katanga
    and the Space Race 138-140
    medical inspections 29, 33
    origins and history 26
    photographs of earthwork 138
    stabilisation 29, 39
    time at 36-37
    women at 66-67
Van Reybrouck, David 21, 35-36, 91, 97-98
Vansina, Jan 53-54, 55
Vellut, Jean-Luc 29
Venice Biennale 16, 19
video
    and the experience of time 44
    endurance 76-77
    loop 44, 63, 64-65, 76, 77
La Voix du Congolais (journal) 90
waste/recycling 121, 143
Western views of the Congo 21, 133, 136, 147-148
WIELS 18
women's oppression under colonialism
    education 51, 71
    legal structures 51
    religion 51
women's political participation 60
women's role as wife/mother
    la maman zaïroise 54
    Zairian propaganda 64
women's work/labour
    agriculture 50-51, 66-67
    ancestry 72-73, 75
    domestic work 51, 70-71
    endurance 76, 77

Colour Plate Gallery

Plate 1: Sammy Baloji, *The Album (Pauwels's Album, p.7 installation detail)*, 2013. Digital photograph on archival paper. © Sammy Baloji. Courtesy of Axis Gallery, New York. (Figure I.1, p. 9)

Plate 2: Sammy Baloji, *Untitled 3* from *Mémoire* series, 2006. Archival digital photograph on satin matte paper, 60 × 159.38 cm. © Sammy Baloji. Courtesy of Axis Gallery, New York. (Figure 1.1, p. 25)

Plate 3: Sammy Baloji, *Untitled 17* from *Mémoire* series, 2006. Archival digital photograph on satin matte paper, 60 × 167 cm. © Sammy Baloji. Courtesy of Axis Gallery, New York. (Figure 1.2, p. 28)

Plate 4: Sammy Baloji, *Untitled 10* from *Mémoire* series, 2006. Archival digital photograph on satin matte paper, 60 × 178.56 cm. © Sammy Baloji. Courtesy of Axis Gallery, New York. (Figure 1.4, p. 31)

Plate 5: Sammy Baloji, *Untitled 9* from *Mémoire* series, 2006. Archival digital photograph on satin matte paper, 60 × 159 cm. © Sammy Baloji. Courtesy of Axis Gallery, New York. (Figure 1.6, p. 38)

Plate 6: Sammy Baloji, Sammy Baloji, *Untitled 8* from *Mémoire* series, 2006. Archival digital photograph on satin matte paper, 60 × 160.18 cm. © Sammy Baloji. Courtesy of Axis Gallery, New York. (Figure 1.7, p. 38)

Plate 7: Sammy Baloji, video stills from *Mémoire*, 2006. © Sammy Baloji. Courtesy of Axis Gallery, New York.
(Figures 1.8–1.10, pp. 40-41; 1.12–1.14, pp. 42-43)

Plate 8: Michèle Magema, video stills from *Oyé Oyé*, 2002. © ADAGP, Paris and DACS, London 2021.
(Figures 2.1–2.3, pp. 48; 2.6–2.8, pp. 59-61)

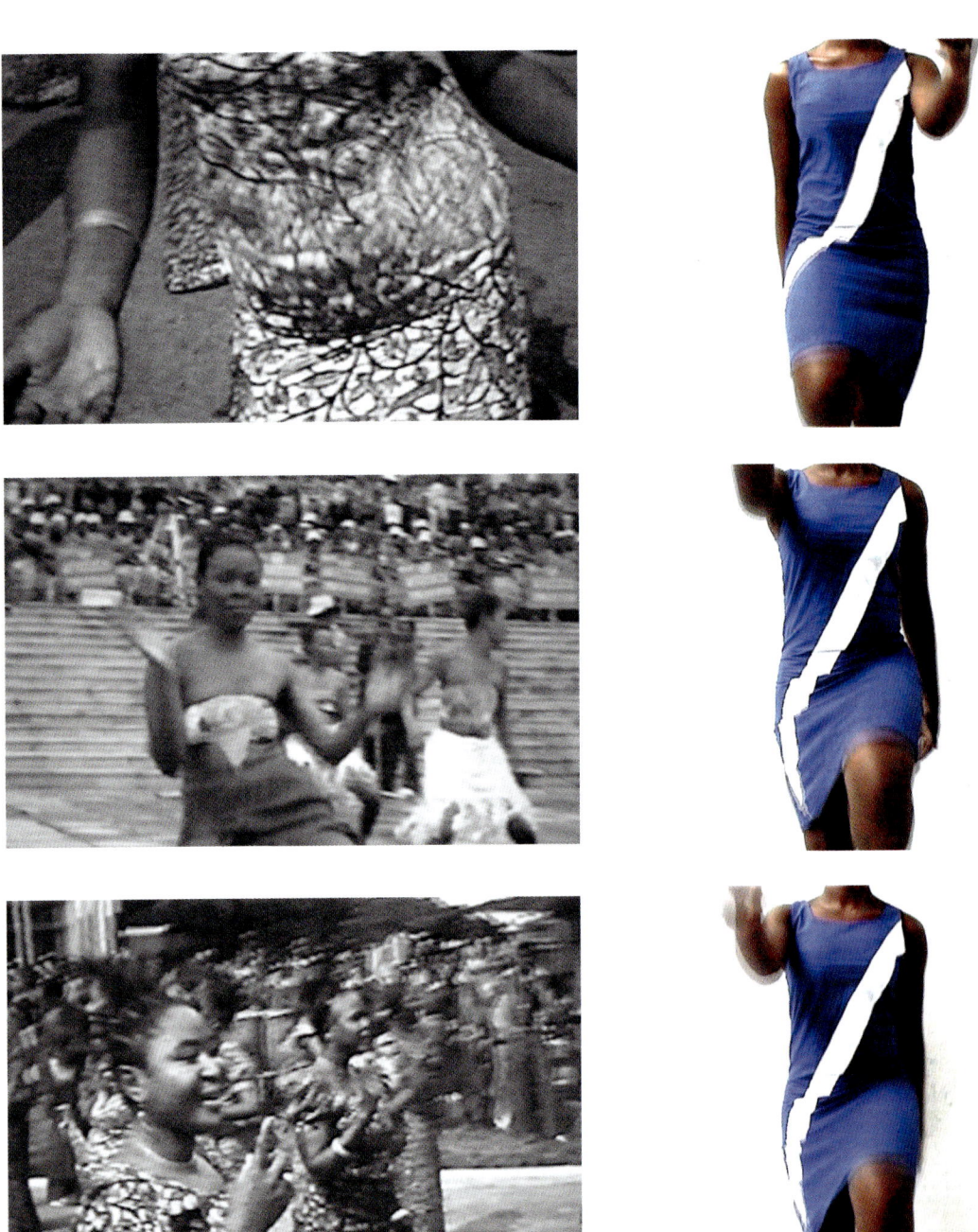

Plate 8 – continued

Plate 9: Sammy Baloji, *Untitled 7* from *Memoire* series, 2006. Archival digital photograph on satin matte paper, 60 × 191.79 cm. (Figure 2.9, p. 65)

Plate 10: Sammy Baloji, *Untitled* 6 from *Memoire* series, 2006. Archival digital photograph on satin matte paper, 60 × 170 cm. (Figure 2.10, p. 65)

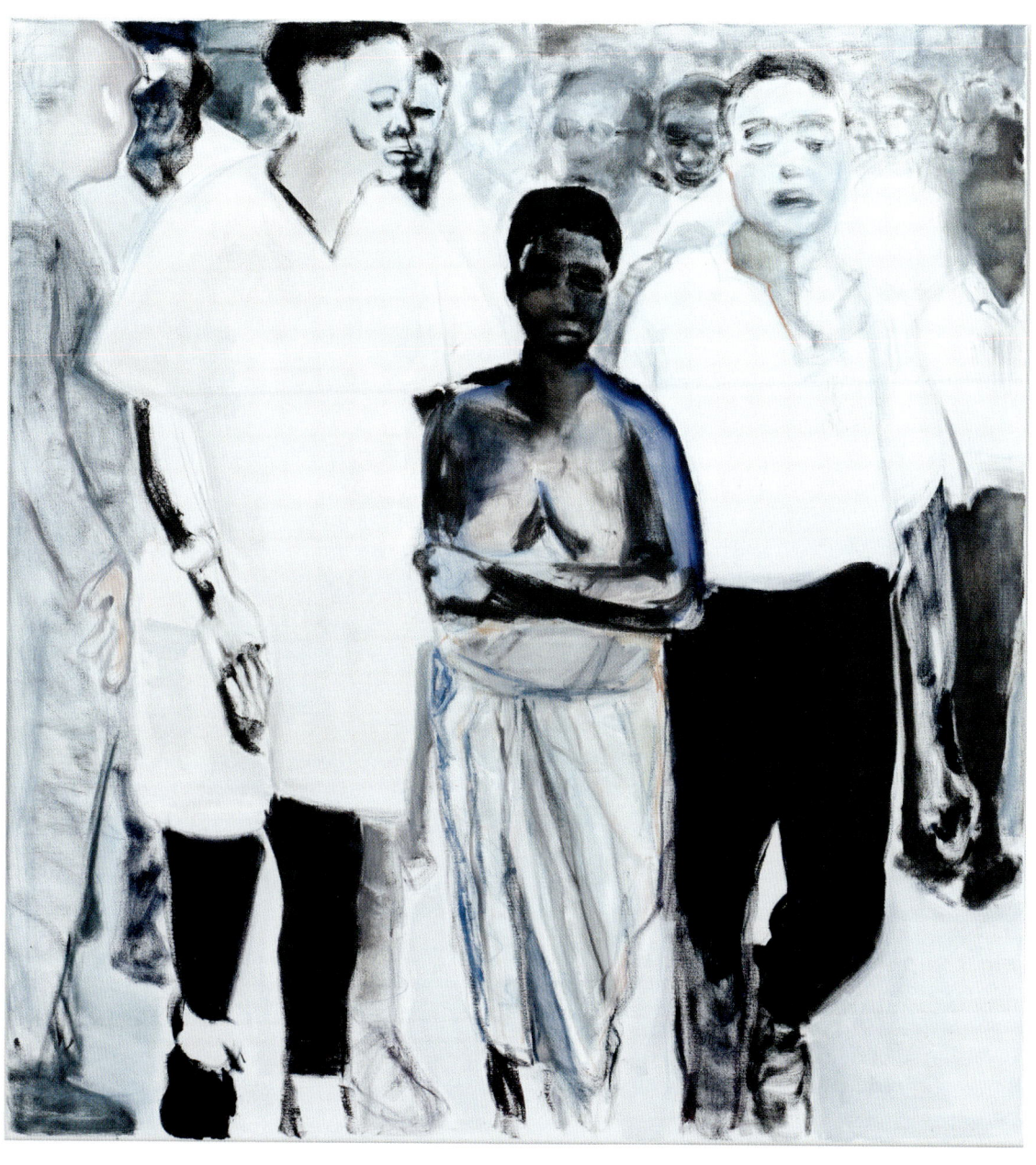

Plate 11: Marlene Dumas, *The Widow,* 2013. Oil on canvas, 150 × 140 cm. Collection Defares. © Marlene Dumas. Photo: Peter Cox. (Figure 2.13, p. 74)

Plate 12: Guy Tillim, *A traditional dancer and crowd salute Jean-Pierre Bemba as he walks to a rally from the airport, Kinshasa, 2006* from the series *Congo Democratic*, 2006. Archival pigment ink on 300g cotton paper, 91 × 133 cm.
© Guy Tillim. Courtesy of Stevenson, Amsterdam/ Cape Town / Johannesburg. (Figure 2.16, p. 80)

Plate 13: Guy Tillim, *Lumumbiste Party supporters prepare for a meeting, pinning up pictures of Patrice Lumumba and their leader Antoine Gizenga, who was a deputy to Lumumba after the first elections in 1960, 2006* from the series *Congo Democratic*, 2006. Archival pigment ink on 300g cotton paper, 91 × 133 cm. © Guy Tillim. Courtesy of Stevenson, Amsterdam/ Cape Town / Johannesburg. (Figure 2.17, p. 81)

Plate 14: Georges Senga, *Une vie après la mort*, 2012. Inkjet on Baryta paper, 170 × 60 cm. Courtesy of the artist.
(Figure 3.1, p. 87)

Plate 15: Georges Senga, *Une vie après la mort*, 2012. Inkjet on Baryta paper, 170 × 60 cm. Courtesy of the artist.
(Figure 3.2, p. 87)

Plate 16: Georges Senga, *Une vie après la mort*, 2012. Inkjet on Baryta paper, 170 × 60 cm. Courtesy of the artist.
(Figure 3.5, p. 96)

Plate 17: Georges Senga, *Une vie après la mort*, 2012. Inkjet on Baryta paper, 170 × 60 cm. Courtesy of the artist. (Figure 3.7, p. 98)

Plate 18: Georges Senga, *Une vie après la mort*, 2012. Inkjet on Baryta paper, 170 × 60 cm. Courtesy of the artist.
(Figure 3.8, p. 99)

Plate 19: Georges Senga, *Une vie après la mort*, 2012. Inkjet on Baryta paper, 170 × 60 cm. Courtesy of the artist. (Figure 3.9, p. 101)

Plate 20: Tshibumba Kanda-Matulu, *Discours du 4 janvier 1959, Les Martyrs de l'Indépendance*, ca. 1970–73. Acrylic on flour sack, 38.42 × 73.03 cm. Virginia Museum of Fine Arts, Richmond. Eric and Jeanette Lipman Fund. © Virginia Museum of Fine Arts. Photo: Travis Fullerton. (Figure 3.14, p. 106)

Plate 21: Burozi (signed Tshibumba), Lumumba, Master of the World, ca. 1970s. Oil on fabric, 45.72 × 31.75 cm. Source: Bogumil Jewsiewicki, *A Congo Chronicle: Patrice Lumumba in Urban Art* (New York: The Museum for African Art, 1999). (Figure 3.17, p. 108)

Plate 22: Georges Senga, *Une vie après la mort*, 2012. Inkjet on Baryta paper, 170 × 60 cm. Courtesy of the artist.
(Figure 3.18, p. 115)

Plate 23: Georges Senga, *Une vie après la mort*, 2012. Inkjet on Baryta paper, 170 × 60 cm. Courtesy of the artist. (Figure 3.19, p. 115)

Plate 24: Georges Senga, *Une vie après la mort*, 2012. Inkjet on Baryta paper, 170 × 60 cm. Courtesy of the artist.
(Figure 3.20, p. 116)

Plate 25: Kongo Astronauts, *Untitled [-6]* from *Capital SCrashed.exe* series, 2021.
© Kongo Astronauts. Courtesy of Axis Gallery, New York. (Figure 4.2, p. 120)

Plate 26: Kongo Astronauts, *Untitled [-3]* from *Capital SCrashed.exe* series, 2021. © Kongo Astronauts. Courtesy of Axis Gallery, New York. (Figure 4.3, p. 125)

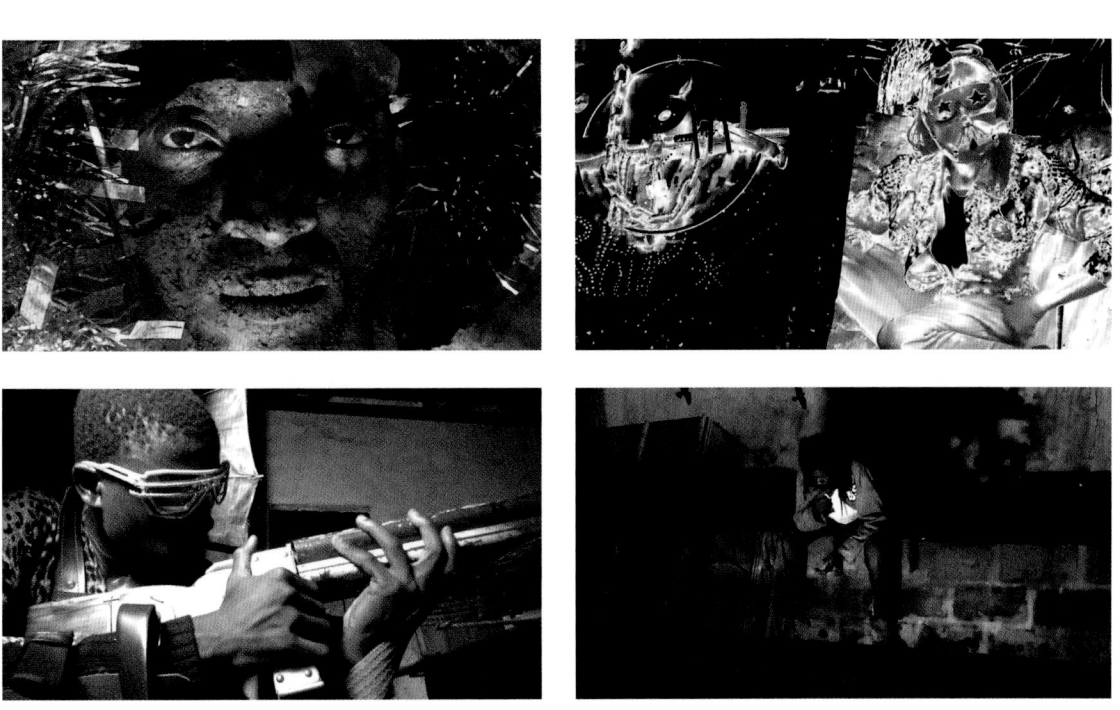

Plate 27: Kongo Astronauts, film stills from *Postcolonial Dilemna #Track4 (Remix mix)*, 2019. © Kongo Astronauts. Courtesy of Axis Gallery, New York. (Figures 4.8-4.11, pp. 131-132)

Plate 28: Kader Attia, *Independence disillusion*, 2014. Oil on canvas, 40 × 31.97 cm. Courtesy of GALLERIA CONTINUA. Photo: Miguel Ángel Emérico. (Figure 4.13, p. 135)

Plate 29: Kongo Astronauts, *Untitled [-4]* from *Capital SCrashed.exe* series, 2021. © Kongo Astronauts. Courtesy of Axis Gallery, New York. (Figure 4.19, p. 144)